A History of Fair Trade in Contemporary Britain

A History of Fair Trade in Contemporary Britain

From Civil Society Campaigns to Corporate Compliance

Matthew Anderson
Senior Lecturer, University of Portsmouth, UK

palgrave
macmillan

First published 2015 by
PALGRAVE MACMILLAN

Palgrave Macmillan in the UK is an imprint of Macmillan Publishers Limited, registered in England, company number 785998, of Houndmills, Basingstoke, Hampshire RG21 6XS.

Palgrave Macmillan in the US is a division of St Martin's Press LLC, 175 Fifth Avenue, New York, NY 10010.

Palgrave Macmillan is the global academic imprint of the above companies and has companies and representatives throughout the world.

Palgrave® and Macmillan® are registered trademarks in the United States, the United Kingdom, Europe and other countries.

ISBN 978–0–230–30381–2

This book is printed on paper suitable for recycling and made from fully managed and sustained forest sources. Logging, pulping and manufacturing processes are expected to conform to the environmental regulations of the country of origin.

A catalogue record for this book is available from the British Library.

A catalog record for this book is available from the Library of Congress.

Typeset by MPS Limited, Chennai, India.

Contents

Acknowledgements

This book is based on research funded by the Economic and Social Research Council (ESRC). I am also grateful to the University of Birmingham for the award of a Universitas 21 travel scholarship for research at the University of Melbourne. The final stages of writing were supported by an award from the Society of Authors and the K Blundell Trust.

I would like to take this opportunity to thank all the staff and volunteers from Oxfam, Christian Aid, CAFOD, the Methodist Development Relief Fund, Traidcraft, Twin Trading, the Trades Union Congress, the Co-operative and the Fairtrade Foundation, who put their own time and effort into assisting this research project. And I would like to extend my thanks to these organisations for agreeing to open their archives for academic research.

In particular, I would like to thank Richard Adams, John Boyle, Barbara Crowther, Bruce Crowther, Rosie Dodd, George Gelber, Brad Hill, Gillian Lonergan, Roy Scott, Michael Taylor, Chrissie Webb and Carol Wills for their help and support.

Special thanks to Prof Matthew Hilton for his expert advice and guidance and to Dr Sophie Bostock for her encouragement and friendship.

List of Abbreviations

AAM	Anti-Apartheid Movement
ACP	African Caribbean and Pacific countries
ATO	Alternative Trade Organisation
CA	Consumers' Association
CAFOD	Catholic Agency for Overseas Development *(formerly Catholic Fund for Overseas Development)*
CAP	Common Agricultural Policy
CI	Consumers International
CTS	Co-operative Tea Society
CU	Consumers' Union
CWC	Ceylon Workers' Congress
CWS	Co-operative Wholesale Society
DFID	Department for International Development
ECRA	Ethical Consumer Research Association
EFTA	European Fair Trade Association
ELTSA	End Loans to Southern Africa
ETI	Ethical Trading Initiative
EVS	European Values Study
FLO	Fairtrade International (*formerly Fairtrade Labelling Organizations International*)
FTAANZ	Fair Trade Association of Australia and New Zealand
FTF	Fairtrade Foundation
FTM	Fairtrade Mark
GLC	Greater London Council
GNI	Gross National Income
GNP	Gross National Product
HbS	Helping by Selling
HDI	Human Development Index

ICA	International Coffee Agreement
ICA	International Co-operative Alliance
ICFTU	International Confederation of Free Trade Unions
IFAD	International Fund for Agricultural Development
IFAT	International Fair Trade Association *(formerly International Federation for Alternative Trade)*
IGD	Institute of Grocery Distribution
IOCU	International Organisation of Consumers Unions (later CI)
ISEDC	International Small Enterprise Development Centre
ITUC	International Trade Union Confederation
NEWS	Network of European World Shops
NIC	Newly Industrializing Countries
NIEO	New International Economic Order
NGO	Non-Governmental Organisation
MCC	Mennonite Central Committee
MDG	Millennium Development Goals
MNC	Multinational Corporation
OA	Oxfam Activities
OECD	Organisation for Economic Co-operation and Development
OT	Oxfam Trading
OXFAM	Oxford Committee for Famine Relief
STABEX	Stabilisation of Export earnings
TEAR Fund	The Evangelical Alliance Relief Fund
TGCA	Toledo Cacao Growers Association
TNC	Transnational Corporation
TUC	Trades Union Congress
TWIN	Third World Information Network
UNCTAD	United Nations Conference on Trade and Development
UNDP	United Nations Development Programme
WCC	World Council of Churches
WCL	World Confederation of Labour

WDM	World Development Movement
WFTO	World Fair Trade Organization
WFTU	World Federation of Trade Unions
WTO	World Trade Organization

Introduction: A New International 'Moral Economy'?

Fairtrade has been hailed as one of the retail success stories of the past decade.[1] Sales of Fairtrade products in Britain have significantly outperformed retail analysts' most optimistic predictions in recent years, reaching £1.78 billion in 2013.[2] Britain is now firmly established as the leading European Fairtrade market,[3] fuelling media speculation as to why Fairtrade has taken root so firmly. Many commentators have looked to the British consumer in answering this question. Journalists have reported that: 'Britons over the past decade have become a nation of ethical shoppers'.[4] Some have looked to investigate 'how consumer power sparked a Fairtrade revolution on our high streets'.[5] Fairtrade's success in mobilising consumer support has certainly been impressive, but is this the full story?

The aim of this book is to consider whether consumer demand provides an adequate explanation for the growth of Fairtrade in Britain. By adopting a methodology that looks beyond the 'ethical shopping trolley', a wider Fair Trade social movement is revealed, grounded in the work of non-governmental organisations (NGOs) and alternative trade organisations (ATOs). I will argue that the emergence of Fair Trade in late twentieth-century Britain has only partly been the result of 'the market' responding to consumer demand. Of greater significance, although often overlooked, was the role of the social movement that successfully began to integrate political consumerism within its international development campaigns.[6] This approach presents an opportunity to consider a theory of change that places less emphasis on individual behaviour change and opens up space to explore ideas about collective consumption, public procurement and corporate compliance.

Public surveys of consumer behaviour in relation to Fair Trade and ethical foods have attempted to define 'the ethical consumer' based on socio-demographic factors such as age, gender and social class.[7] Market research studies tend to define the purchase of Fair Trade products as a lifestyle choice for those who can afford it, highlighting the importance of the more affluent 'middle-classes', with greater access to disposable income.[8] Respondents may be asked about price, quality, brand image and product attributes, but surveys rarely offer a sense of the consumer's 'world view'. It is rare in commercially focused market research for studies to investigate Fair Trade shoppers' political views, religious beliefs or the extent of their involvement with related organisations and networks. Deciphering this social and cultural data may not have direct commercial application, but an understanding of these networks offers potential for a deeper insight into the motivations of Fair Trade supporters. By broadening the scope of the analysis beyond the individual consumer, the dynamics of the Fair Trade social movement take on a greater significance. This movement has contributed to all aspects of Fair Trade from launching international trading ventures, providing assistance to producers, setting up church stalls, campaigning on the streets and lobbying government.

Prominent in much of the recent academic work on Fair Trade have been studies into the operations of global supply chains and impact assessments of Fairtrade certification on the livelihoods of producers in the global South.[9] But this has led to something of an imbalance in terms of understanding the workings of Fair Trade companies and organisations. There is now an opportunity for more detailed academic studies of those groups engaged in Fair Trade in the global North. This book is not a traditional business history, although it does include detailed case studies of Fair Trade businesses; instead what it explores is a history of ideas. The motivation for this research has been to understand what has made Fair Trade, to use Chip and Dan Heath's phrase, a 'sticky idea'.[10] It was this capacity for the idea of Fair Trade to be easily understood and remembered that has been so important in its success to date. In their book, *Made to Stick*, Chip and Dan Heath outline six principles nearly all 'sticky ideas' have in common: (1) Simplicity; (2) Unexpectedness; (3) Concreteness; (4) Credibility; (5) Emotions; (6) Stories. Fair Trade's success as a 'sticky idea' is perhaps most clearly demonstrated in its ability to motivate behaviour change. Working across global supply chains, the idea of Fair Trade has successfully encouraged producers to adopt new business models, retailers to stock new lines, consumers to support new products, governments to assist new programmes.

Revisiting the existing historical narrative of Fair Trade in contemporary Britain, provides a valuable opportunity to explore alternative approaches to some of the key questions that have faced the movement.

These include: Should Fair Trade represent an alternative model of trade, or act as a transformative force within the market? What is the relationship of Fair Trade to the wider global justice movement? How can Fair Trade expand its market recognition and still maintain its founding values? As different organisations worked to address these questions how they responded shaped the experience and model of Fair Trade. Over time alternative trading practices were adapted and refined, producer partnerships evolved and deepened, and development education programmes were updated to include new ideas and practices. For some organisations these changes happened gradually as their experience of Fair Trade evolved, for others there were significant 'tipping points' that fundamentally changed the nature of their engagement with Fair Trade.[11]

This research investigates the motivation of those organisations that pioneered Fair Trade and looks to understand the political, religious and intellectual ideas behind the movement and how these ideas shaped the model of alternative trade. The story of Fair Trade in modern Britain encompasses a surprisingly broad spectrum of civil society groups, and this book tracks their efforts from the early 1970s to shape what was to become perhaps one of the most diverse social movements of the twentieth century. Led by development agencies, faith-based groups and campaign organisations, Fair Trade was formulated as a powerful critique of global trade relations and promoted as a genuine opportunity for reviving international development efforts. But there were also tensions. Many within the NGO community assumed that they would find natural allies in the co-operative movement, the trade unions and consumer organisations; but in practice these relationships proved complex and at times conflicting. Fair Trade was in competition with another 'sticky idea' – Free Trade.[12] The dominance of Free Trade as *the* economic orthodoxy of the late twentieth century was such that even actors critical of neoliberal economics found that the terms of debate had been framed within the intellectual and political confines of this model. It is perhaps not surprising that there was resistance to ideas that required engaging with the concept of a new economic order. These institutionalised power dynamics represented a barrier to 'intrapreneurs'[13] and creative thinking, making it difficult for new ideas, such as Fair Trade, to gain traction or 'stick'.

Defining Fair Trade (and Fairtrade)[14]

The wider social movement behind Fair Trade has campaigned collectively to embed the concepts of justice and sustainable development at the heart of trade structures and practices.[15] This philosophy has evolved through experience and dialogue over the last 40 years. The most widely accepted definition of Fair Trade is found in the Charter of Fair Trade Principles:

> Fair Trade is a trading partnership, based on dialogue, transparency and respect, that seeks greater equity in international trade. It contributes to sustainable development by offering better trading conditions to, and securing the rights of, marginalized producers and workers – especially in the South. Fair Trade Organizations, backed by consumers, are engaged actively in supporting producers, awareness raising and in campaigning for changes in the rules and practice of conventional international trade.[16]

Rather than dogmatically following a single approach the influences and practices of Fair Trade have been diverse and have evolved over time, constantly updated and renewed. In responding to the *Charter of Fair Trade Principles*, agreed in 2009, Ian Bretman stated, 'For decades, Fair Trade initiatives all around the world have been focussed on addressing the practical problems faced by producers, rather than trying to make a theory work in practice.'[17] The different approaches to Fair Trade are most clearly seen in the two distinct channels: the independent product certification route as operated by Fairtrade International[18] and the integrated supply chain route as supported by the World Fair Trade Organization (WFTO)[19] (using its own Guarantee System). Despite these different approaches, both WFTO and Fairtrade International have agreed on the core principles of Fair Trade. These include: (1) Market access for marginalised producers; (2) Sustainable and equitable trading relationships; (3) Capacity building and empowerment; (4) Consumer awareness raising and advocacy; (5) Fair Trade as a 'social contract'.[20]

As the Fair Trade movement, and particularly certified Fairtrade, looks to 'tip the balance' and move further into mainstream markets, its alternative trading model has received increased critical attention. Questions about the impact and effectiveness of Fairtrade have intensified with the rise of alternative sustainability standards.[21] Specific aspects of Fairtrade certification have been criticised for failing to integrate temporary workers and not delivering benefits for marginalised employees who are neither co-operative members nor covered by the Hired Labour Standards.[22] More broadly the ability of Fairtrade to increase wages, improve production processes and strengthen gender relations have been challenged in recent studies.[23] Many impact evaluations are showing mixed results; however, with the challenges that exist in relation to appropriate design, methods and rigour, it remains difficult to isolate and measure impact.[24] On balance, findings from academic impact studies suggest that producers within the Fairtrade system achieve 'significant though not universal positive changes' in economic and social outcomes compared to conventional trade.[25] While Fair Trade may not be sufficient to address structural issues of trade and inequality, as a dynamic model, it has demonstrated an ability to evolve and adapt based on stakeholder consultation and dialogue. The research objectives of this book are not focused specifically on the impact of Fair Trade, but the intention is to contribute to the wider discourse about ownership, governance and theory of change.

Most studies of Fair Trade in Britain include some overview of the formation of the Fairtrade Foundation and the standard biographical details are reasonably well-known: the Fairtrade Foundation was set up in July 1992 by CAFOD (Catholic Fund for Overseas Development), Christian Aid, New Consumer, Oxfam, Traidcraft Exchange and the World Development Movement, and later joined by the Women's Institute. The role of the Fairtrade Foundation is to monitor and license the FAIRTRADE Mark in the United Kingdom.[26] The Fairtrade Foundation identified its joint goals: 'to challenge the conventional model of trade, and offer a progressive alternative for a sustainable future.'[27] And, 'to empower consumers to take responsibility for the role they play when they buy products from the third world'.[28] Beyond these details there is only limited academic consideration of the roles played by these founding organisations. Although several of these organisations are established household names, others are not (in particular New Consumer).[29] This has raised some questions about the legitimacy and governance of the Fairtrade Foundation – to what extent are its members qualified to act as guardians of the movement? For the Fairtrade Foundation its credibility is based on the perceived experience and independence of its member organisations, and this high level of trust is particularly important given public scepticism about the proliferation of social labels.[30]

In 2006 representatives of the Philippine and Asian Fair Trade organisations stated that they were 'tired of being lectured and dictated to from the North countries [*sic*]'.[31] They argued that there was an imbalance in the Fair Trade system and that 'labelling companies have to be challenged because the power they have to exclude small producers is awesome. To be certified by them is success in the markets to be refused or shunned is a one way ticket to oblivion.'[32] Questions were also raised about governance and ownership of the movement. Shay Cullen, founder of PREDA,[33] argued that, 'No one knows where the authority to make and impose their rules on others came from. They seem to be self-appointed.'[34] The Fair Trade movement and the labelling initiatives have been mindful of this critique and there is evidence of increasing engagement with a wider debate about authentic partnerships and who represents 'authentic' Fair Trade.[35] Fairtrade International launched a New Standards Framework in 2011 and has also revised its General Assembly to give producers a greater role in the governance of the organisation.[36] For its part the WFTO has looked to strengthen its regional membership and has restated its commitment that small farmers and artisans should be the main focus in all governance structures and decision-making within the Fair Trade movement.[37] But despite these recent developments, some critics argue that Fair Trade has yet to adequately address the conceptual and practical challenges that have been raised.[38] Given this context, a historical reassessment of the basis and evolution of the Fair Trade model is particularly timely.

Consumer demand and the politics of consumption

Alex Nicholls and Charlotte Opal in their influential book, *Fair Trade: Market-Driven Ethical*, define Fair Trade as 'a consumer-driven phenomenon, underpinned by the growth of "ethical" consumption more generally'.[39] They further argue that: 'Fair Trade is entirely a consumer choice model, it operates within the larger free trade model of unregulated international commerce'.[40] In contrast, Clive Barnett, Nick Clark, Paul Cloke and Alice Malpass question whether Fair Trade really represents a triumph of market logic. They argue that 'the growth of ethical consumerism is not simply about spontaneous changes in consumer demand being met by more or less elastic market supply; nor is the politics of this activity primarily about the aggregation of myriad privatised preferences'.[41] They have attempted to develop a broadly political, rather than a narrowly economic approach to Fair Trade and ethical consumerism. This has led them to highlight the role of organisations involved in Fair Trade which seek to embed ethical purchasing in wider programmes of mobilisation, activism, lobbying and campaigning. Using the activities of Traidcraft as an example, they argue that 'agency needs to be located not in the activities of consumers but in the articulation of intermediary organisations, social networks, and everyday practices of social reproduction'.[42]

Embracing a longer view of consumption and consumer studies, Daniel Miller declared that 'consumption has become the vanguard of history'.[43] Miller was optimistic about the potential of ethical or 'progressive consumption'. He argued that, 'what is required is a "middle-range" morality, which re-inscribes on to the surface of commodities their consequences for producers, often from the developing world'.[44] But despite extensive academic research and media coverage, the concept of 'the consumer' remains hard to pin down. Tim Lang and Yiannis Gabriel have shown that, 'consumers come in millions of forms, broken down and divided by class, income, family, gender, taste, lifestyle, aspirations, etc.'.[45] They have suggested that this diversity therefore makes it misleading to talk of 'the consumer'.[46] While the diversity of consumer interests should not be underestimated, Matthew Hilton's research offers a nuanced assessment of the history of consumer politics that argues, 'consumerism has shown its greatest potential as a movement for historical change when it has attached itself to a broad set of social democratic principles that coalesce with other interests in society'.[47] Fair Trade's success as a 'consumer movement change' needs to be understood as highly contingent on its connection to wider social networks that defined these 'everyday practices of social reproduction' in relation to global issues of trade, poverty and international development.

Intellectual origins of Fair Trade: A longer history

Frank Trentmann, in his history of Britain as a *Free Trade Nation* has argued that 'the moral view of the world according to Fair Trade has a historical blind spot'.[48] This, he argues, is illustrated in the failure of the Fair Trade movement to recognise that in the late nineteenth and early twentieth centuries, 'morally energized civic-minded consumers opted for Free Trade'.[49] Although Trentmann acknowledges that 'there is no direct line between this kind of racial stereotyping and the ethical consumerism of more recent years', he contends that the Buy Empire Goods campaign 'occupies an intermediary stage towards Fair Trade'.[50] He concludes his description of Empire Day in Oxford in 1927, by declaring that, 'here was an imperial precursor to the international Fair Trade movement that would spring up half a century later'.[51]

But these attempts to demonstrate an element of continuity from the consumer support for the Empire Marketing Board to Fairtrade Foundation significantly underplay the extent to which the Fair Trade movement of the late twentieth century represented a 'switch [of] moral tracks'.[52] Trentmann argues that Fair Trade needs to be placed in 'a longer more troubled genealogy of consumption and power'.[53] This may be true, but at the same time Fair Trade's origins as a protest movement need to be clearly articulated. Fair Trade did not develop *from* the Buy Empire Goods campaign rather Fair Trade emerged (somewhat belatedly) *in opposition* to this 'conservative imperial consumerism'. Arguably, the modern Fair Trade movement developed as a historically specific, internationalist vision that was shaped by the experiences of the anti-apartheid movement, was motivated by solidarity with socialist countries such as Nicaragua, was informed by liberation theology and was articulated in consumer activism such as the fair tea prices campaign. If one seeks to uncover a longer history of Fair Trade that encapsulates the experiences of the eighteenth and nineteenth centuries, there are more fruitful parallels to explore in the philosophy and practices of the social critics and protest movements of the time.

The politicization of consumption in Britain has a long and well-documented history dating back to at least the eighteenth century. E. P. Thompson in 'The moral economy in the English crowd in the eighteenth century,' developed an analysis of traditional rights and customs that would encourage scholars to rethink their interpretation of 'food riots'.[54] The concept of the 'moral economy' has been applied to research in numerous fields and historical periods – the study of Fair Trade is no exception. Although Thompson himself was uneasy about the extension of the concept beyond 'eighteenth-century crowd action' it has proved a valuable tool for numerous academic debates.[55] Gavin Fridell has argued that, 'Whereas the old moral economy in England described by Thompson asserted the right of the poor consumers to gain access to the means of life, the new international moral economy of Fair Trade asserts the right of poor producers to get a fair price for what they sell on the market'.[56] Rather than the threat of riot as its political force, the Fair Trade moral economy is seen to rely on activist and consumer pressure – and the threat of bad publicity challenging the reputation of brands owned by multinational corporation's (MNC's).[57]

If crowd action in Thompson's 'moral economy' had primarily been about consumers imposing their rights to food at fair or 'customary level', social thinkers during the nineteenth century started to articulate a concept of consumer duty. John Ruskin, the nineteenth-century social thinker, believed that strengthening relations between the consumer and producer was central to moralising the market. Ruskin believed that value of goods and human labour had been undermined by the industrialisation of production and that the market could not be relied on to reflect the true value of goods or labour. Ruskin wrote in *Unto This Last* (1862), 'What anything is worth it [the market] can not tell you; all that it can tell is the exchange value.'[58] Ruskin articulated what he believed was the consumers' responsibility: 'In all buying, consider first, what condition of existence you cause in the producers of what you buy; secondly, whether the sum you have paid is just to the producer, and in due proportion, lodged in his hands.'[59] The challenge for Fair Trade was how to integrate these simple sounding lessons into the commercial practices of international business.

Taken together the concepts of 'market failure' and 'consumer duty' have been fundamental to Fair Trade campaigns. The failings of international markets have been highlighted by fluctuating commodity prices which at times have left producers receiving less for their goods than the cost of production. Ruskin saw the relations between consumer and producer breaking down; with the introduction of the factory system in England the home was no longer the centre of production. The Fair Trade movement also looked to bridge the gap between consumer and producer; but in the global markets of the twentieth century, this meant reconnecting with producers in the 'Third World'.

From the early nineteenth century, Peter Gurney argues that co-operators had developed 'a democratic, ethical model of consumption – a "moral economy of co-operation" – that depended on an associated, active membership rather than the gullible mass consumers preferred by capitalist manufactures and advertisers'.[60] Gurney's work was a clear extension of the analytical discourse outlined 30 years earlier. E. P. Thompson concluded his now famous thesis by arguing that, 'The moral economy of the crowd took longer to die: it is picked up by the early co-operative flour mills, by some Owenite socialists, and it lingered on for years somewhere in the bowels of the Co-operative Wholesale Society.'[61] A number of revisionist studies have sought to highlight the persistence of a socially progressive co-operative philosophy. Stephen Yeo stated that, 'The fact the world did not go their way should not be allowed to conceal what Holyoake called the "world-making" project of co-operators' and that, 'results need not be allowed to erase struggles, nor need defeat be equated with failure.'[62]

Building on this understanding of the Co-operative movement as a pioneer of ethical consumerism, recent studies on Fair Trade have frequently looked to the Co-op in their historical assessments of the movement. Tim Lang and Yiannis Gabriel situated the Co-operative movement within the first wave, of what they describe as 'active consumers'. In

Lang and Gabriel's model of consumer activism the first wave, 'took note of, helped and began to adopt the vitality and appeal of the fourth wave [alternative consumerism] by making new commitments to position co-operatives as more trustworthy sources of the necessities of life'.[63] Alex Nicholls and Charlotte Opal have developed an alternative model for understanding Fair Trade based on the commercial growth of the market. Within this model the Co-operative Group is also identified as a 'naturally sympathetic retail business' and situated in the third wave of development, building upon the work of ATOs.[64] But while the model of co-operative trade has been an important inspiration, international co-op to co-op trade in the nineteenth and twentieth century was not necessarily a direct precursor of Fair Trade.[65]

Christian led 'consumer-orientated activism' also has interesting historical precedents in popular campaigns of the eighteenth and the nineteenth centuries.[66] The most well-known example of this form of Christian moral critique of consumption is the boycott of slave-produced sugar, led by Thomas Clarkson and supported by Christian shoppers. From 1791, the Abolitionists encouraged consumers to switch to honey instead of sugar or to buy sugar from the East Indies which was free from slavery. One grocer from Birmingham reported that his sugar sales halved in just four months.[67] It is estimated that during the boycott approximately 300,000 consumers abandoned slave-produced sugar.[68] But despite the success of this campaign, revisionist studies have shown that other factors including commercial pressures on plantations and the impact of slave revolts were probably of equal importance.[69]

Perhaps less well-known is the White List Movement instigated by the Christian Social Union (CSU) from 1887 to 1914. The White Lists were a form of retail certification that guaranteed that products made in Britain had been manufactured under at least minimum working conditions. Although focused on conditions in British factories, the organisation and certification of the 'human rights content' of goods, exhibited features in common with the internationally directed model of twentieth-century Fairtrade labelling.[70] By 1908, Oxford, Birkenhead, Leeds and Leicester all had White Lists of over a hundred firms. And in Manchester, the White List included 700 firms from 40 different trades. But the expansion of the White List Movement was curtailed by the First World War and it was never successfully revived in post-war Britain. Julien Vincent, political and social historian, has argued that through the CSU's involvement in the White List campaigns 'the Christian ideal was not secularised, but that economic life became re-sacralised, and re-enchanted'.[71]

One of the most vivid critiques of nineteenth-century colonialism can be found in Eduard Douwes-Dekker's novel *Max Havelaar*.[72] The story follows the experiences of Max Havelaar, a Dutch colonial administrator who sought to improve conditions for coffee farmers in Indonesia, but was hindered in his mission by the indifference shown by the Dutch colonial government and coffee traders.[73] When it was first published in 1860, it was reported to have 'sent a shiver through the country'.[74] The main object of Havelaar's criticism was the Kultuurstelsel (Cultivation System) which was used by the Dutch to justify the compulsory cultivation of export crops. The book was discussed in the Dutch Parliament and was championed by those already opposed to the Cultivation System. By 1862, two years after the publication of *Max Havelaar* the Cultivation System was abolished for pepper, in 1863 for cloves and nutmeg, in 1865 for tea and in 1866 for tobacco. But one remnant of the Cultivation System persisted into the twentieth century – the compulsory cultivation of coffee, which continued until 1917.[75] Interest in the story of *Max Havelaar* was renewed when the first Fair Trade certification scheme, set up in the Netherlands in 1988, choose 'Max Havelaar' as the name for their certification label.

Modern Fair Trade and the twentieth-century development agenda

In 2006, the European Parliament adopted a resolution on Fair Trade that stated, 'while international trade agreements fail to deliver for the poor countries, the Fair Trade system has proved to be effective in poverty reduction and sustainable development'.[76] This policy agenda is backed by academic assessments critical of standard economic approaches to trade and economic growth. Professor Tim Jackson has argued that, 'Far from raising the living standard for those who most needed it, growth let much of the world's population down over the last 50 years. Wealth trickled up to the lucky few.'[77] Nowhere is the failure of economic growth more clearly evidenced than in the knowledge that 1 billion people across the world are living on less than $1 a day – half the price of a small cappuccino in Starbucks.[78] Building on public and academic interest there has been a shift in recent years towards greater institutional support and recognition for Fair Trade at an intergovernmental policy level.[79] But for much of its early history Fair Trade had been on the sidelines of major conferences and debates about the future of trade and development. While the Fair Trade movement had sought to influence this agenda, until recently, it had been dismissed as a coalition of well-meaning volunteers, poorly equipped for the serious business of trade and international negotiations.

The past 50 years have witnessed significant shifts in development politics, philosophy and economics. But the impact on Fair Trade has been somewhat ambiguous and remains open to academic discussion. Gavin Fridell in his work on Fair Trade coffee sets out with the ambitious task of studying 'the structures of global capitalism' and providing 'a framework for situating Fair Trade within the "big questions" of a historically informed development theory'.[80] Fridell's broad reading of the influence of the development agenda on Fair Trade leads him to conclude that 'the reorientation within the fair trade network away from the state-led development promoted by the broader fair trade movement represents an overall setback for the network and its vision'.[81] While this assessment has the descriptive appeal of a grand narrative, there are aspects that do not seem to fit with the empirical evidence emerging from national studies of Fair Trade.[82] In particular there has been a tendency to conflate the 'fair trade movement' with the programmes of the United Nations Conference on Trade and Development (UNCTAD) and the United Nations Development Programme (UNDP), and in so doing present an assessment that overstates the extent of Fair Trade's statist orientation.

Rather than a macro-level approach, focused on raising official aid and restructuring international trade relations, the Fair Trade movement primarily looked to encourage a greater understanding among citizen-consumers in the North of the working conditions faced by producers in the global South. The aim was to recalibrate questions of international development so that they could be understood on a human scale. Instead of a state-led development programme, Fair Trade was pioneered and coordinated by a network of NGOs and ATOs. Talking more broadly about the rise of the NGO sector, Akira Iriye described its growth as 'one of the most impressive developments of twentieth-century world history'.[83] But he argued that in general historians have been extremely slow to recognise the contribution of this 'third sector'. So rather than acting as a standard bearer for official development slogans such as 'trade not aid', the Fair Trade movement represented an alternative vision of trade and development that favoured practical action and direct engagement with producers and communities in the South.[84]

The 1960s: First UN Development Decade

The launch of the first UN Development Decade raised hopes that the 1960s would witness a transformation in the Third World on a scale comparable to the Marshall Plan's post-war European reconstruction. Official development assistance (ODA) increased from $5.2 billion in 1961 to $6.6 billion in 1967, but this was still significantly short of 0.7% of gross national product (GNP).[85] In 1968 Britain, (although not at the bottom of the table), had only contributed official aid to a value of 0.42% of GNP. Even at this level, the political nature of assistance was underscored by the fact that 43% of Britain's aid was wholly tied and another 16% was partly tied.[86] At this time France was considered among the leading donors of development assistance (with official aid at 0.72% of GNP).[87] But this figure somewhat overstated the level of French aid assistance, since it also included flows to France's overseas departments and territories – now excluded from ODA calculations.

The 0.7% target found strong backing in the shape of the Pearson Commission, appointed by World Bank President Robert McNamara in 1968. The Commission's 1969 Report proposed that ODA 'be raised to 0.70% of donor GNP by 1975, and in no case later than 1980'.[88] The 0.7% target was formally recognised in October 1970 when the UN General Assembly adopted a resolution including the goal that 'Each economically advanced country will progressively increase its official development assistance to the developing countries and will exert its best efforts to reach a minimum net amount of 0.7% of its gross national product at market prices by the middle of the Decade.'[89] It is worth noting that with the revised System of National Accounts in 1993, GNP was replaced by gross national income (GNI), an equivalent concept. Organisation for Economic Co-operation and Development (OECD) Development Assistance Committee members' performance against the 0.7% target is now measured in terms of ODA/GNI ratios.

The 1960s also witnessed growing momentum around the potential of international trade. Following the second UNCTAD conference in New Delhi in 1968, the phrase 'trade not aid' quickly gained popularity as a way of expressing the need to bridge the gap between foreign exchange available to developing countries through their exports and foreign exchange needed for their imports.[90] But international trade did not have a particularly good track record when it came to Third World development. Between 1953 and 1967, world trade as a whole increased by an average of 6.9% per year, but the gains from international trade continued to be amassed disproportionately by the industrialised countries of the North.[91] As a result, low-income countries' overall share of export earnings declined from 27% in 1953 to 19% in 1967.[92] For example, between 1953 and 1961 Brazil expanded its coffee exports by 90% in volume, but revenue fell by 35%.[93] The modest (and somewhat simplistic) target of 5% annual growth rate in the GDP of developing countries was only achieved by a handful of countries and even then the benefits of economic growth failed to trickle down to the community level.

The objectives of Fair Trade were to provide micro-level trade interventions designed to support small-scale farmers and artisan producers disadvantaged by the failings of intergovernmental economic policies.[94] The movement was not state sponsored but led by international development agencies, campaign groups and Christian agencies.[95] While some academics have identified examples of what resembled early Fair Trade initiatives during the 1960s, in reality most of these operations were closer to commercial ventures than genuine Fair Trade companies. There were organisations such as Oxfam's Helping by Selling (HbS), that were operating trading companies and buying goods from producers in developing countries, but at this relatively early stage they were not offering wages any better than the market rate, they did not make advance payments and did not give producers any commitment to long-term development. This trading model arguably represented only 'a very limited "fair-trade" importing programme'.[96]

The 1970s: Second UN Development Decade

Development studies have characterised the 1970s as the decade when the South's power seemed to be growing.[97] Gilbert Rist, reflecting on the hope and enthusiasm of the time, described how 'the decade began in an almost revolutionary atmosphere marked by support for liberation movements, the growing influence of dependency theory, and hopes in Tanzania's original model of self-reliance'.[98] The oil crisis was perhaps the defining moment of the decade. Following the Israeli–Egyptian conflict of October 1973, the oil-exporting countries (OPEC) retaliated against Western support for Israel by quadrupling the price of crude oil. It seemed that for the first time the balance of economic power had tilted slightly towards the developing countries.[99] But for non-oil exporting Third World governments these measures only worsened their economic position. The price of imported Western manufactured goods increased dramatically while their earnings from exports of raw materials stagnated. Added to increased petroleum prices, the double burden vastly inflated Third World debt.[100]

In April/May 1974 the UN General Assembly held a special session to study the 'problems relating to raw materials and development'.[101] Following this session the UN General Assembly issued a Declaration on the Establishment of a New International Economic Order (NIEO) that set out to recast the rules of the international economy. The NIEO was based on the ideas of 'equity, sovereign equality, interdependence, common interest and cooperation among all States'.[102] Despite this progressive agenda, the NIEO was arguably still underpinned by a belief in market expansion that largely ignored ideas about dependency theory and self-reliance.[103] The opportunity to develop the NIEO was short-lived as the 'Third World' began to break up in the mid-1970s. It seemed that, 'at the very moment when it [the Third World] was vigorously expressing its collective demands, it ceased to exist as an entity with a common destiny'.[104] New divisions emerged between the rich countries, the 'least developed countries' (LDCs) and the 'newly industrializing countries' (NICs).[105] The common interest between these groups in pursuing a collective project for the future had completely disappeared.

The 1970s also witnessed a global expansion of MNCs. As MNCs strengthened their hold on the world economy, their trading activities led to accusations of exorbitant profits and exploitation in countries in the South. By the end of the decade MNCs controlled between a quarter and a third of world production and with the proliferation of 'transfer pricing' one-third of world trade consisted of exchanges within these companies.[106] Brian Wren, Coordinator for Third World First,[107] described the expanding operations of MNCs to campaigners by drawing on economist Richard Barnet's analogy of the multinational company as a giant.[108] Wren vividly illustrated the global workings of a MNC: 'The brain lives in skyscrapers in New York, London, Frankfurt and Tokyo. Blood is capital, pumped through the system by global banks. The world's financial centres are the heart, while the hands reach out into Third World for cheap labour to make goods mostly for sale in industrial countries.'[109]

From the early 1970s Fair Trade represented a new and distinctly modern approach to 'alternative trade' that incorporated the principles of: 'fair prices', pre-financing, longer-term contracts and producer dividends or social premium. The Fair Trade movement emerged in Britain as NGOs and ATOs (in particular Oxfam, Christian Aid, CAFOD, Campaign Coffee and Traidcraft), looked to fill the vacuum left by government and business reluctance to genuinely engage citizen-consumers on issues of international trade and development. Although building on a longer history of political action, the messages and organisational structure of Fair Trade identified it as more closely aligned with the 'new social movements' than traditional labour or consumer politics. It was here that the politically neutral figure of 'the consumer' proved a valuable tool in allowing development agencies and Christian voluntary organisations to move beyond the social, cultural or religious affiliations of their core supporters. However, beyond the politics of consumption, the objectives of Fair Trade were inspired by a diverse set of ideas that combined elements of co-operative principles (democratic member control), religious teachings (liberation theology) and development thinking (small is beautiful) and this translated into a focus on development education in the North and a practical action in the South.[110]

The 1980s: 'the Lost Decade of Development'

In contrast to the optimism that greeted the early 1970s, the 1980s has been seen as, 'the end of development' or even the 'lost decade'.[111] In Britain, the political landscape was shaped by Margaret Thatcher's determination to roll back the welfare state at home and internationally to reduce government spending on overseas aid. Within a month of holding office Thatcher cut the aid budget by 6% and further cuts followed. Funding cuts announced in March 1980 to be implemented for the following three years amounted to a 32.6% reduction on Labour's planned figures.[112] The diminished priority of overseas aid was evident as it fell from 1.06% of government expenditure in 1979/1980 to 0.95% in 1982/1983.[113] This caused alarm within Oxfam, as the Director General stated, 'We know no other aid-giving country which is planning such cuts in its aid expenditure.'[114] The quality of aid was also undermined. The Development Minister, Neil Marten said in February 1980 that government policy was to give 'greater weight in the allocation of our aid to political, industrial and commercial considerations alongside our basic development objectives'.[115] Oxfam responded that this was likely to make it more difficult to 'achieve the aim of more aid to the poorest'.[116]

In February 1980 the Brandt Commission presented its report to the Secretary-General of the United Nations.[117] The Commission's terms of reference had specified three main areas of study: the past record of development in the Third World; the prospects for the world economy; and the creation of a new economic order.[118] Published in March 1980, the report achieved record sales in Britain but internationally the reception was mixed: it was fiercely debated in Tanzania, ignored in Canada and unobtainable in Mexico. In the United States it was eclipsed by the Soviet invasion of Afghanistan, the presidential election and the Iran hostage affair.[119] The Brandt report's main recommendations highlighted the need to increase aid, reduce debt burdens of Third World countries and to work towards fairer international trade. But critics argued that the Brandt report actually represented a retreat from the New International Economic Order (NIEO), because it ignored the potential of producers' associations and 'self-reliant development' in favour of increased aid to boost industrial export from South to North.[120]

Established in 1962 with the backing of the US government, the International Coffee Agreement (ICA) was designed to guarantee stable coffee prices and promote political stability in Central and South America. Throughout the Cold War period, the importance of coffee as a cash crop ensured that the commitment to the ICA was seen as central to protecting US interests in the region. But by the late 1980s, with Soviet influence diminishing, the ICA was no longer seen as consistent with US geopolitical strategy. Backed by Britain and Holland, the United States pulled out of the ICA and effectively engineered its collapse in pursuit of free market deregulation. The ICA finally collapsed in July 1989 with dramatic repercussions for both producers and traders. Within hours average 'green' coffee prices fell from the guaranteed $1.26 per pound to 65 cents per pound. The loss to import earnings for Third World producer countries in the following six months was reported to be as high as £2.5 billion.[121]

The 1980s represented a period of expansion and increased international networking across the Fair Trade movement driven by the growth of world shops and ATOs. From the mid-1970s there had been a series of informal meetings every couple of years among Fair Trade organisations, but in an effort to build on these networks more formal representative structures emerged: in 1984 the first European World Shops conference was convened; in 1987 EFTA[122] (the European Fair Trade Association) was established; in 1989 IFAT[123] (the International Federation of Alternative Trade) was founded. The late 1980s also saw the first moves towards product certification, with the Max Havelaar label launched in the Netherlands in 1988. The concept caught on, and within a year coffee with the Max Havelaar label had a market share of almost 3%.

The 1990s: Third Disarmament Decade

The 1990s began on an optimistic note. After the fall of the Berlin Wall in 1989 and the implosion of the USSR, it was hoped that the South might, as the UNDP proposed, be able to cash in on the 'peace dividend'.[124] The Report of the South, published in 1990, seemed to offer an opportunity for the people of the South to make a distinctive contribution to the dominant theories of development. Led by former Tanzanian President Julius Nyerere, the Report affirmed the importance of self-reliance, both individually and collectively. The Commission clearly restated the view that, 'development has therefore to be an effort of, by and for the people. True development has to be people-centred.'[125] But critics argued that the Report lacked consistency and ultimately reaffirmed the development orthodoxy by identifying 'rapid and sustained economic growth' as the 'development imperative'.[126] Arguably an inherent weakness of the Report was found in an approach that considered the poverty of the South without seriously examining the wealth of the North.[127]

In parallel to the work of the Commission of the South, in 1990 the UNDP Secretariat supported work on a series of annual reports that further elaborated on the concept of 'human development'.[128] Led by Mahbub ul Haq, the Human Development Reports set out to provide an alternative to conventional measures of national development and central to this approach was the new 'human development indicator' (HDI). The HDI represented a push for a broader definition of well-being and provided a composite measure of three basic dimensions of human development: health, education and income. The significance of the HDI was that it offered an alternative measure of growth to GDP and it was able to take account not only of total income but also how it was distributed. The reports and their recommendations continue to raise public awareness of ideas about human development, 'The HDI trends [still] tell an important story both at the national and regional level and highlight the very large gaps in well-being and life chances that continue to divide our interconnected world.'[129]

Building on the recommendations of the Brundtland Report, more than a hundred heads of State and thousands of delegates (including representatives of a thousand NGOs) assembled in Rio de Janeiro in June 1992 to take part in the 'Earth Summit', The United Nations Conference on Environment and Development (UNCED).[130] Five documents emerged within the framework of the official UNCED: (1) Rio Declaration or 'Earth Charter'; (2) The Convention on Climate Change; (3) The Convention on Biodiversity; (4) The Principles of Forest Management; (5) Agenda 21.[131] Agenda 21, often referred to as the 'bible of sustainable development', was designed as a practical framework to promote the idea of 'thinking locally, while acting globally'.[132] While the Rio Conference created widespread interest in 'environmental problems', the ambiguity of 'sustainable development' as a guiding principle led critics to argue that the warnings of radical environmentalism had been sidelined by a political agenda that continued to promote economic growth and industrialisation at all costs.[133]

Building on the success of Max Havelaar in the Netherlands, the 1990s saw the growth of 'Fair Trade' labelling schemes across Europe. Although the structure of the Fair Trade market varied considerably, by the end of the decade most European countries had established Fair Trade labelling bodies that were certifying consumer products: France (Max Havelaar France, 1992), Germany (TransFair Germany, 1992), Switzerland (Max Havelaar Switzerland, 1992), United Kingdom (Fairtrade Foundation, 1992/94), Italy (TransFair Italia, 1994), Denmark (Max Havelaar Denmark, 1995), Sweden (Föreningen för Rättvisemärkt, 1996).[134] Outside of Europe, national labelling schemes developed along similar lines: Fairtrade Label Japan was set up in 1993; TransFair Canada was established in 1997; TransFair USA was set up in 1998 and began certifying coffee in 1999; Fair Trade Association of Australia and New Zealand (FTAANZ) started operating in 2003.[135] In moves towards greater collaboration, Fairtrade Labelling Organizations International (FLO) was established in 1997 to coordinate international Fairtrade standards, certification and audit of production, and the labelling of products.

The 2000s: Mainstreaming Fair Trade and responding to the MDGs

The growth of Fairtrade labelling was not without its critics, particularly in relation to the certification of products sold by some MNCs. By the early 2000s, over two-thirds of Fair Trade products were sold by mainstream catering and retail outlets.[136] But despite some controversies, the success of Fairtrade labelling was shown in its ability to adapt the Fair Trade principles in order to engage with mainstream business. Growing sales and public awareness of Fair Trade also translated into achievements in the area of political lobbying, in particular: the adoption of resolutions on Fair Trade by the European Parliament (in 1994, 1998 and 2006), a Communication on Fair Trade by the Commission (1999), mention of Fair Trade in the Cotonou Agreement (2000).[137] In the United Kingdom, the House of Commons switched to Fairtrade tea and coffee throughout the Palace of Westminster in November 1997, and between 1999 and 2008 the Department for International Development (DFID) provided grants totalling approximately £1.9 million to support the work of the Fairtrade Foundation including: education programmes in schools, community campaigns with Fairtrade Towns, new product development and the promotion of Fairtrade in the 'out of home' sector.[138]

The United Nations Millennium Declaration, signed in September 2000 committed world leaders to achieving the eight Millennium Development Goals (MDGs) by 2015.[139] The Fairtrade Foundation has highlighted the importance of Fairtrade Premiums in mitigating the severe volatility in food prices and contributing towards the MDGs by enabling investment in food storage, productivity and quality improvement, and vital community amenities.[140] The findings of the Asian Development Bank Institute broadly supports this assessment: 'Fairtrade contributes directly to MDG8 (develop global partnerships in development), in particular targets 12 and 13, that address the needs of the poor in developing countries under rule-based, non-discriminatory trading systems.'[141] As discussions move to the post-2015 development framework, the Fair Trade movement has positioned itself as 'the best practice partnership for sustainable development'.[142] However, analysts suggest a note of caution: 'While both organic and fair-trade certification have significant poverty reduction potential, so far their large-scale impacts on poverty have yet to be realized. This is due to the high costs associated with certification, particularly for organic certification, which does not have built-in mechanisms to assist smallholders with certification costs.'[143]

Book outline

The structure of the book is essentially thematic but also broadly reflects the chronological development of the movement. Chapter 1 investigates Oxfam's involvement in Fair Trade and provides an opportunity to revisit the question of 'what is Fair Trade?'. The story of Oxfam shops in 1959, selling pincushions made by Chinese refugees in Hong Kong, is often identified as the beginning of Fair Trade in Britain.[144] However, as this chapter explains, if we understand Fair Trade to mean more than simply charities running commercial trading ventures – then it was not until the early 1970s that Oxfam developed a genuine model of Fair Trade. This reassessment should not detract from the significant contribution of Oxfam, but again challenges a chronology that depicts the 1960s as a uniquely progressive period of British social history.[145] From the early 1970s, Oxfam undertook a restructuring of its trading practices and the initiative that evolved (although not as progressive as some within the organisation were promoting) became the benchmark for subsequent Fair Trade operations.

Chapter 2 examines the involvement of religious groups (particularly Christian development agencies) in establishing many of the earliest

North–South links that developed into Fair Trade ventures. In particular, this chapter investigates the work of three Christian development agencies that played an important role in establishing the Fairtrade Foundation: Christian Aid, CAFOD and Tearfund. The involvement of religious agencies within the Fair Trade movement calls for a reassessment of the assumption, found in much of the broader historical literature of this period, that post-war Britain witnessed a fundamental secularisation of social action. This chapter does not set out to characterise Fair Trade as an exclusively Christian mission, but looks to establish the role of Christian teachings and organisations in the context of an emerging network of organisations converging around the ideas of Fair Trade.

Chapter 3 considers the claims that the Co-operative movement could be seen as 'naturally sympathetic' to Fair Trade.[146] This chapter explores the tensions that existed within the Co-operative movement over how to conduct its international trading. From the late nineteenth century, the consumer co-operative members of the International Co-operative Alliance (ICA), such as the British movement, expressed a desire to realise the ideals of international co-operation. However, when it came to a choice between demonstrating solidarity with producer co-operatives from the South and maintaining the consumer dividend, invariably it was the producer co-operatives that lost out. Faced with increased commercial pressure from supermarkets during the 1960s and 1970s, the Co-op resisted moves by its members to support NGO led campaigns such as the Anti-Apartheid Movement or the fair tea campaign. It was not until the early 1990s that the Co-op management recognised that Fair Trade was a viable proposition and offered an opportunity to reconnect the management of its global supply chain with the wider ideals of the movement.

Chapter 4 investigates the role of the Trade Union Congress (TUC) on the international stage, particularly in relation to conditions of workers in the Third World. By using Fair Trade as a focal point, this chapter looks to understand how (and if) the TUC incorporated the concerns of Third World workers into its international agenda. What emerges is a discrepancy between the ideals of international trade unionism, which articulated a philosophy consistent with the main principles of the Fair Trade movement, and the reality of the TUC's international programme that prioritised the job security of its members sometimes at the expense of workers in the Third World. This resulted in a situation whereby NGOs and Fair Trade campaigners, largely unaware of the TUC's internal politics, believed that the TUC would be receptive to campaigns focused on raising international labour standards. But as will be shown, those organisations that hoped to build alliances with the TUC were left bewildered and disappointed by the lack of leadership and commitment in advocating on behalf of workers in the 'Third World'.

Chapter 5 looks at how the concept of the 'ethical consumer' became a contested site within the Fair Trade movement and how this shaped the character of the Fairtrade Foundation. The controversial decision to certify Nestlé's Partners' Blend coffee is examined within the historical context of Fair Trade's move towards mainstream markets. This was not the first time that the Fairtrade Foundation had entered into negotiations with an MNC, nor was it the first time that the movement seemed to be facing a 'crisis of identity'. Conceptually, Chapter 5 aims to empirically test Mitchell et al.'s theory of stakeholder salience and provide a historical assessment of the key stakeholder relationships as Fairtrade entered the mainstream.[147] Drawing on case studies of Typhoo Tea, Cafédirect, Green & Black's, Divine Chocolate and Nestlé this chapter investigates the strategies adopted as the Fairtrade Foundation entered into negotiations with its first commercial licensees and built networks with its NGO partners.

The final chapter considers the main drivers of change within Fair Trade and explores a new direction for consumer politics. This assessment does not imply that Fair Trade campaigners should immediately discard consumer activism; conversely there may be real value in widening definitions of consumer politics in order to address the question of living standards of Fair Trade producers from a new perspective. In responding to this challenge Fair Trade may begin to find ways to define trading networks more holistically so that producers are empowered, also as consumers, and as citizens. Recent developments around Fairtrade consumer labelling in the global South also show the potential for the Fair Trade movement to reimagine how it positions debates over minimum price and living wages. And as the Fairtrade International develops its Theory of Change, there may be an opportunity to articulate a more nuanced understanding of the ethical consumer – one that better represents the complexities of the market reality and provides new frames to challenge and explore meanings of Trade Justice.[148]

1

Oxfam 'Helping by Selling': Charity, Trade and Advocacy

The Fair Trade movement has defined itself as, 'driven more by the desire to make a practical difference to the lives of people', than by, 'a need to conceptualise generic solutions to the problems of trade and development'.[1] For an international development agency such as Oxfam, this practical focus on poverty relief has been central to its institutional vision and values, and is enshrined in its charitable objects. But Oxfam's Fair Trade programme also developed and evolved alongside a sharpening intellectual and political critique of trade and development. Oxfam's Commercial and Deputy Director throughout the 1970s, Guy Stringer, recognised the potential of Fair Trade as a new form of advocacy.[2] He argued that 'it will almost certainly be impossible to dramatically change western-based, capital-serving trade systems merely through critical attack.'[3] As Oxfam's trading operations developed there was a growing belief that its international trading partnerships could be reinvented as a practical demonstration of the possibilities of a 'socially ideal' trade system.[4] Although Oxfam was not always able to articulate a consistent or generic solution, its ambition to offer a genuine alternative to the increasingly dominant free trade, market-led ideology, was fundamental in shaping its involvement with Fair Trade. For Oxfam, Fair Trade offered both a practical demonstration of 'alternative trade' and a political challenge to the status quo.

Oxfam, through its subsidiary Oxfam Trading, was directly involved in 'alternative trade' or 'fair trade' for over 30 years.[5] During this time Oxfam's trading model evolved and adapted to take account of commercial pressures, political constraints and shifts in development thinking. By the mid-1970s Oxfam had established a set of principles that would guide its international trading operations and provide a model for Fair Trade. These principles covered four main areas: (1) payment of fair prices; (2) pre-payment of up to 40% of the value of the purchase order; (3) distribution of profits in the form of dividends and grants; (4) a programme of producer services.[6] Negotiating the complexities of international trading, often hampered by limited resources and poor communications, was a challenging operation. And as Oxfam staff were only too aware, 'the reality does not always meet up to ideals and practising fair trade is fraught with difficulties'.[7]

The history of Oxfam's involvement with Fair Trade has been a surprisingly neglected field. While many academic studies of Fair Trade include some reference to Oxfam, few have critically engaged with the empirical evidence found within the extensive archival sources. This is a missed opportunity to investigate and contextualise the intense internal debates about the direction and function of its commercial policy. The result is an overly idealised portrayal of Oxfam's early trading programme and this is particularly problematic when Oxfam is then identified as a potential benchmark to consider contemporary questions about 'authentic' or 'alternative' Fair Trade.[8] While Oxfam has undoubtedly played a pivotal role within the wider story of the Fair Trade movement, the existing narrative is too often simplified and therefore overlooks many of the challenges and complexities involved in realising a model of trade that represented a genuine alternative. A detailed historical assessment of Oxfam's Fair Trade company presents an opportunity to explore a range of discussions that inform contemporary political debates about Fair Trade, such as: How efficient is Fair Trade at delivering international development? Is Fair Trade able to engage with the poorest producers? To what extent is Fair Trade 'charity'?[9]

Oxfam Trading and the historical narrative of Fair Trade in Britain

The historical narrative presented in the current academic literature broadly argues that the 1950s and 1960s represented a new approach to international trade and that the post-war period was the moment that 'the concept of Fair Trade began to take shape'.[10] The story of Oxfam's trading ventures has frequently been cited to illustrate this narrative. Gavin Fridell, for instance outlines how, 'In Europe, Oxfam UK was at the head of the Fair Trade network. ... In 1950 [*sic*], it began selling crafts made by Chinese refugees, and in 1964 it created its first alternative trade organisation (ATO) to import crafts and commodities directly from artisans and producers in continental Europe'.[11] William Low and Eileen Davenport, investigating the 'alternative' character of

Fair Trade argued that, 'The principal of linking income generation for marginalized groups through the sale of their own handcraft products had become the dominant paradigm by the late 1950s. Oxfam, for example, used a network of second hand shops to raise money for its relief efforts, and in the late 1950s started to sell crafts made by Chinese refugees alongside second hand goods'.[12]

As has been identified in the accounts above, Oxfam's international trading can be traced back to the late 1950s when pincushions, made by Chinese refugees seeking asylum in Hong Kong, were brought to the United Kingdom and sold to Oxfam supporters. In December 1964, these relatively ad hoc trading arrangements were formalised with the establishment of Oxfam Activities Ltd. And in 1967 Oxfam's imports from the 'Third World' were consolidated to form Helping by Selling (HbS). While the story is familiar, the retelling of these events, both within Oxfam and publicly, has been affected by a type of 'institutional teleology'.[13] This is not an institutional failing of Oxfam per se, indeed research by Tom Buchanan has shown that a certain 'mythologisation of events' is commonplace in the foundation of voluntary sector and human rights organisations.[14] The role of the historian is therefore to go beyond the ambiguities of 'official' history; but too many academic accounts of Fair Trade have accepted this 'founding myth' uncritically.

Some accounts have credited Leslie Kirkley, the then Director of Oxfam, as personally delivering this first suitcase of pincushions and embroidered boxes.[15] However, in reality the story is probably more complex.[16] Following the communist revolution in China, an influx of Chinese refugees to Hong Kong meant that the population of the city had expanded from 1.6 million in 1941 to 3 million in 1960.[17] With many refugees homeless and living in miserable conditions, the Lutheran World Federation Department of World Services established centres to provide food, clothing and vocational training.[18] When the German-born, director of the Federation's relief work in Hong Kong, Pastor Ludwig Stumpf was invited by Oxfam to speak at the World Refugee Year Conference in 1959, he brought with him a suitcase of pincushions and boxes made by the Chinese refugees.[19] Initially, Oxfam staff showed little interest in these handcrafts. But conference delegate Elizabeth Wilson, one of the founders of Huddersfield Famine Relief Committee, was more enthusiastic.[20] She took these items to sell in the north of England and thereafter successfully imported further handcrafts from Pastor Stumpf. It was a further year or two before Oxfam also began importing from Pastor Stumpf. Lynn Ten Kate, a Gifts organiser and later Executive Secretary at Oxfam, was keen to expand the programme and persuaded Jimmy Betts, Oxfam's first Field Director, to bring back handcrafts including: beads, bowls and ornaments from producers in Southern Africa.[21]

While it is true that the 1950s and 1960s witnessed the formation of new trading ventures run by major charities such as Oxfam, this historical perspective only offers a limited insight into the business philosophy, practices and impact of these trading operations. A starting point for a reassessment of Oxfam's trading activities is an understanding that buying from producers in the 'Third World' does not, in itself, represent an alternative model of trade. And the fact that Oxfam, a charity, owned the trading company is not synonymous with Fair Trade. A more detailed and nuanced assessment is required. For Oxfam, the justification for operating an importing company throughout the 1960s seemed to be a straightforward case of responding to the desperate need for employment that existed throughout the developing world. A campaign leaflet stated that: 'One in every three people in need of work in the so-called developing countries of Africa, Asia and Latin-America is unable to get a regular job.'[22] These sentiments were consistent with the first UN Development Decade's focus on 'trade not aid'. But this uncritical stance regarding the mutual benefits of trade with developing countries was not that different to those arguments used by multinational corporations (MNCs) to justify their presence in oppressive regimes including South Africa.[23] A closer evaluation of the terms of trade operated by Oxfam Activities and HbS during the 1960s, reveals a commercial outlook not entirely compatible with modern definitions of Fair Trade.[24]

Oxfam Activities: Christmas cards and corporation tax

A government review of charity tax exemptions included in the Finance Act of 1965 ruled that charities would be liable for income tax on trading activities, unless they set up subsidiary trading companies which would then covenant to pay profits back to the charity. Oxfam was one of the few charities that had acted relatively swiftly in forming a new trading company. The Guardian reported, in November 1966, that most of the 150 charities selling Christmas cards had not yet set up trading companies and would therefore be liable for 40% corporation tax on their net profits.[25] The timing of the formation of Oxfam Activities, in 1964, actually had more to do with the pressure from the Charity Commission and the Inland Revenue, than efforts to pioneer 'trade not aid'. Many charities resented the pressure to form trading companies.

Some charity organisers were concerned that: 'Once trading companies are organised ... charities may be tempted to expand trading beyond the traditional Christmas card.'[26] Oxfam did indeed extend its trading activities beyond Christmas cards and its expanding retail programme represented only one sector of its commercial portfolio. Throughout the 1960s and 1970s Oxfam Activities was responsible for the growth of a number of new ventures that aligned commercial consumer services and charitable fundraising for Oxfam.[27]

Helping by Selling (HbS) was set up in 1967 to coordinate Oxfam's relatively ad hoc international trading arrangements and was soon able to capitalise on Oxfam's growing high street presence. Peter Burnell, in his survey of development charities in Britain noted that: 'The Oxfam shops, which sell Third World handcrafts as well as donated goods, are crucial. Not only do they help shape the general public's perception of the charity, but they also consistently generate around 30 per cent of its income.'[28] Oxfam's growing network of shops, from only 4 in 1962 to 136 by 1967, were a significant factor in driving Oxfam's early international trading programme and not only in commercial terms. Maggie Black, in writing Oxfam's official history argued that, 'in opting for shops as the fundraising way forward, Oxfam subconsciously made a choice about what kind of organisation it would be in terms of character of its support and broad public perception of its activities'.[29] This assessment, often overlooked in academic literature, offers an insight into both the internal challenges faced by Oxfam in balancing trading and fundraising, and the wider public challenge of engaging consumers and charity supporters.

The import programme run by HbS focused mainly on handcrafts that utilized low-level technology and could provide employment for large numbers of people. HbS favoured what it described as 'appropriate "labour-intensive" rather than "capital intensive" industries'.[30] This practical response fitted with the hands-on nature of Oxfam's charter, 'When there is so much we can do now we don't intend sitting around talking about it.'[31] But beyond the immediate benefits of providing employment, there was only limited consideration of the wider impacts of the business. Issues of working conditions, pay, community involvement and the environment were not directly addressed and therefore effectively remained 'externalities'. The idea that the 1960s was a time when, 'Northern ATOs did not seek to make a profit that would accrue to private pockets, but instead sought to cover operating costs and direct all remaining profits into the hands of Southern producer groups', underestimates the difficulty in making this vision a reality and conflicts with contemporary accounts that describe the challenges faced by ATOs such as Oxfam.[32] In 1970 Guy Stringer, the newly appointed Commercial Director, noted his concern that 'it is necessary to persuade our organisers and supporters to be less worried about the profit from this operation and to see it much more clearly as a form of aid'.[33]

By the late 1960s HbS was established as a commercially successful venture and by the mid-1970s had also become an important source of income for Oxfam – representing 47% of Oxfam Trading's total sales and returning profits of £90,000 on sales of £343,564 in 1974.[34] But this level of profitability also strengthened calls from some staff that Oxfam should consider a systematic review of the trading principles and practices of HbS. Although it had set out to assist producers in the 'Third World' by developing trade partnerships, there were few guidelines as to how this could be achieved. What was required was a clear framework that would allow Oxfam to assess its own performance and provide greater transparency for supporters and shoppers.

An internal evaluation of Oxfam's international trading programme, undertaken in the mid-1980s, offered an opportunity to review key achievements and reconsider the position of trade within the wider context of Oxfam's work. The author of the report, Jonathon Stockland, argued that although Oxfam's rationalisation of its trading operations in the 1960s was clearly a pragmatic response, it represented a 'missed the opportunity to explore the wide range of possibilities inherent in the trading operation that was growing out of Oxfam's other relief work and which could, if so conceived, become a conscious extension of that work in fundamental agreement with Oxfam's own principles of existence'.[35] In practice, throughout the 1960s, Oxfam's HbS programme was trading along essentially commercial lines. Products imported from the 'Third World' were to be stocked in Oxfam's shops and sold for a profit which would then contribute towards Oxfam's international relief and development work.

Oxfam Bridge: The search for a 'Socially Ideal' model of trade

In 1972, Roy Scott, a manager at Oxfam Trading, began work on creating a new type of trading venture. Scott believed that Helping by Selling (HbS) was only, 'a very limited "fair-trade" importing programme'.[36] He argued that HbS was too close to the trading values of commercial importers and in a drive to make profit they were ignoring the development potential of international trade. Scott identified the following failings of HbS: they paid wages that were no better than the market rate, they did not make advance payments, and they gave producers no commitment to long-term development. He argued that Oxfam's trading operations should act as a practical demonstration of 'the kind of socially "ideal" trade system most supporters of the Third World believe is necessary'.[37] It was this critique of Oxfam's existing trading programme, and detailed proposals for an alternative, that laid the groundwork for establishing the key principles of 'alternative' – or 'fair' – trade. In terms of Oxfam's ability to link trade and development this new venture 'Oxfam Bridge' represented Fair Trade 2.0.[38]

Roy Scott outlined his concerns about HbS and proposed a new direction for Oxfam Trading's importing programme in May 1972, *The Future of the Helping by Selling Project*. Scott argued that the limiting factor for 'Third World' development was not simply lack of jobs, but a trade system weighted against the poorest, which revealed remnants of colonial exploitation. Scott maintained that: 'The present international trade structures prevent the average producer in the Third World from gaining even his minimum living from the work of his own hands.'[39] At the heart of Scott's critique was the condemnation of the involvement of 'profit-seeking employers, middlemen, agents and exporters'.[40] Scott framed the problem as one of exploitation by the middleman of those left vulnerable by an unregulated marketplace. There are parallels here with E. P. Thompson's moral economy of the eighteenth century – except that the moralising element is not found within the community but is imposed from outside.[41]

Scott put forward three proposals to the Oxfam Executive for consideration. The name of the new trading venture would be Oxfam Bridge, but how this would fit within Oxfam's existing structure was a contentious issue. Each proposal set out a distinct vision and purpose for the new organisation: 'Bridge as an Oxfam enterprise', 'Bridge as an Oxfam programme', or 'Bridge as an Oxfam initiative'.[42] The first proposal, 'Bridge as an Oxfam enterprise', would keep the HbS structure intact and prioritised HbS' fundraising function. Oxfam's trading partnership was seen as 'a means not an end' and what was outlined was an extension of 'Helping by Selling without any major new policies or structural changes.'[43] Proposal two, 'Bridge as an Oxfam programme', was for a totally independent organisation established with an Oxfam aid grant but then expected to be self-financing.[44] The management board would be made up of democratically elected representatives of producers and consumers. This proposal was sold as a 'brave independent movement liberating producers entirely from continuing charity support'.[45] The third proposal 'Bridge as an Oxfam initiative' was a compromise. A new subsidiary company would be established with its own board of management, but control would remain firmly with Oxfam.

It was the second, more ambitious, proposal that Scott believed had the greatest potential. Scott's solution was to remove the middleman and form an international co-operative, 'a "bridge" linking worker-producers of very poor countries with the ordinary shopper here in Europe'.[46] Scott's plans envisaged an organisational structure that would eventually lead to Bridge being run jointly by the consumers and producers independent of Oxfam. Scott outlined four stages of development, from the initial phase when the Board of Trustees represented the joint interests of all producers and consumers, through to the theoretical absolute situation, whereby a poll of Bridge producers counted for 50% of the total vote and equally Bridge consumers would make up 50% of the voting strength.[47] In this final model, the Board of Trustees would have no voting rights and Bridge would be organised as an independent co-operative. The role of the consumer was not envisaged by Scott as charity or paternalism. He argued that Bridge should, 'guarantee a fair price to producers, and the availability of their products also at a fair price to the common man in the consumer's country'.[48] The equality in the proposed consumer/producer relationship was most notably demonstrated by the existence of dividends not only for producers but also for consumers as well. The consumer dividend was to be 10% and would be allocated by the Bridge Committee for publications and educational activities that would 'increase internationalism, understanding and appreciation of the world community'.[49]

When Bridge was launched in June 1975, it was as a new subsidiary company with its own board of management, but control remained with Oxfam. This was not the progressive model outlined in Scott's original vision, but Bridge did represent a genuine attempt to prioritise a more equal relationship between the producer and consumer. Bridge's mission statement from November 1975 stated that it was 'dedicated towards providing the best possible employment, earnings, working and social environments for producers; and fair prices, quality and service for customers'.[50] Oxfam was now committed to an international trade programme that went beyond the considerations of commercial buyers in order to ensure that those producers making goods, imported and sold by Oxfam, would receive a 'fair' return for their work. In the first year of trading (May 1975–April 1976) Bridge achieved sales of over £500,000 which translated to a net profit of £81,296 to be made available for dividends.[51] Oxfam's Commercial and Deputy Director, Guy

Stringer, described this first distribution of the producer dividend, as 'a very significant advance in the history of Oxfam Activities, and in my view of Oxfam'.[52] If the 1960s represented a 'beta version' of Fair Trade – then, by the mid-1970s, the majority of the major fixes and revisions had been addressed and the programme was now 'fit for purpose'.

In September 1976, as Bridge seemed to be succeeding in its joint aims of development and profitability, Roy Scott made the shock announcement that he was resigning, apparently unhappy at the way the trading philosophy had been diluted.[53] The story was reported in the Sunday Times,: 'The Oxfam executive charged with building up Bridge, Roy Scott, has just resigned. He feels that corruption and exploitation have, perhaps inevitably, crept into the project.'[54] Scott believed that Oxfam had essentially shunned the ideals of Bridge in a bid for short-term growth, 'Oxfam couldn't cope with the idea of Bridge as an international co-operative.'[55] At the moment when the Fair Trade model offered so much potential as a 'brave independent movement', it seemed that Oxfam's instinct was to step back and retreat to the more familiar and conservative role of charity support. But Oxfam's reluctance was not simply a rejection of the 'radical' – its vision for the new trading programme was a nuanced blend of the pragmatic and the political. It is clear that there was some uncertainty within the Oxfam Executive Committee about the idea of an international co-operative. First, there were practical concerns about how Oxfam would oversee the operations of the co-operative in its early years. Secondly, (as explored in Chapter 3), by the mid-1970s doubts were being raised within Oxfam about the effectiveness of the co-operative model in promoting international development. But arguably, the decisive factor was that Oxfam recognised the value of maintaining its own international trading company. This was not judged to be purely in terms of raising income, but also that it provided Oxfam with a justification for engaging with Third World development in a manner that may otherwise have been judged to be beyond its charitable remit.

From the early 1960s, Oxfam had received an increasing number of repudiations from the Charity Commission challenging Oxfam's right to provide 'development' aid and questioning the objectives of its campaigns.[56] The 1962 Charity Commissioners Report clarified its position that: 'Propaganda and advocacy for legislation, whether in this country or overseas, have been described by the courts as political, and not charitable; so, too, has the promotion of international friendship'.[57] Although Bridge, as a trading subsidiary of Oxfam, was not beyond the regulatory interventions of the Charity Commission, in practice the producer dividend scheme gave Oxfam a considerably freer rein in its support for community development projects. A review of Bridge producer dividends for 1975–1976 demonstrated the range of projects that were supported, including: loans for seeds and fertilizers, subsidies for sewing machines and co-operative and vocational training.[58] As the Bridge programme expanded, an increasing number of applications were submitted that called for funding for infrastructure development. In September 1980, Oxfam approved a £14,445 application for a new warehouse and workshop for the Palam Rural Centre, a group of leather workers producing leather sandals and belts in Tamil Nadu, India.[59] Support for these programmes, via producer dividends received little public attention, but had these projects been directly funded by Oxfam grants it is conceivable that the Charity Commission could have questioned whether they represented a direct response to tackling 'observable poverty'.[60]

It was not only in supporting producer development projects that Bridge was able to make an impact on Oxfam's work. Bridge's campaigning work was equally significant. A Bridge leaflet from 1975 stated that:

> The biggest reason why people earn so little is *exploitation*. With so much unemployment and poverty around it's very easy to pay people virtually nothing for a day's work ... Bridge openly admits it's here to break this: to give a better deal to the mass of ordinary working people.[61]

The political implications of this campaign would have almost certainly been judged to have gone too far had it been produced by Oxfam in its charitable capacity. But by focusing on the need for consumer action, rather than the agency of the citizen or voter, Bridge was able to engage with a more openly political discourse.

Oxfam Bridge: Expansion and consolidation

Throughout the 1970s and 1980s Oxfam Bridge had focused primarily on importing handcrafts. The emphasis was on utilitarian articles that were thought to have a better chance of repeat sales and therefore offer greater job security. Products purchased fitted within two main categories of home goods: furniture, kitchen utensils, children's toys, mats, rugs and other textile products; or personal accessories: scarves, ties, belts, gloves, footwear, jewellery, bags, baskets, wallets and purses.[62] The success of handcrafts in Oxfam shops was part of a wider consumer trend for handcrafted products during this period. It was estimated that European countries imported more than $500 million worth of handcrafts in 1978–1979.[63] This reflected a growing interest in artisan-made decorative and household goods that illustrated the creative and artistic skill often lacking in the mass produced goods of modern consumer societies.

Oxfam also had some experience of importing food products, but this had not been straightforward and served to highlight the complexity of trying to operate an alternative model within existing commodity markets. Oxfam Bridge had begun importing tea in 1977, in response to consumer campaigns for fair tea prices.[64] The tea was sourced from several co-operatives in Darjeeling, Assam and Nilgiris and was blended and packed in India.[65] But in 1989, the Bridge management decided to stop importing tea from the Tea Corporation of India because it had become impossible to guarantee a 'Fair Trade' supply.[66] Owing to the variation in quality from estate to estate and from harvest to harvest it was necessary to blend from different sources to produce an acceptable year-round product.

Virtually all tea produced in India was sold at auction, which made it difficult to guarantee the exact origin. Buying directly from small co-operatives was equally problematic since this tea tended to be of lower quality and needed to be blended with 60% of higher quality tea from other estates. Bridge buyers were forced to admit that 'Oxfam's tea is purchased from the same tea auctions as that of multinational companies.'[67] If Fair Trade was to rely on the goodwill of the consumer it was suggested that Bridge should be more honest with consumers about the difficulties of international supply chains. Bridge management acknowledged that the withdrawal of tea would lead to questions from consumers, but they remained committed to be 'as honest and open as we can about the difficulties of trading fairly in commodity industries such as that of tea'.[68]

The popularity of Bridge handcrafts continued to build throughout the 1980s with sales growing from £900,000 in 1980 to £2.4 million by 1985. Bridge was also becoming increasingly important within the Oxfam Trading representing 52% of total sales in 1985 compared with 36% in 1980.[69] With Oxfam's high street presence becoming well-established, it is perhaps surprising that Bridge was achieving strong sales despite only being stocked in 389 of Oxfam's 777 shops in 1985 – and only operating three specialist Bridge stores.[70] The initial reluctance to promote Bridge more widely was partly a cautious approach by managers not wanting to expose Oxfam to undue commercial risk, but primarily it was a strategic response to the charity regulations and guidance surrounding rate relief. Oxfam shops represented an important stream of fundraising revenue and many shop managers were reluctant to offer space to the less profitable Bridge goods. This tension was heightened by the fact that shops could claim charity rate relief if they were able to satisfy the local authority that the shop was occupied by the charity 'mainly' for the purpose of selling the donated goods.[71] By 1990, following the recommendations of the Stockland evaluation, distribution of Bridge products was expanded to cover 600 of the 850 shops operating at that time. Stockland had argued that Oxfam Trading should view Bridge more clearly as a form of 'visible aid'.[72]

How to support the poorest producers and be commercially viable?

As Bridge expanded, a debate developed within Oxfam about who Bridge should be buying from. The debate centred on how to support the poorest producers and still run Bridge as a viable enterprise. It was Oxfam's field staff that had the task of classifying producer groups as either 'priority' or 'non-priority'. Priority groups were judged to have 'clear social objectives' and 'encouraged producer participation in the running of their organisation'.[73] Non-priority groups did not place an emphasis on social objectives or producer participation, but were regarded by the Oxfam Trading staff as being 'reasonable employers'.[74] The distinction was reinforced in February 1988, when it was decided that only priority groups should receive dividends. But even with the best intentions, it was not always a straightforward task for Bridge buyers to determine the true merits of a particular producer organisation. Jeremy Shaw, in his report on India, stated that he was surprised, 'how difficult it is to determine sometimes whether a producer is "true Bridge" or commercial, even when one is actually on the site'.[75] These difficulties were not unique to Oxfam, but they were given greater emphasis as a result of first-hand experience 'in the field'. This sometimes translated into heated internal debates. Bridge management accepted that producers they dealt with 'may not be the poorest of the poor by Oxfam's criteria in the field'.[76] But they argued that in the context of crafts production, orders and assistance were still being targeted to 'very needy people indeed'.[77]

Central to defining Bridge's objectives for helping the poorest producers was the geographical focus of its trading programme. In 1980, Maurice Zinkin, a commercial consultant, was employed to investigate these issues. Zinkin's assessment warned of the pitfalls of expanding too rapidly and reducing the effectiveness of the operation and the quality of producer assistance. Zinkin argued that: 'If we do not confine ourselves to a limited number of producers, preferably concentrated in specific geographical areas, we will find our effort is too diffused to be effective'.[78] Tensions about the geographic focus of Bridge imports continued to surface throughout the early 1980s. Zinkin reiterated his opposition to further expansion into Africa and South America and recommended that Bridge continue to focus its efforts on India where there was a strong crafts tradition and skilled producers, 'who are sufficiently poor for us to do so with a clean conscience and who benefit greatly from proper quality control'.[79] For those producers where the quality of craft was inadequate for export, it was suggested that assistance with the local market should be given. While this approach was no doubt pragmatic given Oxfam's limited resources and the higher risks associated with trade in Africa and South America, the majority of the Bridge Committee continued to support further expansion.

Despite the commercial challenges, the second half of the 1980s saw a sustained attempt to focus Bridge's trade on those geographic regions seen to be in greatest need. Backed by Stockland's evaluation, the Bridge Committee pushed for an extension of 'positive discrimination towards the least advantaged producers' and proposed that 'geographical sourcing is extended to Africa and the Americas'.[80] Edward Millard, Marketing Manager at Bridge was clear that: 'The main argument for developing in Africa was that great need existed and few other ATOs had the resources or the will to respond'.[81] In 1986, South Asia was still the main source of orders accounting for 60% (India alone made up 50.9% of all orders). In contrast, the whole of Africa only represented 1% of orders.[82] By 1990 there were signs of a gradual geographic diversification. Bridge had begun to reduce its dependence on South Asia as a reliable supplier of goods (its share of total orders fell to 42.4%) and this enabled greater capacity to be directed towards importing from African producers with their share of orders gradually rising to 5.2%.[83]

From handcrafts to food products: Support for IFAT and FLO

As discussed in the previous chapter, Fair Trade developed as a range of approaches and by the late 1980s two distinct channels were emerging: the independent product certification route as operated by Fairtrade International and the integrated supply chain route as supported by the

IFAT/WFTO.[84] In the United Kingdom, in contrast to the clear dividing lines that emerged in the United States and parts of Europe (particularly France, Spain and Italy), British-based ATOs and Fair Trade companies have not tended to align exclusively with a particular approach to Fair Trade. Leading Fair Trade companies including: Traidcraft, Cafédirect, Divine Chocolate and People Tree, have all, at various stages, been both members of the WFTO and also supporters of the Fairtrade Mark.[85] While Oxfam's support for both Fairtrade-labelled food products and 'fairly traded' handcrafts was not particularly controversial among the general public, it did prompt some internal discussion about Oxfam's priorities and the merits of handcraft production versus food products and commodities.

In July 1989, Oxfam joined the International Federation for Alternative Trade (IFAT).[86] This reflected a commitment by Oxfam to extend the benefits of producer support and networking across the Fair Trade movement. The Bridge committee recommended that, as the largest ATO, it seemed 'appropriate for Oxfam Trading to participate in the movement even though because of our resources we probably had more to give'.[87] As well as linking ATOs, forming IFAT was a significant step in advancing consumer/producer relations. Producer representatives were involved in the second IFAT conference. The IFAT Secretariat described this initiative as a 'watershed in forging more equitable North/South trading links'.[88]

By the early 1990s food products were beginning to be seen as increasingly important to the development of Oxfam's Fair Trade commitment. Bridge management argued that farmers, 'as much as any craft group, desperately need marketing support, to be able to sell their product directly overseas'.[89] With the successful launch of Max Havelaar coffee in the Netherlands, extending the offering of alternative food products sold in Oxfam shops was seen as consistent with Oxfam's wider Fair Trade goals. This was not just about capitalising on a growing niche market, instead it was argued that 'the really compelling reason for Oxfam Trading's commitment lies in the need for us to be a central participant in the Fair Trade debate. It is around food products much more than crafts that this is taking place.'[90] Although Bridge food sales only accounted for 7% of total sales in 1990, because of the relative size of the operation compared with other ATOs, sales of £600,000 still made Bridge one of the biggest food importers within the European Fair Trade Association (EFTA).[91]

The lessons of Oxfam Trading's experience importing tea from India persuaded them that future ventures should focus on coffee, where the source would be easier to guarantee. In 1989, Oxfam worked alongside Traidcraft, Equal Exchange and Twin Trading, to develop an 'ethical' coffee. Cafédirect would become the first joint initiative by leading British ATOs to create and market a Fair Trade product.[92] Bill Yates, Oxfam's head of campaigns, encouraged by developments at Cafédirect believed that Oxfam should support moves towards creating a Fair Trade label for use in the United Kingdom. Yates described the plans under discussion for a Fair Trade label as essentially a continuation of what ATOs had been doing for the past 15 years. He stated, 'of course, Twin Trading, Oxfam Trading and other Alternative Traders are already conducting their business on these lines'.[93] For Yates, the only real significance of the Mark was 'the sheer scale of the order quantities and the number of consumers and producers who would be affected'.[94]

Not everyone in the alternative trading community supported the move towards Fair Trade food products, some saw this as a step backwards. Roy Scott commented:

> Bizarre isn't it, you get countries away from cash crops by arguing value should stay with the producer – and now we have the wonderful rigmarole about how great all these food products are – all that is going on is we in Europe import the raw materials and do all the processing.[95]

Scott believed that Bridge's original focus on handcrafts had been for a good reason. Unlike cash crops, most handcrafts were not subject to import duties and this meant that producers could benefit from the value added in the manufacture process. Handcrafts were also a way of supplementing earnings from home and were a particularly valuable source of independent income for women.

During the early meetings of the steering committee, Oxfam Trading had remained 'largely peripheral to the FTM [Fairtrade Mark] project' and took only a minor role in planning wider campaign initiatives.[96] Oxfam recognised that support for the Fairtrade Mark could cause a dilemma for the operation of its own handcrafts programme. It was thought likely that 'many of the most vulnerable producers would who most needed the alternative market would fail to meet the criteria'.[97] They would then be overlooked by buyers, even alternative buyers. This potentially would lead to an awkward position where Oxfam would be a leading supporter of the Fairtrade Mark but not using it. It was agreed that for handcrafts that 'Oxfam's name itself could be the guarantee'.[98] As a result, at this early stage in its development, the criteria for Fairtrade certification was restricted to farmed products and commodities.[99]

In December 1989 the Bridge committee was asked 'whether expansion into Africa was a higher priority than putting resources and energy into the Fair Trade [*sic*] Mark initiative'.[100] Oxfam had been making regular grant contributions to the Fair Trade Mark steering committee (later renamed the Fairtrade Foundation) from 1990/91 but there were still some doubts within Oxfam about the direction of its Fair Trade programme. Internal discussions at Oxfam focused on the possible tensions between backing a scheme that offered the scale and impact of mainstream markets and their role in capacity-building working with marginalised producer communities in Africa. There was some justification at the time for reasoning that the immediate benefits of the Fairtrade Mark were more likely to be seen by producers in South America than Africa, as had been the case with the Max Havelaar certification of coffee.[101] Despite some reservations, by March 1991 support within Oxfam for the idea of the Fairtrade Mark was consolidating. Publicly, Fairtrade labelling was now endorsed as 'wholly in line with Bridge policy of seeking conventional commercial markets for producers'.[102]

OXFAM Fair Trade Company

In 1996 with growing public awareness of Fair Trade, Oxfam's international trading initiative 'Bridge', was renamed the 'Oxfam Fair Trade Company'. Three years later, the Oxfam Fair Trade Company, with a turnover of €10.7 million, was still recognised as one of the 'big four' European Fair Trade importers alongside: GEPA €29.8 million, Fair Trade Organisatie €15.9 million, Traidcraft €12.4 million.[103] With 1,700 product lines stocked in 400 of its high street shops, Oxfam Fair Trade Company represented over 15% of the total UK Fair Trade market.[104] But by the end of 2002, Oxfam's own Fair Trade products were no longer stocked in Oxfam shops and the trading company had been wound up. What had happened to Oxfam's Fair Trade programme – why did it decide to exit the market just as consumer demand appeared to be taking-off?

At the time, Oxfam chose not to make a public statement explaining its decision to stop importing Fair Trade products. The story was only picked up, somewhat belatedly, by *The Observer* in January 2003. But this article did little to clarify Oxfam's position and only raised more questions. The report stated that: 'Oxfam had decided to scrap the brand for "commercial" reasons'.[105] Retail analyst, Alison Clements, was called upon to provide an explanation. She argued that 'persistent public indifference to ethical concerns had finally proved insurmountable'.[106]

It was noted that just 3% of UK shoppers regularly bought Fair Trade products, despite the majority being aware of the scheme. Clements concluded that 'price is becoming more important than ever'.[107] The Fairtrade Foundation, attempting to set the record straight, highlighted the fact that sales of Fair Trade goods in the United Kingdom had grown from £43 million in 2001 to £53 million in 2002. The Foundation argued that: 'Oxfam's decision is not because there isn't an interest in the market, it's because the market has grown.'[108]

So was Oxfam bowing to market indifference or was its decision an indication that Fair Trade was coming of age? Oxfam did face commercial pressures, but this was driven more by the declining fashionability of handcrafts rather than consumer indifference to ethical concerns. By the late 1980s, with the trend for 'ethnic crafts' declining Oxfam recognised that the food sector looked likely to emerge as an important market for Fair Trade. But the dilemma for Oxfam Trading managers was that Oxfam shops did not seem well-positioned to expand their range of Fair Trade food products. Despite stocking tea and spices from the late 1970s and supporting Cafédirect from its launch in 1991, a survey conducted in 1996 found that only 3% of shoppers knew that Oxfam sold food and even among regular customers only 27% were aware of Oxfam's Fair Trade food range.[109] The structure of the Oxfam Fair Trade Company was evolving – but slowly. On one side of the business there was a lack of retail engagement with consumers about Fair Trade food, and on the other, there were Oxfam buyers with long-term trading relationships and contracts with handcraft producers. So by 2001, the balance of the business was still firmly towards handcrafts – representing over 70% of the organisation's turnover.[110]

However, 'commercial reasons' only partly explain the changes in Oxfam's Fair Trade programme. As shown earlier Oxfam's involvement with Fair Trade had always been closely connected to its campaigning agenda, and operating a trading company had successfully allowed Oxfam to engage in longer-term development work. Given this wider 'political' context, Oxfam's positioning of its advocacy role and the requirements of UK Charity Law were an equally important consideration. Throughout the 1990s there were signs that the Charity Commission was beginning to adopt a more broadly defined approach to the alleviation of poverty overseas (as reflected in the Fairtrade Foundation's successful application for charitable status in 1995). For Oxfam this raised questions about the impact and benefits of its direct involvement with Fair Trade – could its advocacy work be expanded in this area without operating a trading company?

In 2000, Oxfam commissioned an independent impact assessment of its Fair Trade programme. The report, conducted by Raul Hopkins an economist at the International Fund for Agricultural Development (IFAD), focused on the impact of Oxfam's trading links with 18 producer groups. The remit of the study was wide-ranging, 'to investigate the claim that Fair Trade alleviates poverty and improves the well being of producers and their families'.[111] The main emphasis was given to the analysis of handcrafts (in the final sample there was only one food producer group).[112] The report found that craft production was, for many families, a vital source of complimentary income to subsistence farming, and that for many groups the additional income received from Oxfam Fair Trade made a significant impact to their overall well-being. The findings showed that in more than 40% of the producer groups, the increase in income was above 45%, and the average increase was 28%.[113] Overall it was recommended that the positive, and measurable, impact on income and well-being of producer groups demonstrated good reason for continuing support for the Oxfam Fair Trade Programme.[114]

The report also identified some areas where there was scope for improved 'institutional learning'.[115] Perhaps most significantly, it was clear that despite extensive efforts aimed at a capacity-building, little had been achieved in terms of accessing the mainstream international market. Oxfam's ambition was that by empowering producer groups and assisting with product development, producers would develop the market knowledge and business skills required to deal with commercial buyers independently from Oxfam Fair Trade. But the impact assessment found that there was little sign of this diversification and many producer groups remained dependent on Oxfam for at least half of their sales. On average, 75% of sales went to Fair Trade organisations (including Oxfam Fair Trade), 21% went to the domestic market and only 4% went to commercial markets. The report's conclusion called for a new consideration of Oxfam's role in relation to global markets. Hopkins proposed that 'the aim cannot be limited to accessing mainstream markets but, in addition, to influence the terms in which this market operates. This implies a greater role for advocacy work within Oxfam's Fair Trade agenda.'[116]

Rather than the commercial challenges, it was the bigger conceptual and political questions emerging from this assessment that preoccupied Oxfam. Accessing mainstream markets would not necessarily lead to better incomes and improved producer well-being without structural changes to the global market. This suggested that a new theory of change was required – one that more directly addressed issues of power and politics. A renewed focus on campaigning and advocacy was not incompatible with running a Fair Trade programme, but there was a sense within Oxfam that its resources and expertise could make a greater impact directed towards research and policy interventions. The increased profile of the Department for International Development (DFID) under the Labour administration (1997–2010) and broad cross-party support for Fairtrade within the House of Commons, offered an opportunity for further political progress at a national and international level. This new campaigning focus was in evidence in 2005 as the United Kingdom geared up to host the G8 Summit. Make Poverty History and Live 8 made the headlines as the most high profile and media-friendly events, but behind the scenes Oxfam GB (Great Britain) had been building support for Oxfam International's Make Trade Fair campaign. Oxfam's 'Big Noise', the popular mobilisation element of the Make Trade Fair campaign, had by December 2005 received the backing of 17.8 million people internationally – making it one of the world's largest ever petitions.[117]

Oxfam's withdrawal from Fair Trade importing happened relatively quickly, but most producers were able to find alternative buyers either in Europe or in local markets.[118] But what impact did Oxfam's decision to withdraw from its Fair Trade importing programme have on the Fair Trade movement in Britain? On one level this move represented a step towards a more corporate mainstream identity for Fair Trade and shifted the balance towards certified Fairtrade food products. But it would be a mistake to characterise this decision as the end of Oxfam GB's involvement with Fair Trade. Oxfam continued its membership role as a charity shareholder of the Fairtrade Foundation and retained its founder role as a Guardian of Cafédirect Gold Standard.[119] Although no longer importing its own range of Fair Trade products, Oxfam shops still offer an 'alternative' outlet on the UK high street for Fair Trade shoppers and stock a wide range of products from 100% Fair Trade companies including: Traidcraft, Cafédirect and Divine Chocolate.

Conclusions

Oxfam has been an important part of the Fair Trade story both in Britain and internationally. By applying its practical experience of poverty alleviation Oxfam was able to go beyond general statements of 'trade not aid' and implement an alternative model of trade that brought benefits to the producers and communities it worked with. In 1970, Oxfam's Public Charter positioned its advocacy role clearly in terms of positive campaigning and engagement: 'Oxfam is "for" not "against". To be "anti" is to risk appearing to know only what one does not want.'[120] For the most part, this approach was aligned with a Fair Trade programme that sought to improve pay and working conditions for producer communities – but could this strategy really challenge the wider injustices in the global trade system? Perhaps more than any other organisation, Oxfam has shown the potential and limitations of an approach to Fair Trade that sought to unite commercial, political and charitable objectives.

Over the last 40 years the social, economic and political context of international development has changed dramatically, and Oxfam's Fair Trade programme has adapted to, and at times influenced, the re-evaluations and changes in development philosophy, business ethics and charity law. Perhaps the most significant change in recent years has been Oxfam's engagement with the political dimensions of trade and international development, (and the general acceptance by the British public and government of this role). It is still too early to judge whether the reappointment of William Shawcross as Chairman of the Charity Commission will substantially affect the regulatory environment, but if there are changes Oxfam's response will no doubt be closely followed by supporters and political commentators alike.[121] Under the current charity law, (Charities Act 2011), it seems unlikely that Oxfam would be required to make significant changes to its operations or charitable remit. However, it is interesting to note that in 1979 Brian Walker, Oxfam's Director at the time, felt it necessary to discuss with the Charity Commission the 'possibility of Oxfam becoming a non-charitable body'.[122] It is unclear how far this might have gone, but the Charity Commission did appear to take the matter seriously and responded that 'there would be serious repercussions both for Oxfam and the charitable world as whole. We hope that this step will not be taken for the sake of pursuing activities, such as land-reform, which are essentially political.'[123]

Oxfam's current approach to development thinking is most clearly expressed in *From Poverty to Power*.[124] This book represents a genuine attempt to consider how change happens and Oxfam's role in what is recognised as a complex and unpredictable world.[125] Duncan Green, Oxfam GB's Senior Strategic Advisor, sets outs Oxfam's position on key development issues including: income inequality; women's rights and political development; economic growth; climate change; and international systems of finance, trade and aid.[126] In a thesis that would have not been possible ten years ago, Green directly addresses political and philosophical issues previously considered beyond the scope of 'charity'. Government-led redistribution and employment programmes are assessed favourably in case studies of Taiwan, Vietnam and Brazil, and the role of progressive taxation and radical land reform are also considered as part of broad-based understanding of development.[127]

The marginal consideration afforded to Fair Trade within Oxfam's new theory of change and food justice campaigning is perhaps surprising given the historic importance of Oxfam's Fair Trade programme. While recognising the growing consumer market, Oxfam ultimately characterises Fair Trade as a 'niche solution'. Green argues that: 'Fair trade is neither a panacea, nor a substitute for wider reform of international trading systems'.[128] Launched in 2011, Oxfam's GROW campaign represented the start of a new high-profile campaign on global food justice.[129] To focus consumer attention on the world's biggest food brands Oxfam developed an online 'Behind the Brands' company scorecard.[130] However, in collating this data, Oxfam chose to award FLO certification only a marginally higher weighting than either Rainforest Alliance or UTZ Certified.[131] Was this simply a clerical oversight? Perhaps, but it may also suggest that unless Fairtrade International is able to communicate a theory of change that engages with Oxfam's understanding of active citizens and effective states – Fairtrade, as an idea, may be in danger of losing some of its 'stickiness'.

2
Christian Ethics and Economics: Voluntary Organisations and Alternative Trade

'Only vicars would be mad enough to buy them.'[1] This was the reason given by one supermarket chief for not listing Fair Trade products in the early 1990s. Retailers argued that paying a Fair Trade premium would only appeal to a niche demographic. This response has been used by commentators to illustrate how out of touch many supermarkets seemed about the potential for Fair Trade and ethical goods. However, while the market for Fair Trade was clearly not only limited to vicars, the support of Christian groups has played an important role in the progression of the Fair Trade movement and this has yet to be properly addressed in the academic literature. The limited research in this area is perhaps a wider reflection of how the role of religion has been downplayed in order to 'package' Fair Trade to fit with conventional consumer marketing. In countering this imbalance, this chapter does not intend to characterise Fair Trade as an exclusively Christian mission; this would be a step too far. Instead, the aim is to investigate how contemporary Christian perspectives about ethics, justice and fairness developed, and to better understand the role of Christian voluntary organisations within the growing network of Alternative Trade Organisations (ATOs) and campaigners working on Fair Trade.

Internationally, many Fair Trade companies that are now household names can trace their origins to the work of religious groups and Christian development agencies. In the Netherlands, Fair Trade Organisatie (the first ATO to bring coffee to Fair Trade markets in Europe) was set up by Dutch Catholics.[2] In Germany, GEPA (one of 'the big four' European Fair Trade importers) was jointly financed by Protestant and Catholic Churches through 'Bread for the World' and 'Misereor'.[3] In Australia, TradeWinds was the inspiration of Father Emmett Devlin, a Dominican

Priest.[4] In the mid-1970s, with financial backing from the Australian Catholic Relief and World Christian Action, TradeWinds began importing tea from Sri Lanka.[5] In North America, Ten Thousand Villages was started by a Mennonite Central Committee (MCC) worker who brought embroidery from Puerto Rico to sell in the United States.[6] In the early 1970s the project was established as an official MCC programme. And in the United Kingdom, Tearcraft (with the financial backing of Tearfund) began importing jute handcrafts from producers in Bangladesh in 1974.

The participation of Christian groups with early Fair Trade ventures has been reasonably well documented, but what has not been properly investigated is the wider impact of this involvement on the ideas and practices of Fair Trade. Moving beyond immediate church-based networks offers an opportunity to consider important social and cultural questions such as: What role have Christian beliefs and teachings played within the Fair Trade movement and did this change as Fairtrade entered the mainstream? Can the success of Fairtrade be linked to a resurgence of support for Christian ethics? Or, to borrow the terminology of social historian Alan Gilbert, did 'worldly standards' become, 'the arbiters of Christian ethics'?[7]

Charity and Christian voluntary organisations

Historically, charity has been closely aligned with a religious sense of duty towards helping others and has been identified as, 'a markedly Christianized concept'.[8] The mission statements of Christian charities refer to Bible passages from both the Old and the New Testament, that declare the responsibility of Christians to be the salt and light (Matthew 5), to love thy neighbour (Luke 10:27) and to bring about God's justice and mercy (Micah 6:8).[9] And in turn, these teachings are positioned as central to the Church's purpose and vital to the Church's role as an agent of change. Today there are approximately 30,000 charities on the Charity Commission's Register with aims that include advancing religion.[10] William Shawcross, Charity Commissioner recognised that:

> People of faith – particularly Christians – have formed the backbone of civil society and charitable giving in this country for at least a thousand years. Not only are millions of individuals motivated by their faith to give of their time and money to charities right across the register. There are also tens of thousands of registered charities with the specific purpose to advance religion.[11]

This sense of moral action as the driver of charity has been criticised for reinforcing the hierarchical distinctions between donor and recipient.[12] However, the nature of this relationship is more complex than simply the depoliticisation of long-term political and economic struggles. The work of Christian voluntary organisations offers a multifaceted perspective on charity and moral action in the conceptual development of Fair Trade.

The history of charity as a Christian mission and the role of Christian voluntary organisations as 'service providers' has, for the most part, been surprisingly overlooked in studies of modern Britain. This omission is also reflected in studies of Fair Trade. Social historian, Frank Prochaska, commenting on the limited literature on Christian voluntary organisations, has stated that: 'Whenever one thinks about the ongoing debate on secularization, the role of charity in the equation remains something of a mystery'.[13] Prochaska's opinion was that Christian voluntary organisations would maintain the upper hand over state assistance, 'only so long as Christianity provided a compelling explanation for the ills of society – and the capacity and commitment to combat them'.[14] For Prochaska, the post-war creation of the welfare state signalled that there was 'a decisive winner in the debate over social policy'.[15]

If the relevance of Christian charity at home had diminished by the late twentieth century, public support for the work of Christian agencies overseas proved surprisingly resilient. Prochaska, explained that Christian agencies such as Christian Aid and CAFOD were perhaps well placed, 'to pioneer ahead of government or to work in areas in which the state had little interest'.[16] This assessment was backed up by the findings of the 1990 European Values Study (EVS). In response to the question: 'Do you think it is proper for churches to speak out on Third World problems?' 76% of European respondents answered – yes.[17] While the Church may have lost its preeminent position as arbiter of individual morality, on issues of aid and international development, it seemed that the majority of the general public still viewed the Church as making a significant and relevant contribution. And in Britain, support for the Church's public role on Third World issues was even higher, showing a level of support slightly above the European average.[18]

As the official overseas development and relief agencies of the Christian Churches: Christian Aid, CAFOD and Tearfund, have operated their international development programmes backed by the public support of the major Christian denominations represented in the United Kingdom. All three of these agencies are current member organisations of the Fairtrade Foundation, and both Christian Aid and CAFOD were founding members.[19] Throughout this chapter the work of these

Christian development agencies (and their related trading organisations) will be investigated in order to explore how far Christian values and teachings have shaped the ethics, business practices and consumer understanding of Fair Trade. The following section provides a brief historical sketch of the post-war establishment and growth of Christian Aid, CAFOD and Tearfund and outlines their mandates as leading Christian charities.

Christian Aid

Christian Aid's mandate defines its work as, 'founded on Christian faith, inspired by hope and acts to change an unjust world through charity – a practical love and care for our neighbours'.[20] Started in 1945, 'Christian Reconstruction in Europe', the precursor to Christian Aid, grew up as the aid and development division of the British Council of Churches.[21] From 1949, the movement became the Inter-Church Aid and Refugee Service; this marked a broadening of its stated purpose to include longer term development. In 1957, Inter-Church Aid and Refugee Service held a door-to-door collection in 200 towns and villages across the United Kingdom. This was the first Christian Aid Week and in total raised £26,000.[22] The concept of Christian Aid Week proved a very effective way of raising not only funds, but awareness. Reflecting the widespread public recognition of Christian Aid Week, in 1964 the organisation changed its name to Christian Aid. Christian Aid's most recent accounts show that the charity now has an income of £103.6 million and is supported by a staff of 872 and 100,000 volunteers.[23]

CAFOD

CAFOD's values and mission are founded in the teachings of Catholicism: 'We are inspired by Scripture, Catholic Social Teaching and by the experiences and hopes of people who are disadvantaged and living in poverty. We work with people of all faiths and none.'[24] In March 1960, the National Board of Catholic Women organised the first 'Family Fast Day' in response to a request from the people of Dominica for help with a mother-and-baby healthcare programme. Around 600,000 hand-made leaflets were distributed around parishes in England and Wales, asking people to 'go without, so that others may have'.[25] During this first campaign £6,673 was raised for a clinic in Dominica.[26] Two years later, the Catholic Fund for Overseas Development (CAFOD), was officially established by the Catholic Bishops of England and Wales, to facilitate Catholic participation in the Freedom from Hunger Campaign.[27] In 1965, CAFOD became a member of Caritas Internationalis and its development work expanded to include 74 international projects.[28] CAFOD's most recent accounts show that the charity now has an income of £51.3 million and is supported by a staff of 460 and 3,100 volunteers.[29]

Tearfund[30]

Tearfund's values set out its commitment, 'to work with and through a worldwide network of local churches – forming one global church – to end poverty'.[31] Tearfund owes its origins to the World Refugee Year (1959–1960). Heightened awareness of the plight of refugees resulted in a flow of unsolicited donations to the British Evangelical Alliance. Many of these donations were sent with requests that the money be sent to Christian missionaries working with refugees. These donations were recorded in a file marked Evangelical Alliance Refugee Fund (EAR Fund).[32] In 1968, the decision was taken to develop EAR Fund and go public under the leadership of Rev. George Hoffman. In November 1968 the name was changed to The Evangelical Alliance Relief Fund, or Tear Fund.[33] Hoffman in the first *Tear Times*, speaking of Tear Fund's objectives, stated, 'we believe we have an added responsibility – like the Catholic and Quaker agencies to their constituencies – to arrest the attention of Evangelicals in this country, and inform them of the needs, requirements and the opportunities to help'.[34] Tearfund's most recent accounts show that the charity now has an income of £59.4 million and is supported by a staff of 1,139 and 3,200 volunteers.[35]

In recent years, Fair Trade campaigners have been at pains to emphasise that the ambitions of the movement should not be limited by the boundaries traditionally associated with 'charity'. Bruce Crowther, Fairtrade Towns Co-ordinator at the Fairtrade Foundation, has argued that: 'People see it as charity, but it is not, it is justice. We have to get rid of the charity way of thinking.'[36] Academic accounts of the mainstreaming of Fair Trade have also reinforced the idea that 'Fair Trade is not about charity or aid'.[37] However, despite the public distancing of modern Fair Trade from charitable 'good works', the historical links to charity and charitable institutions remain and continue to inform the character of Fair Trade in the United Kingdom. It should be remembered that the Fairtrade Foundation is a registered UK charity and its charitable objects are defined as: '1. To relieve poverty suffering and distress in any part of the world; 2. To promote research into and education concerning the causes and effects of poverty.'[38]

During its application for charitable status the Fairtrade Foundation recognised that it was 'pushing against the boundaries' of what the Charity Commission considered 'the relief of poverty' under the Charities Act 1960.[39] However, there was also an understanding that being structured as a charity would provide the 'clearly defined altruistic status' that would reinforce public confidence and remove any doubt about the financial, structural or representative support of other charities.[40] Following prolonged negotiations with the Charity Commission, it was almost a year after the launch of the FAIRTRADE Mark that the Fairtrade Foundation was granted charitable status in February 1995.[41] The Foundation had successfully argued that the Fairtrade Social Premium represented a direct response to 'observable poverty'.[42]

Defining fairness: Christian teachings and precedents

'Fairness' as ethics and morality

Fairness should perhaps be understood as an intrinsically human trait. Recent research has shown that from as early as 19 months toddlers understand right from wrong and can apply the concept of fairness appropriately to different situations.[43] Psychologist, Stephanie Sloane, has suggested that this shows that children are born with 'a skeleton of general expectations about fairness', but these principles and concepts are then shaped in different ways depending on the culture and the environment they are brought up in.[44] The socially constructed dimensions of fairness are particularly relevant when addressing issues of inequality and entitlement that have become prominent features of a modern globalised society.[45] So, while fairness is not a uniquely Christian concept, teachings about morality and responsibility for our 'global neighbours' can be seen as an attempt to offer a Christian approach to countering the global North–South 'empathy deficit'.[46] Empathy is increasingly seen as a 'social glue', and the absence of empathy has been linked to a range of social, economic and environment issues: from widening inequality and social disconnectedness, to the overconsumption of goods and resources.[47]

In recent years, the Fair Trade movement has worked hard to lose its 'sandals and brown rice' hippy associations, while still maintaining its environmental and sustainability credentials. The early discourse about sustainable consumption in the 1970s was often framed in terms of 'simpler living' – a concept that owed much to the Christian teachings of frugality and simplicity. While newly formed campaign groups, such as Friends of the Earth, advocated simpler living on environmental grounds; for Christians it represented an individual and collective moral challenge to the 'false ideologies' of materialism.[48] One of clearest statements that positioned a Christian response to simpler living came at the first Lausanne Congress in 1974. Headed by US evangelist Reverend

Billy Graham, the committee addressed questions of Christian evangelicalism, social responsibility and simpler living. The Lausanne Covenant, often seen as providing the theological and collaborative strategy for worldwide evangelism during this period, declared that: 'Those of us who live in the affluent circumstances accept our duty to develop a simpler lifestyle in order to contribute more generously to both relief and evangelism.'[49]

In the United Kingdom, the idea of simpler living was used by a coalition of Christian development agencies, (including Christian Aid, CAFOD and Tearfund), to integrate a consumer campaign into a wider critique of European trade policy during the early 1970s. In petitioning the European Community Commissioners on reforms of its trade relations with the 'Third World' they called for 'an international environment where the basic needs of the majority of human mankind get the highest priority'.[50] Recommendations included stricter limits on the operations of multinational companies (MNCs), greater support for international commodity agreements, and reform of the Common Agricultural Policy.[51] But this economic critique was also communicated as a call for simpler living. The Christian development agencies recognised that little progress would be made in reducing the gap between rich and poor, 'unless the EC [European Community] are prepared to sacrifice the unrestricted advance in their living standards and increased consumption of resources'.[52]

Building on this critique, a Christian Aid leaflet from 1977 titled *'A Look at Lifestyle from a Christian Viewpoint'* asked the question, 'What can simple living achieve?' In reply, two main points were made: first, that savings could be donated to Christian Aid and 'would bring benefit to a few of those most in need'.[53] But possibly more significantly, a simpler lifestyle was meant as 'a sign of the sort of change we wish to see in the economic structures of the world – change designed to help the poorest'.[54] It was hoped that this example would contribute towards changing public opinion and Government policies on fairer trade and aid. On a personal and household level Christians were challenged to look at their own circumstances and consider the wider implications of their consumer lifestyle choices. The handbooks and leaflets produced during this period were designed to challenge any sense of entitlement felt by Christians in the global North. This discourse represented an important precursor to more secular discussions that would later identify the social implications of a 'Money-Empathy Gap'.[55]

The publication of the special British edition of Ronald Sider's book, *Rich Christians in an Age of Hunger*, in November 1978 generated considerable interest and caused some controversy.[56] The Rev. David Watson, wrote in his foreword to the second edition of the book, 'It contains the most vital challenge which faces the church today'.[57] Sider argued that consumers, and particularly Christian consumers, should take responsibility for the consequences of their consumption. He stated: 'We are implicated in a structural evil. International trade patterns are unjust ... Unless you have retreated to some isolated valley and grow or make everything you use, you participate in unjust structures which contribute directly to the hunger of a billion mal-nourished neighbours.'[58] Sider argued that to rectify this situation a structural change in global economic relations was required, and that Christians should be at the forefront of this change. He recommended three courses of action: the giving of tithes, the reintroduction of the jubilee principle and a commitment to fairer trade.[59] The logic of this argument would motivate Christian development agencies in the United Kingdom to question the economic orthodoxy of free trade and support trading initiatives that pioneered 'alternative economic spaces'.[60]

II 'Fairness' as justice and liberation

While simpler living may have been an important precursor to sustainable and ethical consumption, it was apparent that for Fair Trade to represent the perspectives of the global South, it would need to address issues of poverty and inequality. This required a theory of change that saw fairness not only as an issue for individual morality, but one of justice and liberation. Christian Aid's recent strategy document, 'Partnership for Change' states that: 'Our generation has the tools and know-how to deliver [the vision of justice and peace]. Christian Aid's task is to inspire the will to make that happen.'[61] Reflecting on this task Christian Aid recognised that: 'The theological perspectives of the global South will have a significant part to play in inspiring that will'.[62] During the 1960s theologians in the global South, predominantly from Latin America, began to describe the reality of extreme poverty as an issue of social justice rather than charity. The dual concepts of 'structural sin' and the 'preferential option for the poor' were the central tenets of what became known as 'liberation theology'.

In Britain, from the early 1970s, Christian voluntary organisations began to build links with groups founded on the principles of liberation theology.[63] This new theological understanding opened up the political and economic sphere of international trade and development to a religious and social critique that redefined the role of Christian development agencies. Increasingly these North–South links were envisaged in terms of solidarity and partnership, rather than charity. In turn, this was reflected in a shift from campaigns for increased international aid to a greater emphasis on the need for trade justice. Conservative members of the church viewed this new theology with scepticism, believing it to be a radical departure from the principal Christian mission. However, by 1980 the World Council of Churches (WCC) declared that: 'Churches are once again realising that it is not possible to be the church of Jesus Christ if they fail to respond with love and justice to the challenge of the poor.'[64]

Gustavo Gutierrez, the Peruvian theologian, is credited with popularising the term 'theology of liberation' or 'liberation theology' sometime between 1964 and 1968.[65] Gutierrez argued that liberation theology was best understood not as a new theme for reflection but 'a new way to do theology'.[66] He described it as 'a theology which opens itself – in the protest against trampled human dignity, in the struggle against the plunder of the vast majority of humankind, in liberating love, and in the building of a new society of justice and fraternity – to the gift of the kingdom of God.'[67] At the 1969 Joint Committee on Society, Development and Peace (SODEPAX) conference in Cartigny, Switzerland, Gutierrez gave a paper on the meaning of development.[68] He argued that charitable support given by wealthy nations for limited projects left the distribution of resources basically untouched. Gutierrez challenged Christians in the rich world to make a genuine commitment to justice in the South.

In Brazil, Archbishop Dom Hélder Câmara called for a church that would unambiguously declare its solidarity with oppressed peoples and would accept the probable loss of state financial support. In 1964, Câmara established 'The Church of the Poor' and eventually this Church grew to number 86 Bishops including 16 Brazilians.[69] But Dom Helder's efforts to utilise the Church to advance social justice within Brazilian society did not go unchallenged. Any attempts to do more than provide charity were met with severe criticism, both from the state and conservatives within the Church. Câmara stated, 'when I feed the poor, they call me a saint; when I ask why they are poor, they call me a communist'.[70] In *Revolution through Peace* (1971) Câmara contributed to the widening debate about 'Trade not Aid'. He argued: 'It is not aid that we need ... If the affluent countries, East and West, Europe and the United States, are willing to pay fair prices to developing countries for their natural resources, they can keep their aid and their relief plans.'[71]

It was not only the Roman Catholic faith that articulated a Biblical perspective on political liberation. In 1974, delegates at the Lausanne

International Congress on World Evangelization agreed a public statement that set out a worldview that emphasised the need for cooperation. The fifth paragraph of the Lausanne Covenant was dedicated to Christian Social Responsibility and discussed the case for 'socio-political involvement'. The Lausanne Covenant affirmed that:

> Although reconciliation with other people is not reconciliation with God, nor is social action evangelism, nor is political liberation salvation, nevertheless we affirm that evangelism and socio-political involvement are both part of our Christian duty. For both are necessary expressions of our doctrines of God and man, our love for our neighbour and our obedience to Jesus Christ.[72]

While not as radical as liberation theology, the Lausanne Covenant made it clear that the duty of Christian evangelicals extended beyond individual reconciliation with God and also required Christian action in the world.

It was no coincidence that the values of partnership, respect and equity that were central to the discourse on 'liberation theology' and social political action, resonated strongly with the founding principles of Fair Trade.[73] Drawing on Catholic Social Teachings and statements of evangelical mission, Christian Aid, CAFOD and Tearfund succeeded in articulating a concrete vision of how Christians in Britain could effectively contribute towards a people-centred development model.[74] Based on the example of Dom Helder, Christian voluntary organisations began to shift the debate on trade, from an exclusive focus on trade volumes, to a more reasoned and ethical consideration of the value of fair prices. Likewise, Gutierrez's work demonstrated the importance of connecting Christian teachings on justice with structural issues of inequality, poverty and trade. This understanding allowed Christian organisations to pursue an approach that was both 'in and against the (secular) market'.[75] Christian Evangelical teachings on social responsibility highlighted the duty of individuals and provided Christian voluntary organisations with a Biblical underpinning to the wider public discourse on ethical consumption.

Christian economics and social investment

On 20 October 1961, the *Daily Mail* reported with some enthusiasm how Sir Malcolm Trustram Eve, the Church Commissioners' senior executive, had successfully doubled its income by courageously investing the Church's millions into, 'the great jungle of Ordinary-share Stock Exchange dealing'.[76] With an investment portfolio comprising shares in 284 industrial and commercial companies and 126 investment trusts, the Church's income had risen from £8 million in 1954 to a record figure of £16 million in 1961.[77] With such a broad portfolio the Church had financial interests in a wide range of British-made goods from shipping, steel and electronics to tobacco and frozen food.[78] The only investment officially banned was in breweries.[79] By the late 1960s this 'embarrassment of riches' was quietly being questioned and at the same time there were calls for a more proactive policy of social investment, particularly in regards to developing countries. In the autumn of 1968, the Church Assembly report on 'Christians and World Development' was supported by an amendment calling upon the Church Commissioners to increase investments in developing countries.[80] Despite reservations about the whole question of overseas investments, there was a growing recognition of the positive moral possibilities offered by investments in poorer economies.[81]

In 1969, CAFOD and Christian Aid jointly commissioned a working group, led by the Overseas Development Institute, to address the question of 'whether the capital accumulated in the Trusts of the Churches could be used also to benefit the economies of the less developed countries'.[82] The report, published in 1972, was titled: *A Third force for the Third World: A Study of the channels for investment of Church Trust Funds in economic development*. The starting point of the report was a resolution passed at a World Council of Churches (WCC) Conference in October 1969. This resolution set out the objective that: 'The British churches should take the lead in creating an independent fund for investment in the creation of wealth in developing countries by devoting, before the end of 1972, 5% of their invested funds for that purpose.'[83] The report concluded that the institutions that existed in the late 1960s allowed only limited scope for investment in Third World development and that there was potential to establish a trust for that specific purpose. The report stated that Church funds should be 'something different from government investment on one hand and private investment on the other'.[84] They further proposed that church investors could, 'pioneer the use of investment money with a moral purpose, and thus become a third force in the Third World'.[85]

In the early 1970s, the WCC started to question their investment policy in South Africa.[86] In particular, they focused on loans to South African government. They argued that: 'Even those that sincerely believe, unlike the WCC, that investment can benefit black South

Africans are unable to make out any remotely plausible case for arguing that loans to the South African Government and its agencies can do anything but strengthen apartheid.'[87] In 1973, the WCC sent out questionnaires to ten banks to assess their involvement with South Africa. These questionnaires were essentially an early form of social audit. One of the banks that responded was Midland Bank, their statement read: 'We believe we should be guided by our responsibility to our shareholders, customers and staff.'[88] The WCC responded by closing its account with Midland Bank. The WCC justified this decision stating that 'banking and all commercial life – and all life itself – come under moral judgement, and there is no place where we may go and hide and say we have escaped the eye of God. The WCC has argued that corporate ethics are no different from private ethics.'[89]

The campaign against loans by Midland Bank gained momentum in 1974 when End Loans to Southern Africa (ELTSA) was established by the Reverend David Haslam.[90] A campaign pamphlet from 1975 stated: 'Midland bank has always been considered a relatively "clean" bank with respect to involvement in Southern Africa and many church and anti-apartheid organisations bank with Midland for this reason.'[91] But it continued, 'no longer is this the case – Midland, along with the whole banking system, is up to its eyes in supporting apartheid in Southern Africa'.[92] In March 1976, at the Midland Bank AGM, the Methodist Church set an important precedent when it tabled a shareholder resolution to End Loans to South Africa. This was the first shareholders' resolution to a British company or bank to be tabled on a social issue.[93]

The resolution, supported by the Anglican Church Commissioners stated that they found bank loans to the South African Government morally unacceptable and called for the Midland Bank to withdraw the loan facilities.[94] A letter explaining ELTSA's objections was sent to shareholders signed by three Anglican Bishops: David Sheppard of Liverpool, Kenneth Woollcombe of Oxford, and Trevor Huddleston of Stepney. As a result of this letter 109 shareholders agreed to sign the resolution (there was a minimum requirement of at least 100). The resolution achieved three million share-votes, only about 6% of the total; however the action was still considered a success due to the level of publicity and media interest that it generated.[95]

The use of this direct form of shareholder activism was seen by some Church leaders and institutional shareholders as too political; as a result, the dioceses of Birmingham, Northampton, Clifton and Southwark, and Liverpool Cathedral did not support the ELTSA resolution.[96] However, the ELTSA shareholder resolution was just a starting point and over the following 20 years the support and momentum behind the idea of ethical Church investments and the potential of people-centred economics would steadily build. The work pioneered by the WCC on church investment for Third World development would later prove an important foundation for the activities of the ethical investment co-operative – Shared Interest.[97] By linking UK social investors and Fair Trade organisations needing finance to improve their livelihoods, the idea of 'investment money with a moral purpose' would become a reality.

Business ethics: Christian alternative trade organisations

In contrast to the research and planning that characterised the Church investment programmes, moves into trading began as relatively ad hoc ventures. Tearfund was the first Christian agency to become directly involved with alternative trading. In 1974, in response to the unfolding crisis in Bangladesh, which had been left devastated by civil war and a cyclone, Tearfund agreed to start importing local handcrafts to sell in Britain.[98] The programme was implemented through the work of Ian Prior, on the Tearfund staff, and Richard Adams, a greengrocer who had been supporting farmers in the Third World by importing their surplus produce. Richard Adams flew out to Bangladesh and filled a cargo plane (on its return leg to Britain after a Tearfund relief mission) with £10,000 worth of jute handcrafts from local producers. Tearcraft was then registered as a business on 23 December 1974 and the first catalogue went out in February 1975.[99]

Tearfund's development work was shaped and motivated by Christian evangelicalism and this commitment also characterised Tearcraft's approach to international trade. At a practical level, for Tearcraft this meant working with and through evangelicals. Stephen Rand, the Communication Director of Tearfund, explained that 'a holistic view of the gospel required that each producer group should have some key input from evangelicals'.[100] This close connection between Christian faith and business was at times difficult to implement. Some within Tearcraft, including Richard Adams, believed that a focus on handcraft production as a practical mission of the Church was overly restrictive and damaging to the commercial viability of the enterprise. Before long, these tensions led to growing disagreements and in 1979 Richard Adams left Tearcraft and established a new trading venture called Traidcraft. Traidcraft maintained a Christian outlook and its founding principles declared that: 'Traidcraft is a Christian response to poverty'.

However, in contrast to Tearcraft, it actively sought to work with 'all those who share our commitment to fighting poverty, whatever their faith commitments'.[101]

While it may be too simplistic to view the subsequent business fortunes of these two organisations as a direct reflection of the commercial success of a secular brand positioning over that of a more traditional Christian message, it is clear that Traidcraft did adopt a more mainstream approach to Fair Trade.[102] Richard Adams, reflecting on the influence of Christian faith on the Traidcraft, stated that there was 'no area of our work where there was not endless scope for applying our faith yet few areas where we could lay claim to a definitive approach'.[103] Although 85% of Traidcraft's staff were Christian, when operating outside Christian networks Traidcraft's approach was not overtly Christian. Adams acknowledged this and stated that: 'I was very conscious of how "Christian language" might alienate people.'[104] Traidcraft's success in engaging both Church congregations and community groups can be seen in the rapid growth of its network of Traidcraft representatives, or 'Fair Traders'. In just three years this network had expanded from 120 Fair Traders in 1979 to more than 400 in 1982; and by 1988 there were 1,500 Fair Traders active – achieving annual sales of £1.5 million (41% of Traidcraft's turnover).[105]

From the early 1980s, Christian voluntary organisations began to view ATOs as increasingly significant to Third World development. The non-evangelical basis of Traidcraft's mission allowed it to engage successfully with both Christian Aid and CAFOD. In 1983, Christian Aid and Traidcraft announced new links between the two organisations. A special version of the Traidcraft catalogue was sent out to Christian Aid's 60,000 supporters.[106] In return for this support, Traidcraft donated 10% of the retail price to Christian Aid for its development programmes.[107] In 1983–1984 Christian Aid received a dividend of £17,022 from its sales of Traidcraft products.[108] Following its success with Christian Aid, in 1984 Traidcraft produced a mail order catalogue for CAFOD. One of the items featured in the first catalogue was Nicaraguan Coffee. Commenting on its support for Nicaragua, CAFOD stated that 'new Nicaragua', 'raises fundamental questions as to the role of the Church and Christians in the construction of a different kind of society outside the capitalist or communist moulds'.[109] CAFOD saw its role in Nicaragua as consistent with its wider goals of presenting Third World countries with, 'a real alternative for development, independent of alignment with either of the power blocs'.[110]

Christian Aid and CAFOD also extended their support to Traidcraft through annual grants to Traidcraft Exchange.[111] Set up in 1986 as a charity with the joint aims of consumer education and producer development, Traidcraft Exchange represented the first time that a UK Fair Trade company had established a subsidiary charity.[112] The charitable objects of Traidcraft Exchange set out two main goals: first, the relief of poverty by providing training and information for producers, suppliers and trading partners in developing countries. Secondly, the promotion of studies on economic, political, social, technical and theological subjects to raise awareness about issues arising from national and international trading practices and the benefits of trading fairly. Traidcraft Exchange's charitable status also meant that it was well-positioned to represent Traidcraft as a member of the Fairtrade Foundation steering committee in 1989, and then as a founder member of the organisation in 1992.

A policy of ethical investment had been investigated by the Churches from the late 1960s, but this was not an option generally open to individual investors. In 1986, Mark Hayes, investment manager at 3i, contacted Richard Adams, managing director of Traidcraft with a proposal for a Development Bank. With the backing of Traidcraft, Shared Interest was successfully registered as an Industrial and Provident Society on 30 March 1990, and Mark Hayes became the first Managing Director. Shared Interest described itself as:

> A Christian initiative which grew out of and continues to express the work and objects of Traidcraft Exchange and in which existing investors in the Ecumenical Development Cooperative Society (EDCS)[113] under the auspices of Scottish Churches Action for World Development (SCAWD) became the major investors. The Society embodies their joint vision of a new economic order based on love and justice, and carries on their work in a new direction.[114]

In 1991, Shared Interest made its first direct investments totalling £77,000. These included: investments in Bridgehead, a trading subsidiary of Oxfam Canada; a loan to Traidcraft to provide advance payments to Fair Trade producers; and finance for Verdin, a Huddersfield-based importer of Peruvian craft products.[115] Alongside Traidcraft and Oikocredit, Shared Interest had shown that Christian finance could be effective in supporting Fair Trade businesses and acting as a force for 'pro-poor' economic development. It was also significant that, with a minimum shareholding requirement of £100, Shared Interest was within reach of most potential investors.[116] By 2001, Shared Interest's membership had reached 8,448 and its membership survey showed that three-quarters of members described themselves as 'active' Christians.[117] In 2003, Shared Interest reinforced its role within the Fair Trade movement when its newly formed charitable subsidiary, Shared Interest Foundation, was accepted as a member of the Fairtrade Foundation.

The Fairtrade Foundation: Early challenges and controversy

As the idea of Fair Trade gained momentum during the late 1980s, Christian voluntary organisations provided the institutional backing and seed capital vital to making the Fairtrade Mark a reality in the United Kingdom. From 1989, when the steering committee was set up, until 1994 when the first Fairtrade labelled product went on sale, the Fairtrade Foundation had to exist without any income from license fees and was reliant on its member organisations for financial support. During this period, in addition to the £100,000 provided by Oxfam, the Christian agencies provided substantial grant funding: Christian Aid contributed £85,000 and CAFOD £30,000.[118] In April 1994, the Foundation faced a potentially serious shortfall of funds to cover expenditure for its first operational year and additional funding was again sought from the agencies: Oxfam £30,000; Christian Aid £20,000; CAFOD £15,000; Traidcraft £2,000.[119] These financial grants helped keep the Fairtrade Foundation afloat and the public backing of major British charities, including the Christian agencies, provided the credibility and consumer guarantee that this was more than just an exercise in 'greenwash'.

In 1990 Christian Aid launched, *Trade for Change,* a two-year campaign aimed at mainstreaming support for 'people friendly' products in the run up to the official launch of the Fairtrade Foundation. An NOP/ Omnibus poll, commissioned by Christian Aid, showed that 74% were willing to 'pay extra for goods produced without exploiting Third World workers' and 78% felt that 'trading fairly with a country was a better way to help that country develop than giving aid'.[120] Peter Madden, author of the Christian Aid publication *Raw Deal*, highlighted how, 'Third World farmers need us all to take people-friendly shopping as seriously as we take buying environment-friendly goods.'[121] Madden focused on the need for consumers and producers to work together to change the trading system. Drawing on historical comparisons with the nineteenth century, he added that, 'the evil of slavery was ended when people of conviction added their voices to the slaves' own demand for the system to be abolished'.[122]

The 16 September 1992 represented a critical moment that would unsettle the Christian development agencies position within the newly formed Fairtrade Foundation. Building on the success of the 'Trade for Change', Christian Aid had decided to develop a consumer campaign focusing on the tea trade. Christian Aid launched the campaign with a full page advertisement in *The Times*. The strapline of the advert read, 'You have stopped using eggs from battery hens, but what about tea from battery tea workers.'[123] Response to the advert proved even more heated than they could have imagined. The timing was particularly significant since the Fairtrade Foundation was in the middle of negotiations with Typhoo tea. The advert sparked an immediate reaction from the other members of the Fairtrade Foundation. Richard Adams, Director of New Consumer and former head of Traidcraft, conscious of the likely impact of this campaign described it as, 'the torpedoing of the most promising initiative of the last twenty years'.[124] Paul Johns, Acting Chief Executive of the Fairtrade Foundation, also condemned the advert outright, 'You have opened your campaign against unfair trade by dropping a bomb on your allies.'[125]

The main criticism of Christian Aid's advert was that it stood to undermine the Fairtrade Foundation's strategy of 'consultation, dialogue and a new, positive approach to campaigning'; it was censured as a throwback to, '1970s-style campaigning'.[126] But was this a valid criticism or an overreaction? The campaign was certainly hard hitting, but rather than calling for a boycott of tea, Christian Aid appealed to consumers to, 'Ask your supermarket to buy goods from sources that provide Third World workers with a decent living.'[127] Although this campaign may have been stretching the limits of 'positive engagement', it was far from a direct attack of Typhoo. Nevertheless, negotiations with Typhoo broke down soon after and this was seen as a missed opportunity to benefit from, 'a Fair Trade advertising and point of sale campaign employing massive resources which would reach millions of people who are normally not touched by the agencies'.[128] Although there were also commercial reasons for Typhoo's withdrawal, the blame was pinned on Christian Aid and the fallout from this incident undermined the Christian agencies position more broadly within the Fairtrade Foundation. At a crucial moment this campaign highlighted the challenges of positioning Fairtrade as a 'critical ally' to mainstream business.

The Christian agencies continued to campaign in support of Fair Trade, but the message became less political. In April 1993, Christian Aid turned attention towards encouraging its supporters to petition supermarkets to put more Fair Trade products on their shelves.

This consumer-focused campaign strategy proved less controversial. Customers handed supermarket managers with vouchers that stated, 'As a customer at your store I would like to see you stocking goods from the Third World which give poor people a fair return for their labour.'[129] The main focus of the campaign was on getting supermarkets to stock Cafédirect. Cafédirect was chosen since it was the most easily recognisable 'fairly traded' product at the time.

Following the launch of the Fairtrade Mark in March 1994, Christian Aid coordinated a consumer campaign aimed at building awareness of newly certified Fairtrade products. The 'Change at the Check-out' campaign encouraged supporters to collect the till receipts from their weekly shop and take them back to the store as an illustration of the volume sales that supermarkets could lose if they ignored calls for Fairtrade. By December 1998, the total value of till receipts collected had reached £14 million.[130] CAFOD launched a co-ordinated campaign calling for a, 'Fair Deal for the Poor'. In just 6 months, 9,000 people signed cards saying 'I don't just want to shop, I want to shop justly'.[131] Tearfund also encouraged its supporters to purchase Fairtrade products as a way of supporting the movement as its commercial viability was tested by the major retailers. An article from *Tear Times*, in 1998, stated that: 'If each of us receiving this magazine (nearly 150,000) switched to Fair Trade coffee, we would double the amount sold in the UK.'[132]

The 'battery tea workers' advert may have represented a 'tipping point' in terms of the strategic positioning of Christian agencies within the Fairtrade Foundation; but the relevance of the Christian message was also facing wider challenges as British society appeared to be moving in an ever more secular direction. By the mid-1990s the internal and external dynamics of the Fair Trade movement resulted in a political and economic policy environment that seemed less compatible with a Christian approach to Fair Trade and trade justice.

Secularisation, charity and 'Third World' development

Over the last 40 years, academic discussions about secularisation have become the mainstay of scholarly articles about faith and religion in modern Britain. The impact of religious teachings and the role of Christian organisations in supporting the Fair Trade movement suggest a resilience (at least up until the early 1990s) that has not been explored in most contemporary accounts. The decline in church attendance and wider Christian association has been well documented, but the trajectory and impact of this decline has not been fully explained.[133] One of the dilemmas raised by recent research into grassroots Fair Trade activism has been the apparent disconnect between the high level of Christian support and the predominantly secular message. Research by Clive Barnett and colleagues found that 70–80% of campaigners actively promoting Fairtrade in Bristol were Christians.[134] However, they also encountered a widespread concern that religion could hinder campaigning among non-faith-based constituencies, and this has led many to Fairtrade Town groups to advocate a 'broad dissociation of Fairtrade from any specific religious identity' within their campaigning.[135] While the endorsement of the Church may not be a guarantee of public support, on a personal level Christian faith continued to be a significant factor in motivating involvement in charitable work, campaign activity and ethical consumption.

Up until the mid-1970s the discussions about the secularisation of modern British society had chiefly engaged sociologists, but Alan Gilbert's work placed this process within a broader historical perspective. Gilbert defined a secularized society as one where, 'to be irreligious is to be normal, where to think and act in secular terms is to be conventional'.[136] Gilbert maintained that areas once dominated by religious teaching had been gradually taken over by secular consciousness. He suggested that two main trends marked the route towards secularisation: a belief in rational science and the industrialization of production. Gilbert claimed that the 'Age of Enlightenment' saw the church's relevance increasingly questioned and, 'human rationality, ingenuity and foresight seemed to be fashioning an institutional environment which openly mitigated symptoms of human insecurity'.[137] In essence the Christian Church had failed to 'elaborate an effective critique of modern secular rationality'.[138]

Gilbert argued that the 'Industrial Revolution' of the nineteenth century was the catalyst for societal change and that 'few aspects, if any, of social organization, cultural reality or human consciousness have escaped profound metamorphosis of industrialization'.[139] In particular, Gilbert argued that the increased material wealth and productive capacity of modern society had, 'encouraged the growth of a modern hedonistic culture'.[140] And this had resulted in the steady decline in influence of the church. By the late twentieth century churches seemed to have lost their claim to be 'influencing the ethical standards of the world'. Instead Gilbert argued that 'worldly standards have become in the modern period, the arbiters of Christian ethics'.[141]

Writing at the turn of the millennium, social and cultural historian, Callum Brown, provocatively declared the 'Death of Christian

Britain'.[142] Arguing that the modern Christian Church had been permanently side-lined, he drew on census figures to show that:

> In the year 2000 less than 8 per cent of people attend Sunday worship in any week, less than a quarter are members of any church, and fewer than a tenth of children attend a Sunday school ... all figures for Christian affiliation are at their lowest point in recorded history.[143]

For Brown, secularization had already happened but he still questioned the main tenets of the secularization thesis. Instead of a gradual process emerging from the 'Industrial Revolution', Brown's contention was that there was 'a short sharp cultural revolution of the late twentieth century which makes the Britons of the year 2000 fundamentally different in character from those of 1950, or 1900 or 1800'.[144] For Brown, the 1960s was the crucial period of change, witnessing the dramatic decline in Church attendance and influence. While this interpretation may broadly describe the social and cultural challenges facing the Christian Church, it still does not account for the formation and successful expansion of Christian development agencies from the 1960s onwards.

In response to Callum Brown, church historian and Anglican priest Jeremy Morris has argued that: 'For the time being it is a strange sort of death that leaves churches still amongst the largest voluntary organisations in the country, and Christianity still notionally the conviction of a majority of the population'.[145] The Fair Trade movement provides an important example of campaigns led by Christian voluntary organisations in post-1960s Britain and their contribution to building support for 'Third World' development programmes. Building on the case outlined by Morris, it also seems a strange sort of death that leaves Christian campaigners as a significant constituent of one the fastest growing grassroots social movements in Britain, and church leaders as prominent supporters and spokespersons for an internationally recognised Superbrand (the FAIRTRADE Mark).[146] The recent history of the Christian development agencies has shown the potential for Christianity to represent a significant moral social force within public debates about global politics and economics.

Hugh McLeod, Emeritus Professor of Church History, has questioned the validity of secularisation as a 'process' and has suggested that it should instead be understood as a 'contest' between 'rival world views'.[147] McLeod has also questioned the inevitability of secularisation and points to the substantial evidence of religious revival in nineteenth century and early-to-mid-twentieth-century Britain. However, McLeod's assessment of religious revival only extends to the 1960s, beyond which he argues that the 'balance tip[s] more decisively in a secular direction'.[148] McLeod's depiction of a contest between rival world views could be extended and applied to the Christian agencies involvement with the Fair Trade movement. Throughout the 1970s and 1980s, support for the Christian message on 'Third World' issues seemed to be gaining ground.[149] But from the mid-1990s, there were signs that the balance was shifting in a more secular direction with the increasing interest of both government and business in Third World development programmes.

A vibrant network of faith communities?

Despite being an organisation with predominantly Christian origins, in recent years the Fairtrade Foundation has looked to open a wider faith dialogue.[150] With 8.4% of the British population identifying with a non-Christian faith, there is an opportunity and a need for Fairtrade to engage with an increasingly plural religious landscape.[151] Increasingly the Foundation now talks about 'a vibrant network of faith communities' rather than singling out Christian support for Fairtrade.[152] This sensitivity about overidentifying Fair Trade with Christian faith is also found among Fair Trade campaigners. Research investigating the motivation and participation of Traidcraft supports found that: 'While often acknowledging that for them personally, faith and church membership were important factors in their fair-trade consumption activities, they just as often insisted that this was not a necessary relationship, either for them or others'.[153]

While 'a shared discourse of faith' has been identified as a successful strategic option open to campaigners, to date, most faith-based Fair Trade campaigns have centred on Christian networks.[154] There are, however, some notable exceptions; for instance, Islamic Relief Worldwide have taken the lead in demonstrating an Islamic perspective on Fair Trade. Ajaz Ahmed Khan, previously the senior policy advisor at Islamic Relief, and Laura Thaut, political scientist, have shown in their policy paper on Islam and Fair Trade that there is, 'a rich heritage in Islam of high moral standards, ethics, values and norms of behaviour, which govern personal, professional and business life'.[155] They conclude that:

> Indeed in many respects, Islamic thinking goes much further than contemporary Fair Trade advocacy efforts, as Islam forbids

> speculation and the hoarding of merchandise in order to increase prices, it prohibits interest as a mechanism of exploitation that reinforces poverty, and prohibits trade in goods that compromises the hearts and minds of consumers, such as alcohol and gambling.[156]

There is also evidence that Fair Trade is engaging the UK Jewish community. In March 2006, the Birmingham Progressive Synagogue became the first Fairtrade Synagogue, and the Fairtrade cotton kippot has become an important symbol of support. However, despite efforts to broaden the supporter base, other faiths (non-Christian) with recognised Fairtrade Places of Worship still represent less than 1% of the total.[157]

Conclusions

Christian Aid's most recent strategy document declares that: 'In Britain and Ireland, our church supporters have repeatedly shown their power as active citizens to rouse the conscience of politicians, and to change the policies of business, large and small, through initiatives such as fair trade.'[158] Evidence for this support can be seen in the 7,000 churches that have now achieved Fairtrade Church status.[159] However, while Christian ethics have continued to motivate individual supporters, and voluntary organisations, they have not been integral to the modern identity of the Fairtrade Foundation. There remains a perception that openly Christian language could alienate the general public, and there is little evidence that the Christian members of the Fairtrade Foundation have been pushing for a stronger Christian message within the Foundation's brand identity.[160]

The influence of Christian belief within Fair Trade has interesting parallels in the life and work of alternative economic thinker and development scholar, E. F. Schumacher. Author of *Small is Beautiful* and founder of the Intermediate Technology Development Group (now called Practical Action), Schumacher's Christianity was not always overtly expressed, but existed as a major influence in his life.[161] In 1977, Schumacher gave an interview with *Christian Century*, in which he discussed his conversion to the Roman Catholic Church in the latter years of his life.[162] Discussing the frequently cited chapter on 'Buddhist Economics', Schumacher acknowledged that *Small is Beautiful* was equally informed by Catholic writers and thinkers. Pondering this apparent theological tension Schumacher's response was characteristically pragmatic, 'Of course. But if I had called the chapter "Christian

Economics" nobody would have paid any attention.'[163] He then went on to explain that 'most people in the West are suffering from what I call an anti-Christian trauma and I don't blame them. I went through that for 20 years myself.'[164]

This chapter has investigated how, on issues of Third World development and Fair Trade, Christian development agencies were able to re-establish the relevance of Christian values in post-1960s Britain. Christian development agencies increasingly entered into a dialogue with their membership about the role of Christians as moral consumers in a global marketplace. A longer historical perspective could position Fair Trade as a revival of a campaigning tradition seen in the nineteenth century (such as the Christian Social Union's White List movement) that sought to re-sacralise economic life. However, what was distinctive about the modern Fair Trade movement was that the social and economic critique was inspired, at least in part, by the theology and activism of the global South.

From the early 1990s, although Christian NGOs and their supporters continued to account for the major constituency of Fair Trade campaigners, there was a shift to towards a more secular message. It was at this point that, to borrow McLeod's terminology, the 'balance tip[s] more decisively in a secular direction'.[165] The Fairtrade Foundation, and the newly created FAIRTRADE Mark, offered mainstream businesses a way of publicly demonstrating a commercial commitment to development; and for consumers, an opportunity to express their support by purchasing certified products. There were also signs of increased government interest in international development and Fair Trade.[166] Under New Labour, the UK Government began to increase the operating budget for the Department for International Development (DFID), and this included modest grant funding for Fair Trade.[167] For Christian voluntary organisations growing mainstream support for Fairtrade represented, somewhat counter-intuitively, a challenge to their institutional legitimacy. It became harder for Fair Trade pioneers such as: Christian Aid, CAFOD and Traidcraft to offer a compelling and distinctly Christian response to the problems of international trade and 'Third World' development.[168] However, at an individual level, Christian faith continued to motivate grassroots campaigners, volunteers and activists, and has underpinned the remarkable success of Fairtrade Towns movement.

3

The Co-operative Difference: Co-operation among Co-operatives?*

In recent years, the Co-op has claimed to be the 'Champion of Fairtrade' in the mainstream.[1] The figures go some way to support this claim: in 2011, the Co-operative Group accounted for 17.5% of all Fairtrade sales through grocery outlets and continues to achieve proportionally higher sales of Fairtrade products for the size of their business than any of their competitors.[2] Total Fairtrade sales at the Co-operative have risen from £100,000 in 1998 to £104 million in 2011 and the value of Fairtrade premiums paid to producers in 2011 reached an estimated £2.2 million.[3] From the early 1990s Fairtrade has been central to identifying the 'Co-operative difference' and promoting a market position separate from the 'big four' supermarkets.[4] The Co-operative Group's new Ethical Operating Plan, launched in 2011, set out its ambition to reinforce its position as the UK's most socially responsible business. A renewed commitment to Fairtrade was a central part of this plan, 'If a primary commodity from the developing world can be Fairtrade, it will be Fairtrade by 2013'.[5]

The connection between the Co-operative movement and Fair Trade can be seen in three distinct ways: firstly, the Co-operative Group's retail support for Fairtrade labelling and conversion of its own brand products; secondly, the involvement of Co-op members in promoting Fairtrade Towns; thirdly, the Fairtrade Foundation's (and Fairtrade International's) support for producer co-operatives through the Small Producer Organization certification standards. At a more abstract level, the apparent ethical and moral links between the original principles of the Rochdale Pioneers and Fair Trade values have also been emphasised.

*An earlier version of this chapter was published in N. Robertson and L. Black (eds.), *Consumerism and the Co-operative Movement in Modern British History: Taking Stock* (Manchester: Manchester University Press, 2009).

The Co-operative Group have stated that, 'Co-operative Values and Principles – such as concern for community and equality – date back to the 19th century, and also resonate with contemporary ideas of corporate responsibility'.[6] Given that the Co-operative movement is now so closely aligned with the Fair Trade movement and has been identified by some academics as 'naturally sympathetic', it could be assumed that the Co-operative movement would have supported 'alternative' or Fair Trade as it developed in the 1960s and 1970s.[7] However, as this chapter shows, the Co-op's support for Fair Trade represented a more recent and significant 'revolution' than has been recognised so far.

This chapter considers how the Co-operative movement addressed tensions that existed over its international trading operations. From the late nineteenth century, the consumer co-operative members of the International Co-operative Alliance (ICA), such as the British movement, expressed a desire to realise the ideals of international co-operation. But when it came to a choice between demonstrating solidarity with producer co-operatives from the global South and maintaining the consumer dividend, invariably it was the producer co-operatives that lost out. In practice, the British movement was operating its trading ventures along the same lines as any other major commercial importer.

What is required, in the context of a widening discussion about the role of the 'ethical consumer' and Fair Trade, is a reassessment of the Co-operative movement's values and principles as operationalized in its international development and trading programme. The Co-op's capacity to support 'alternative' or Fair Trade during the 1960s and 1970s was limited by four factors: firstly, its focus on competition from the major supermarkets; secondly, its complex structure with numerous independent individual societies; thirdly, its failure to recognise the significance of the consumer/producer dynamics within the movement; and finally, its limited communication with its membership. It was not until the early 1990s that the Co-op management recognised that Fairtrade was a viable proposition and had the potential to reconnect the movement with the ideals of international co-operative trade.

Co-op historiography and Fair Trade

There has yet to be an historically focused academic assessment of the Co-operative movement's approach to ethical or Fair Trade in the twentieth century. In part this could be a reflection of the limited academic attention to the Co-op more generally. Some within the movement have argued that this apparent academic exodus was in itself a commentary on the declining dynamism of the Co-op. Rita Rhodes,

Education Officer of the ICA, stated that: 'Both in terms of trading practices and democratic appeal, the movement is not seen to be as radical as once it was. Increasing academic indifference reflects this.'[8] Investigating the Co-operative movement's response to Fair Trade presents an opportunity to explore an important and under-researched aspect of the movement – the significance of Co-operative values as embodied in its international trade relations with developing countries.

By the early twentieth century the established opinion among scholars on the left was that the Co-operative movement had arrived at a position quite different from the idea with which it had begun. Fabians such as Sidney and Beatrice Webb argued that the movement had grown on the basis of self-interest and had idealism grafted on to it.[9] This was a discussion that also exercised G. D. H. Cole, the English political theorist, economist and historian. Cole, himself both a critic and a supporter of the Co-operative movement, recognised that: 'Most socialists and all revolutionaries, until quite recently, have treated the Co-operative movement with patronising contempt. It was a satisfactory grocer's shop and a good savings-bank, but no self-respecting revolutionary would believe that it would ever make a breach in the walls of capitalism'.[10]

Sidney Pollard, British economic and labour historian, building on this early historiography identified in his work two distinct phases of co-operation.[11] The first, 1820–1846, was dominated by Robert Owen and a practical commitment to establishing the Co-operative Commonwealth as the basis of a 'new moral world'. The second phase was initiated by the Rochdale Pioneers in 1846, and was characterised by a slow drift from the ideal of the Co-operative Commonwealth to be replaced by a preoccupation with shopkeeping and the principle of the consumer dividend. In contrast, Professor Stephen Yeo, social historian and associate of the Co-operative College, has argued that the fact the world did not go the co-operators' way, was not academic justification to dismiss their commitment to a 'world-making' project.[12] Yeo showed that as late as 1893 co-operators such as Holyoake were committed to the practical realisation of the Co-operative Commonwealth. Peter Gurney, co-operative scholar and advocate of 'history from below', has also shown that Co-operative ideals were not necessarily squeezed out of the movement as a result of the success of the dividend. He maintained that: 'Late nineteenth century co-operation produced its own brand of utopianism based on the principle of the dividend'.[13]

These debates over the ideals of the Co-op have so far focused almost exclusively on the domestic situation of the movement in Britain and few studies have undertaken a thorough assessment of the international 'world making' potential of co-operation. The concept of international co-operation between co-operatives is essential to linkages between the Co-operative movement and Fair Trade (and is an area that remains under-researched). While research by the sociologist, Johnston Birchall, has looked at how different strands of co-operation, (consumer, worker, credit), developed to form an international movement; there is little discussion about the role of idealism as a uniting force within the movement.[14] In contrast W. P. Watkins, co-operative scholar, adopted a more holistic approach to international co-operative networks, but this study did not extend beyond the 1970s.[15] Contemporary literature on political consumption has to some extent recognised a role for the Co-operative movement in the emergence of the 'ethical consumer' in the late twentieth century, but that role is yet to be fully defined and these linkages require further investigation particularly in relation to the Fair Trade movement in the 1960s and 1970s.[16]

Employee representation and labour relations within British Co-operative Retail Societies has been an important theme within Co-op historiography and remains a pertinent topic.[17] By incorporating an international dimension into this field of research, this chapter will widen the discussion to take account of the Co-op's treatment of workers employed in the global South. The relationship between the national leadership and the ancillaries of the movement will also be examined, specifically the Women's Co-operative Guild (WCG) and their ability to draw on the ideals of the movement to promote a 'radical' or 'socially progressive' campaign. This chapter uncovers the role of the WCG in the consumer activism of the 1960s and 1970s and shows how the WCG was at the forefront in campaigning for fair tea prices and in calling for a boycott of the apartheid regime in South Africa.

Co-operative tea and the campaign for fair tea prices

In 1902, The Co-operative Tea Society (CTS) purchased estates in Sri Lanka, and tea soon became a major import. Tea was virtually the only product imported by the Co-op from developing countries where the Co-operative Wholesale Society (CWS) maintained direct control over the entire supply chain. By 1972, the CTS was making a profit on its operations of £1.1 million, and paid a dividend to the CWS and the Scottish CWS of £650,000. This gave tea a particular significance within the movement and made it the clearest example of the Co-op's international trading principles in practice. So, when the conditions on CWS tea plantations in Sri Lanka and India were openly criticised in the media, in the mid-1970s, many ordinary Co-operative members were shocked by the allegations and some demanded action. Tea became the focus of consumer campaigns, led by non-governmental organisations (NGOs) and joined by many Co-op members, for fair wages for the tea pickers. The politicisation of tea led to a wider questioning of international trade relations, which in turn dealt with many of the ideas that were being developed by groups working on alternative networks and promoting the concept of Fair Trade.

The CWS tea plantations were forced onto the agenda by the public outcry in response to a 1973 World in Action television programme *Cost of a Cup of Tea*.[18] The programme was an exposé of the intolerable working conditions on the tea plantations in Sri Lanka, owned by major household brands including the CWS. The programme stated that, in 1973, tea was about the only item on the shopping list that was still as cheap as in 1970; World in Action set out to investigate 'what it costs others to keep the cost of a packet of tea unchanged'.[19] The Mahouvilla estate, owned by the CTS, was identified by World in Action as having housing that was 'marginally worse' than the Brooke Bond estates, and similarly poor wages and living conditions that resulted in malnutrition, hook worm, vitamin deficiency and high child mortality.[20]

It seems that the international trading obligations and responsibilities of the Co-operative movement had for some time been misunderstood, or idealised, by the membership. One Society member stated that he had, 'always understood that it was in order to ensure that our tea workers were properly paid that the co-ops were obliged to purchase from their own tea plantations'.[21] This unfortunately was not the case. Primarily any obligation to buy from CWS plantations came from the commercial motivation to maintain a consistent supply of cheap tea. Many Co-op members believed that the CWS should operate its trading practices in keeping with Co-op values and principles and not be dragged down by competition with big business. One member responded, 'these are slave conditions which we expect from capitalism and private enterprise, but to see them linked with the Co-operative movement is something which just cannot be left without violent protest.'[22] The scandal of the Sri Lankan tea plantations opened up a previously hidden side of the CWS supply chain and revealed the reality of working conditions on Co-operative owned plantations. In Britain, Co-op members and shoppers responded, 'we don't want cheap "99" tea at that price!'[23]

Conditions on tea plantations proved a significant convergence issue for consumer activists and NGOs throughout the 1970s (ten years later coffee would play a similar role). Several reports were published exposing the poor working conditions on tea plantations, particularly in Sri Lanka.[24] All the big household names came in for serious criticism including the CWS. The activist group, War on Want, called for British manufacturers, retailers and consumers to 'accept responsibility for the conditions which estate workers have to endure'.[25] In 1977 an Oxfam report, *A Bitter Taste to your Cuppa,* was featured in the ICA journal, *Consumer Affairs Bulletin.*[26] The report described how thousands of housewives all over Britain had signed a petition declaring their willingness to pay 'a fair price for tea in order to help poor people in tea growing countries'.[27] In an effort to challenge commercial indifference on this issue, Oxfam looked to Government and argued that public opinion in Britain was sending a message that 'the days of cheap tea at the expense of the poor should be over for good'.[28]

Despite the controversy in Sri Lanka, the Co-operative was still identified as a potential ally for NGOs and consumer activists looking to restructure traditional supply chains. The 'Co-operative difference' meant that it controlled its own brand products from raw material to shelf. The Co-op proudly claimed that 'no other retailer had the same degree of control over the source of its product'.[29] But despite calls for fairer prices for tea, the Co-op, in order to compete with the supermarkets, continued a policy of price cutting. In November 1977 they cut tea prices by 6p per lb and again in March 1978.[30] At the time their adverts ran with the slogan, 'The Co-op: the place to go for a bargain beverage.'[31] As the World Development Movement (WDM) found, the Co-op's price cutting policy was not easy to align with an ethical trading programme. They commented that: 'It has not proved any easier to change the policies of the Co-operative Wholesale Society.'[32] After numerous requests from WDM and pressure from Co-operative members, the CWS finally met with WDM in November 1980. But the meeting achieved little. Ultimately WDM were left with the impression that by this stage the Co-op simply wanted to 'get rid of its estates and responsibilities as soon as possible'.[33]

During the 1970s, the politicisation of tea played an important role in the wider understanding of ethical trade issues among members of the Co-operative movement. Co-op members, in the objections they raised about conditions on CWS tea plantations, referred back to the trading values and principles as established by nineteenth century co-operators, such as Robert Owen and the Rochdale Pioneers, and emphasised how the movement had departed from these ideals. This critique seems consistent with a wider academic assessment of the 1960s as a period of crisis for the Co-op. However, were the conditions on CWS tea plantations really the result of a late twentieth century disconnect from established Co-operative values and principles, or were there underlying structural issues that this critique does not fully address? In order to answer these questions, a longer historical perspective is needed that considers how the ideals of international co-operative trade have been framed and whether this reflects the realities of trade between the British Co-op and co-operatives in developing countries.

International Co-operative trade and the ICA 1895–1970

The British Co-operative movement was a founding member of the International Co-operative Alliance (ICA) in 1895, and for the first 50 years was the dominant force in the organisation. By 1907, over half the affiliated societies were British and they provided over three-fifths of ICA income.[34] The ICA was established as a networking organisation designed to promote co-operation between co-operatives. The founding Objects of the International Co-operative Alliance set out its intention to 'establish commercial relations between the co-operators of different countries for their mutual advantage'.[35] Membership of the ICA brought the British consumer Co-operative into direct contact with other forms of co-operative including worker and agricultural co-operatives. It was this international networking between consumer and producer co-operatives that offered the closest parallel to the trading partnerships that Fair Trade looked to develop.

At the Paris Congress in 1896, it was agreed by ICA delegates that consumer societies should give preference to industrial and agricultural co-ops when purchasing supplies, provided that quality and prices were the same.[36] The International Co-operative Wholesale Society (ICWS), established in 1924, marked the first serious attempt by the ICA to facilitate international trade in the twentieth century, (previous attempts had been hampered by political and economic instability, the result of war and economic depression).[37] But the ICWS was not itself an active trading organisation – it remained solely as a facility for information exchange. Albin Johansson, an ICA delegate, was frustrated at the ICA's inability to challenge capitalism's dominance in international trade. He believed that the ICA had to 'take a step forward from the passing of resolutions to true international constructive work'.[38]

Margaret Digby, Co-op historian and Secretary of the Plunkett Foundation, shared Johansson's belief in the potential of international co-operative trade.[39] In 1928, Digby argued for the 'complete interlocking of the trading interests of producers and consumers,' whereby, 'no consumers' society would purchase goods "outside the movement" while there existed a co-operative marketing society capable of supplying them'.[40] Digby found that, for the most part, a full assessment of the origins of goods imported by the British Co-operative movement was restricted by the limits of the record-keeping. She concluded that, with the exception of tea, it was 'impossible to say how many may be of co-operative origin; others must be from private sources'.[41] The very fact that the CWS were not distinguishing between imports from private suppliers and co-operatives suggests that, in practice, the philosophy of international co-operative collaboration was not prioritised by CWS buyers. This discrepancy between ideology and practice in the CWS' international trade relations was the result of the Co-ops unwillingness to directly address the consumer-producer dichotomy within the movement. Digby argued that nationally the issue of relations between the two sides was being tentatively worked out, but she acknowledged that, 'internationally, it has got little further than the stage of discussion'.[42]

In 1938, the ICA established the International Co-operative Trading Agency (ICTA). This was a direct trading body, but it only traded for two years before the onset of war forced it to suspend business. After the war, the ICTA merged with the ICWS and resumed business in 1946. But in May 1952, the ICTA ceased trading; it had not been receiving sufficient support from its members to cover its expenses.[43] Despite these setbacks, the idea of international co-operative trade remained appealing to many within the ICA and at the 1954 Paris Congress one of the major themes was, 'International Co-operative Trade, the Possibilities of Practical Collaboration between National Organisations and its Development by the Alliance.'[44] In 1966, at the Vienna Conference, the ICA renewed its commitment to international co-operative collaboration.[45] But these statements of intent meant little without the support of the ICA's membership, particularly the British movement. In practice, by the end of the 1960s international co-op to co-op trade between ICA members remained extremely limited.

Multinational co-operatives: an alternative trade model

The Co-op's trading policy during the 1970s was largely informed by a strategy of cost reduction and efficiency savings in order to respond to increased competition from supermarkets and multinational corporations (MNCs). However, an alternative response to the challenge of MNCs was also considered; which had it been pursued, could have led to greater co-op to co-op trade and a genuine structure for 'alternative trade.' Johann Brazda has argued that the context of rapidly integrating markets and fierce retail competition could have led to, 'a new era of international co-operation, with the most active movements engaging in rescue operations for their most endangered counterparts'.[46] For instance, at the 1972 ICA congress in Warsaw, in response to the growing economic power of MNCs, delegates resolved to, 'explore the concept of expanding multinational co-operatives to handle commodities in international trade so as to more closely link producer and consumer co-operatives'.[47]

Some within the British movement believed that the Co-operatives' own label goods could provide the model for restructuring the movement.[48] For instance, in 1972, the CWS own label food range extended to over 665 varieties and had sales of £106 million at wholesale prices. Thirty five of these varieties were made in CWS factories.[49] Charles Job, Director of Royal Arsenal Co-operative Society, argued that the Co-op was undermining itself by stocking numerous goods made by multinationals when CWS alternatives were available. He pointed out that the Co-op's own label instant coffee, which was a bestseller, was actually made by Tenco, a subsidiary of the US giant, Coca Cola. He voiced his concern at Congress that this was not 'a policy which indicates a move towards a Co-operative Commonwealth'.[50] The solution Job advocated was for the CWS to manufacture more, or buy more, from co-operatively owned enterprises abroad.

It seemed that despite initial optimism the practical realities of international co-operative trade were not to be easily realised. One of the main reasons identified by the ICA for the slow growth of inter-co-operative trade was 'the lack of interest shown by co-operatives in developed countries in finding co-operative trade partners from developing countries'.[51] Some international co-op to co-op trade took place, but consumer societies, such as the British Co-op, tended to deal solely with producer co-operatives from developed countries. For instance, there were long-standing trade links between the CWS and the New Zealand Dairy Co-operatives.[52]

One exception was the Japanese consumer co-operative which 'voluntarily sought out trade partners from within the co-operative movement' and 'helped developing co-operatives to improve their international trading capabilities'.[53] For instance, in 1962 UNICOOP Japan agreed on a trading arrangement to import Thai maize from the Thailand COPRODUCT (Bangkok Co-operative Farm Product Marketing Society). It is possible that a forerunner of Fair Trade could be identified among the international co-operative trade in Asia during this period, but to date there has been little academic work exploring these networks. This research agenda has the potential to offer a new perspective on the development of Fair Trade and move beyond a primarily Eurocentric narrative.[54]

By the late 1970s, the Plunkett Foundation, having consistently called for greater co-operation between co-operatives on the issue of international trade, was clearly frustrated by the limited progress. A 1978 report on the extent and prospects of international co-operative trade in Asia concluded that: 'No one would expect co-operatives in developed countries to trade with developing co-operatives on terms less favourable than those offered by competitors in the field. . . However if a buying co-operative does not give due consideration to the competitive offers of other co-operatives because of its reluctance to change trade partners, then there is not much chance for inter-co-operative trade to prosper where developing co-operatives are involved.'[55]

As one of the largest and most powerful Co-operative movements, British support was thought to be crucial to the success of any new venture and it was argued that: 'There can be no effective international co-operative alternative to the Multi-national Corporations without the determined and whole-hearted support of the British movement'.[56] But the British Co-operative movement seemed unable to fully appreciate the significance and the extent of the consumer-producer conflict within international co-operation. This meant that it was not in a position to bring together consumer and producer interests in order to overcome the basic dilemma of price.[57] Conceptually the notion of a 'fair price' may be relatively simple, perhaps deceptively so. But Dr Saxena, former director of the ICA, summarised the challenge when he stated that: 'Consumer organisations are generally interested in the lowest prices, while farmers want the highest.'[58]

The new internationalism: a step too far?

For many civil society groups, the values and principles of the Co-operative movement continued to offer a positive alternative vision of society, and they looked to the British Co-operative, with its 13 million members, for support and leadership. In addition to the campaign for fair tea prices, discussed earlier, there were two further campaigns that prompted the Co-op to respond to civil society-led consumer activism: firstly, the Anti-Apartheid Boycott of South Africa and secondly, Oxfam's Botswana co-operative programme. The Anti-Apartheid Boycott and Botswana co-operative programme offer a useful insight into the Co-op management's thinking, because while they did involve some commercial risk, support for these campaigns did not require a major restructuring of supply chains. In this way they offered an opportunity for the Co-op to demonstrate its wider social purpose without the commitment required of an alternative trade programme. The Co-op's response to these campaigns might be viewed as a test case for the Co-op's values and principles in practice during this period.

I The boycott of South Africa

From the first boycott campaigns of the late 1950s, the Anti-Apartheid Movement (AAM) identified the Co-op as potentially sympathetic to their call for sanctions against South Africa. But the Co-operative Union declined to be involved in the AAM's campaign stating that 'they [did] not think that it [was] practicable or advisable to pursue a policy of boycott of South African goods'.[59] But this did not discourage AAM from trying to gain the support of local Co-operative Societies, and here they had more success most notably with the London, Manchester and Surrey Societies. Some Co-op members championed the calls for a boycott in the Co-operative press and appealed to the ideals of the movement to look beyond the profit motive. They argued that: 'The South African people naturally look to our movement as one that has greater ideals than merely seeking profit and supplying goods whatever the consequences for others less fortunate than ourselves.'[60] In the context of Fair Trade, the boycott of South Africa was particularly significant because it encouraged voluntary organisations and NGOs working on a range of human rights and development issues to join together and advocate consumption as a political act. The British Co-operative movement, despite considerable pressure from the membership, maintained that 'it is unfair to ask the movement to take the lead in this matter when many societies are facing trading difficulties'.[61] Ultimately securing a consistent supply of produce and maintaining market share was prioritised over the ethical concerns of trading with the South African apartheid regime.

It was not only Co-op stores that faced boycott action over business with South Africa. In 1973, the Co-operative Bank's decision to offer its customers Barclaycard credit cards, rather than Access, also made it the focus of consumer action. Barclays was one of the biggest banks in South Africa, officially its stance on apartheid was 'neutral', but, in practice, only 1 in 45 of its clerical bank staff in South Africa were black and it did nothing to oppose apartheid. Activist members of the Co-op stated that: 'Until the bank alters this dangerous decision, we must all refuse to take credit cards through the bank.'[62] This action demonstrated an innovative form of boycott that had not been anticipated by managers at the Co-operative Bank. The *Co-operative News* was also targeted for its continued promotion of South African goods. The CWS had argued that its role was simply to supply a range of goods and let the consumer decide what to buy depending on their own criteria. But campaigners argued that adverts for goods such as Outspan Oranges were, 'aimed at creating a need'.[63] Those that wanted a complete boycott believed that an end to advertising was an important first step. They stated, 'to that end, we firstly want to see an end to promotion of these goods.'[64]

The consumer activism of AAM's boycott of South African products did increase awareness among some Co-op members of the wider implications of their consumer choices, but probably more significantly the boycott gained widespread media coverage and called into question the values and trading practices of those businesses that flouted the boycott. This same values-led consumer activism would also later be called on to demonstrate mainstream demand for Fairtrade certified goods. This was particularly significant given that neither Fair Trade organisations nor the Co-operative movement had the marketing budgets, or the inclination, to employ the services of the so-called 'hidden persuaders'.[65] Growing awareness of Fair Trade would instead rely on a diverse, if somewhat conservative, range of grassroots campaign methods from leafleting and letter writing to petitions and public meetings.

II Oxfam and the Botswana co-operative programme

Graham Alder, writing in the *Co-operative Review* in 1972, provided readers with a detailed account of the changing emphasis in the funding priorities of British voluntary aid agencies. Alder noted that a greater proportion of funds were being directed towards development projects compared to immediate disaster relief and that this represented an opportunity for co-operative development projects.[66] Christian Aid was reported to have increased development funds proportionately from 45.6% in 1968–69 to 55.4% in 1969–70. And Oxfam's development aid, compared to its relief aid, had increased from roughly 3:1 in 1960 to 5:1 in 1970.

One of the first development campaigns to directly partner with the British Co-operative movement was Oxfam's 'Help the Hungry to Help Each Other'. Launched in Birmingham on 4 March 1966, the object of the campaign was to raise money to establish a self-sufficient consumer co-operative in Bechuanaland (Botswana).[67] The plight of Botswana had gained particular attention since it became known that 30,000 men chose to work in South Africa under the conditions of apartheid so that they could send their wages home to their impoverished families.[68]

By 1966 Oxfam was already giving development assistance to 40 co-operative projects in 20 countries.[69] Bernard Murphy, Liaison Officer for Co-operatives and Trade Unions, stated of the Oxfam programme in 1966, 'We do not say that we are the advance guard for co-operative development in the underdeveloped countries but we do say that we have sown the seeds for the nurturing of the co-operative philosophy.'[70] But Oxfam was clear that this was to be a Co-op led initiative. They stated that, 'it is for the British Co-operators to prove the relevance of the co-operative ideal 122 years after the Rochdale Society opened its doors in Toad Lane.'[71]

By 1970 the programme had achieved its main goals, but it had not run completely smoothly.[72] Twenty months after the launch of the campaign, the Co-operative was still short of the £30,000 they had promised Oxfam. Some within the movement, such as Tom Taylor, President of the Scottish CWS, believed that the Co-operative's image had been severely tarnished by its half-hearted approach to the joint programme with Oxfam. Taylor stated that the 'co-operative movement should have some concern for our self-respect and the discharge of our moral responsibilities'.[73] It was proposed that individual Co-operative societies could allocate a 'divi number' to Oxfam as a practical way of raising funds. It was argued that in terms of public perception it could be valuable for the movement to 'identify itself more positively as an organisation with a social conscience'.[74] This initiative had the potential to operate as a type of social premium, a dividend on purchase – not paid directly to producer groups, but providing support for Oxfam development projects. But the Co-operative management rejected the plan and further questioned the feasibility of the whole programme at a time of 'almost unprecedented trading difficulty'.[75]

The Botswana campaign highlighted two main weaknesses of the Co-op during this period that limited its ability to partner with development NGOs effectively. Firstly, the structure of the movement was such that it made it almost impossible to run a well co-ordinated national campaign. Oxfam's Co-op and Trade Union Liaison Officer, Bernard Murphy, commented that, 'despite the fact that (numerically) the Co-operative Movement represents the largest pressure group in the country (13.5 million) it is probably the most difficult to work with.'[76] Secondly, the Co-op management did not seem willing to offer the same level of support to Oxfam as the general membership. The ancillaries of the movement, such as the Co-op Party, the Women's Co-operative Guild, the Education Department and the Woodcraft Folk, were all noted by Oxfam for their contributions. But Murphy stated that: 'If there has been cause for thought it has been that the response from Management Committees has, in the main, been very poor.'[77] The reason given for this was that many societies were 'fighting for survival' and managers were forced to concentrate their energies on 'keeping them afloat'.[78]

The Co-operative difference: towards a 'tipping point'

For much of the 1960s and 1970s it seemed as if there was a growing disconnect between how the Co-op members and the management committees interpreted the Co-operative values and principles. The Co-op was losing market share to the major supermarkets (in 1961 the Co-op accounted for 10.4% of UK retail spend, but by 1980 this had fallen to 6.5%).[79] In response Co-op stores focused on cutting prices in an attempt to win back shoppers. Conceptually this price-based strategy represented a victory of the 'businessmen' over the 'ideologues'.[80] Co-op management committees argued that working-class Co-op members were primarily interested in value for money. Based on this assessment, they could not imagine significant consumer demand for tea that hoped to return a fair price to the producers. Likewise, there was concern that a boycott of South African goods would simply result in members shopping elsewhere, and that customer loyalty would be threatened if dividend payments were directed towards charitable causes.

This commercial focus was seen as a logical management response, and understandable given the context; but only by challenging the business orthodoxy would the Co-op be able to develop an ethical and sustainable business programme. This shift in thinking began in the early 1980s and gathered pace as the decade progressed. There was a broadening consensus within the movement about the need for change, and a recognition among senior figures that the Co-op had been too pre-occupied with economic survival at the expense of its social roots.[81] Hedley Whitehead, President of the Co-operative Union, called for a 'radical re-thinking of the Movement's social purpose'.[82] He argued that otherwise the Co-op may, 'succeed in maintaining a significant stake in UK retailing but on basically no different terms from any of our most prominent competitors'.[83]

Increased public awareness of environmental issues such as global warming and acid rain, proved a turning point for the Co-op and led them to reposition themselves more prominently as a 'green' retailer. They pioneered a number of initiatives such as converting all aerosol products to CFC-free propellants, phasing out plastic egg boxes and promoting the use of biodegradable carrier bags. As well as wanting to 'do the right thing', green initiatives also offered the potential to actively engage a new demographic. Lloyd Wilkinson, Chief Executive of the Co-operative Union, stated that: 'The issues surrounding green consumerism give the movement an unrivalled opportunity to show what "the Co-op difference" really is'.[84] In 1985, the Co-operative Retail Services adopted a statement of social goals that outlined its determination, 'to do everything in its power to protect the environment and ensure the efficient use and protection of natural resources'.[85] The Co-op believed that the consumer could be a positive force for change and highlighted the political nature of consumption. The CWS' *Co-op Action Guide for the Environment* reminded consumers that 'every time you take your supermarket trolley for a spin you're taking part in a referendum about the future of the planet'.[86]

Despite its best intentions, for those outside the movement the Co-op's disparate structure continued to be an obstacle. For instance, *Ethical Consumer,* in its May/June 1989 edition confirmed the Co-op as 'the nearest thing we would recommend as a best buy'.[87] But this praise was somewhat undermined when they conceded that it was hard to generalise about the Co-op policy or practice because it was 'made up of about 100 independent Co-operative societies which collectively operate 1,475 supermarkets and 63 superstores'.[88] Peter Crouchman, Co-op Member Relations Officer and director of Friends of the Earth, also recognised the shortcomings of the Movement's structure. He bemoaned the fact that 'no one person can co-ordinate what we [the Co-op] do. This leads to missed opportunities when centrally-created ideas are lost at the level that matters most – locally'.[89] In contrast, the big supermarkets were much more effective at coordinating national marketing campaigns to highlight their commitment to new environmental initiatives.

It was the Co-operative Bank that was first to (re)introduced, not only environmental issues, but wider social values into the business practices of the movement. In May 1992, they became the first UK bank to publish an 'Ethical Policy'. The Ethical Policy stated that 'given our origins as part of the co-operative movement and its basic values, it is perhaps not surprising that we should be the first bank to respond to people's growing concerns about the quality of life here and in the rest of the world'.[90] Arguably what was more surprising, for many Co-op members, was that the Co-operative Bank (and the wider movement) had not responded sooner.[91] The Co-operative Bank management was finally convinced of the need to prioritise co-operative values in its business mission after conducting market research that revealed 84% of their members felt the bank should have a clear ethical policy.[92] The issues of greatest concern were human rights, armament exports and animal experiments, followed by the fur trade and tobacco manufacture.

There were also signs of change in the Co-operative Retail stores. In May 1992, two years before the launch of the Fairtrade Mark in the UK, the Co-op began stocking Cafédirect coffee – one of the first major UK food retailers to do so. This represented the Co-op's first real move into the Fair Trade market, but commercially it was not an immediate success. Market research had suggested that there was consumer demand for goods produced without exploiting Third World workers.[93] However, by September 1995 Cafédirect only accounted for 1.8% of CWS Retail's ground coffee sales and only 0.1% of the instant coffee market.[94] Bill Shannon, CWS Brands Manager, stated that 'there is no doubt that, had we taken the decision purely on commercial grounds, Cafédirect would have been discontinued by now.'[95] The introduction Cafédirect into Co-op stores had a wider significance, perhaps not fully recognised at the time. Working with Cafédirect, the Co-op business was for the first time, purposefully engaged in a trading partnership designed to support producer co-operatives in the global South including Mexico, Peru and Costa Rica. Despite initial doubts the CWS Retail, encouraged by the success of the Co-operative Bank, believed that they could build a market for Fair Trade products such as Cafédirect.[96]

The concept of building a new 'ethical brand' was not necessarily seen as the most effective way of establishing Fair Trade in mainstream markets. Bill Shannon argued that rather than supporting ethical brands, such as Cafédirect, it would be better for the Co-op to apply the Fair Trade criteria to 'a current, standard, mainstream Co-op Brand product, such as Indian Prince Tea – and doing it in a way that does not add a noticeable increase in cost'.[97] But he conceded that, 'so far it has proved impossible to get such as project off the ground and onto our shelves'.[98] It would be the best part of a decade before this ambition was achieved with all own-brand Co-op chocolate converted to Fairtrade in 2002, to be followed by the certification of all Co-op own-brand coffee in 2003. But it was this type of corporate 'choice-editing' in support of Fairtrade that would become increasingly important to the strategic direction of Fairtrade.

This emphasis on building a market for Fair Trade has been underplayed in much of the academic literature. In reality, the take-off for Fairtrade products at the Co-op was as much about the role of 'social intraprenuers' within the Co-op as consumer demand.[99] In January

1993 a new internal committee was formed, known as the Consumer Issues Group.[100] This was an important moment because it brought together senior management representatives from across the business to work on a strategy that would see the Co-op established as the UK's most ethical retailer. In 1997 the strategic review, that had followed the failed takeover, saw the Co-op focus on its core strength of convenience stores; and responsible retailing was given a greater role in positioning the 'Co-operative difference'. The organisational restructuring also led to the departure of two senior managers and as a result key positions within the revised structure were filled by members of the Consumer Issues Group. By the end of 1997, the respective heads of food retail, marketing, Co-op brand, public relations and corporate affairs were all original members of the Consumer Issues Group and active supporters of the responsible retailing agenda.[101] The tipping point, in terms of Co-op support for Fairtrade, came just 2 years later in 1999 with the introduction of Fairtrade products into all 1,450 grocery stores. Following the successful national roll-out of Fairtrade, the Co-op became the largest stockist of Fairtrade labelled products in Britain.[102] This hugely increased the availability of Fairtrade products and almost overnight propelled Fairtrade from 'the margins to the mainstream'.[103]

Conclusions

The idea of Fairtrade certification succeeded where other attempts to restructure international co-operative trade had failed. By engaging managers, consumers and producers with powerful individual stories and concrete credible facts about trade and development, Fairtrade showed how successful a 'sticky idea' could be in changing both opinions and behaviour.[104] Brad Hill, Fairtrade Strategy Manager for the Co-operative Group, recognised that: 'The principles fitted with the whole values of the Co-op and the Fairtrade Mark gave us the communications tool to talk to consumers about it'.[105]

The potential of an international Co-operative movement had existed from the early nineteenth century. Robert Owen had declared his ambition for an 'Association of all Classes and all Nations' and in 1895 it appeared, with the establishment of the ICA, that Owen's vision had become a reality.[106] But early attempts at encouraging international co-op to co-op trade had soon ended in failure and it was not until the 1960s that there was genuine renewed interest, both from within the movement and wider civil society. During this period, the Co-operative movement, with the international network of the ICA, had enormous potential to develop an alternative trading policy between consumer societies in the 'developed' countries of Europe and producer co-operatives in 'developing' countries of Africa, Asia and Latin America. But the Movement was not able to rationalise the dichotomy between consumer and producer in a way that could make this proposition work. Instead, the British Co-operative movement limited its involvement in international co-op to co-op trade to developed countries, such as New Zealand.

When the Co-op's failings were highlighted by the national media or the Co-operative press there was a strong response from the membership. Co-op members showed a willingness to prioritise ethical values and co-operative principles above consumer priorities of quality and price. Here we see a contrast with the nineteenth century, where it has been argued that the leadership held on to Co-operative values while the average member was more concerned about making ends meet.[107] In the mid to late twentieth century it seems that, for some members at least, the co-operative values proved increasingly relevant, while for the management (particularly during the 1960s and 1970s) the main concern was ensuring the survival of the retail store.

From the 1980s the Co-op began to adopt a more clearly ethical stance and connect more closely with civil society. As discussed earlier there were a number of factors that led to this change in direction: firstly, there was an awareness among the Co-operative Union that as a result of solely focusing on the economic retail competition it had become distanced from its values and principles; secondly, although there was not a 'single Co-operative Society for the UK', the movement was becoming more streamlined; and thirdly, there was a genuine effort to understand the ethical opinions of the membership and the wider public. This showed that there was the possibility of a consumer market for green and ethical products, and from the late 1990s Fairtrade became central to the Co-operative's positioning as a mainstream retailer with a social goal.

With growing support for Fairtrade across its core business functions, the Co-op was now able to overcome many of the consumer-producer tensions that had proved stumbling blocks to its international trade programme in the past. As John Bowes, former Marketing Manager for the Co-operative Group, commented: 'It took the initiative and demonstrated what could be achieved'.[108] However, it is perhaps an indication of the true extent of the Co-op's preoccupation with economic survival during the 1960s and 1970s that Fair Trade (a model of trade that owed so much to the principles of co-operation) was ultimately pioneered by development organisations, Christian agencies and Alternative Trade Organisations rather than the ICA. From the mid-1990s, the 'social intraprenuers' succeeded in situating Fairtrade at the heart of the Co-op's responsible retailing agenda, and in so doing perhaps began to reconnect with its nineteenth-century ideals of a Co-operative Commonwealth engaged in a 'world-making' project.[109]

4
International Trade Unionism: Labour Solidarity?

In responding to the Commons International Development Select Committee report on *Fair Trade and Development*, the Trade Union Congress (TUC) General Secretary, Brendan Barber, stated that, 'Fair Trade is one way that consumers in Britain can make sure people who work in developing countries get a fair day's pay for a fair day's work – so that everyone benefits from globalisation.'[1] But in written evidence to the same Committee the TUC had argued that, 'in the absence of a trade union and a collective agreement in the workplace, labelling the 'human rights content' of goods as having been produced in conditions of respect for worker's rights is unreliable ... So while the trade union movement supports the Fair Trade movement's labelling with regard to price, it believes that labelling against labour standards on Fair Trade products is as premature there as it is in ETI [Ethical Trading Initiative] member companies.'[2] These statements begin to reveal the paradox of the TUC's connection with Fair Trade and more broadly the tensions between trade unions and Fairtrade certification.[3]

This chapter focuses on the interactions between the TUC and Fair Trade in order to build an exploratory case study that investigates both the trade union critique of Fairtrade's Hired Labour Standards and the practical challenges of integrating 'Third World' workers within a model of international labour solidarity. Previous scholarly work has documented the role of the TUC in improving working conditions and securing labour rights for workers challenged by the changing nature of an industrialised workplace in modern Britain.[4] In contrast, the TUC's role on the international stage, particularly in relation to conditions of workers in the global South, has received significantly less academic attention. The aim is to better understand the extent and limits of the TUC's involvement with the Fair Trade movement as it took shape from the early 1970s. Drawing on a range of sources including personal correspondence, committee minutes and published reports, the dynamics of the relationship between the TUC and the British Fair Trade movement will be explored.

The aim of this chapter is to consider the TUC's promotion of 'fair labour standards' and understand how these campaigns related to the political, social and economic agenda being promoted by the Fair Trade movement. Following a broadly chronological structure, this chapter explores how, during the 1970s, the TUC responded to: appeals by 'Third World' trade unions, such as the Ceylon Workers Congress; calls for action from NGOs, in particular War on Want and the Trade Union Committee for International Co-operation and Development; and the funding proposals of the Ministry of Overseas Development. The next section investigates the TUC's involvement with the Brandt lobby from the early 1980s and then looks at how the TUC reacted to the Greater London Council's plans to implement an alternative trade project. The final section focuses on the 1990s and early 2000s, and questions whether the 'plantation vs. smallholder producer debate' provided an opportunity for the TUC to engage with the Fair Trade movement or reinforced the distance between them.

International trade unionism: A new research agenda

In recent years there has been renewed interest in the study of international trade unions among a range of academic disciplines. Perhaps unsurprisingly, the growing volume of literature has produced widely varied assessments of the past contributions and future potential of international trade unions. What remains scarce in the current literature on international trade unions are the detailed case studies that are able to explore the complex relationships between trade unions and new social movements, both nationally and internationally. In this respect, research into the Fair Trade movement can make a valuable contribution in exploring how socioeconomic networks developed between trade unions, NGOs and other civil society groups.

The historian, Patrick Pasture has argued that the international dimension has never been a priority for either the unions' leaders or their constituency. He suggests that the trade union movement has worked, above all, on winning social advances within a national framework and building up national welfare states. Pasture's assessment highlighted the financial fragility of international trade unionism. He argued that 'the resources that unions were and are prepared to invest in international union activity were and are, in fact, ludicrously small compared with either the needs or the resources mustered by other pressure groups.'[5] Commenting on the future of international trade unionism, Pasture argued that it depended on, 'its capacity to free itself from its Western patterns of thought and ideal types'.[6] This Pasture believed, did not seem likely, 'the international union movement has given few signs in the past of possessing just this sort of flexibility. A very Western perspective has always predominated right up to the present day.'[7] But despite this, Pasture concedes that 'the myth of labour-movement internationalism is a stubborn one'.[8]

Robert O'Brien, Professor of Global Labour Issues, maintains that trade unions still have a potentially valuable contribution to make in a globalised economy. He suggests that trade unions are transforming from being a 'supporter of US capitalism, to a brake on neoliberal industrial relations, to potentially advocating a different form of political economy in alliance with other groups'.[9] However, with trade unions largely excluded from the corridors of power, the future significance of international trade unionism is seen to be closely linked with growth of social movements and associated networks.[10] O'Brien argues that trade unions have the potential to make a positive contribution to the development of these alternative networks. He suggests that: 'Labour organizations, particularly trade unions, occupy strategic sectors in the global economy, possess an institutional structure that brings benefits (as well as the often cited costs) and wield traditional forms of influence and power that can complement new social movement activity'.[11]

This optimistic assessment was based on a belief that with the end of the Cold War it might be possible to 'rekindle the spirit of the late nineteenth and early twentieth century internationals', and construct a new form of internationalism.[12] One example of this new spirit of internationalism was found in the trade union presence at the anti-WTO protests in Seattle in 1999. The image of trade unionists marching alongside environmentalists dressed in turtle costumes has been used to illustrate the growing diversity of the global justice movement. O'Brien calls on scholars working on new social movements and civil society to 'give some thought to the old social movement of labour'.[13] While there is a case for further research in order to better understand and contextualise the relationship between trade unions and new social movements, what is also needed are studies that go beyond the drama of these symbolic moments in order to investigate the day-to-day workings and longer-term dynamics of these new networks.

Peter Waterman, labour historian, extended the study of international trade unionism beyond an assessment of Cold War rhetoric to encompass global North–South relations as well as East–West.[14] Waterman is critical of what he sees as the slow progress made by the Westocentric institutions of international trade unionism, such as the International Confederation of Free Trade Unions (ICFTU).[15] He highlights how the weak financial position of the ICFTU has resulted in a dependency on state funding for their development activities. During the 1990s, the ICFTU was only receiving some £7 million per year from affiliation fees of its 113 million members. In contrast, Amnesty International with only 1 million members was receiving £12 million annually and Greenpeace with its 4.3 million members had an income of £110 million a year. The ICFTU's limited funds resulted from it only receiving 1% of membership fees from its members, whereas the Dutch affiliate to Amnesty allocated 38.6% of its annual subscriptions to the international office.

Waterman argued that: 'Given the alternative between reinventing itself as an international solidarity movement and incorporating itself into state-dependent co-operation, it is hardly surprising that the ICFTU has taken the easy option'.[16] But despite his disillusionment with the ICFTU, Waterman remained convinced of the potential of international trade unionism. Throughout the 1970s and 1980s, writing in the *Newsletter of International Labour Studies*, Waterman argued that 'a new labour internationalism would come with the new unionism in the Third World'.[17] This, as Waterman now admits, did not happen but he maintains that a 'breakthrough might yet occur' based on the new union movements in the Third World.[18]

Waterman also questioned the limited recognition of trade unions within the literature on new or alternative social movements. He argued that: 'Much of this literature, moreover, either ignores or writes off labour as an issue – and workers as a potentially progressive force – nationally or internationally'.[19] But in recent years a number of sociologists have responded to this apparent gap in the literature and have sought to incorporate trade unions into studies on social movements. Donatella Della Porta, sociologist and political scientist, argues that trade unions potentially have a valuable role to play as a counterweight and ally to new social movements. Della Porta also identifies the WTO protest in Seattle as a sign of 'the remobilisation of labor'.[20] But taking a wider perspective, she states that: 'Trade unions have often been an important ally for emerging actors, such as the student movement or the women's movement, particularly in Europe. With a wide social base and very often privileged channels of access to institutional decision-makers ... the trade unions can increase the mobilization capacities and chances of success for social movements'.[21]

The prominence of research on the potential of international trade unionism as an ally for new social movements has led to a rather speculative feel to much of the current literature. In contrast, Robert Cox, political scientist and United Nations officer, has adopted a more critical approach to understanding existing relations between trade unions and social movements. This has led him to question the compatibility of trade unions and new social movements. He argues that 'the new social movements have often been suspicious of organized labour, fearing domination by labour's tighter and more hierarchical organization which might not respect the social movements' far more loosely structured and more participatory forms of organization'.[22] Cox is right to highlight the structural differences in organization between trade unions and social movements, but perhaps underplays the significance of trade unionism's perceived poor track-record on socially progressive issues of labour solidarity and international development.

The TUC: An important ally for Fair Trade?

The TUC has been described by Ross Martin as being 'marked out as an organization of distinctive character and apparent influence by its wide-ranging policy concerns, its myriad formal and informal links with government, its close association with the Labour party, its sheer bulk in numerical terms and its capacity for attracting public attention'.[23] The TUC seemed to represent an opportunity to engage with a well-established and influential pressure group. The following section explores the potential for building networks between Fair Trade and trade unionists and identifies three aspects that made the TUC a potentially valuable ally: first, the TUC's broad-based membership; secondly, the TUC's ideals of international solidarity; and thirdly, the promotion by the TUC and ICFTU of 'fair labour standards'.

During the 1970s, the TUC's membership expanded steadily from 10 million members in 1970 to 12 million members by 1979. With 92% of unions affiliated to it, in 1979 the TUC could claim that it directly represented just over half the workforce (52%).[24] But by 1992, TUC membership had fallen under nine million, accounting for 80% of all union members and only just over a third of the total workforce (34%).[25] Despite declining numbers, the TUC's ability to accurately record its membership was still recognised by civil society organisations as an important representative dimension of its political influence. In contrast, many NGOs and voluntary organisations relied on income as an indicator of public support, but this became increasingly problematic with higher levels of state funding.

The international ideals of the TUC seemed to be consistent with the main themes of Fair Trade. Since its formation in 1919, the TUC had played a prominent role in promoting the work of the International Labour Organization (ILO). At the Philadelphia Conference in May 1944, the ILO declared that: 'labour is not a commodity; freedom of expression and of association are essential to sustained progress; poverty anywhere constitutes a danger to prosperity everywhere; the war against want requires to be carried on with unrelenting vigour within each nation.'[26] The TUC's membership of the ICFTU from 1949 provided an opportunity to develop the work of the ILO within the increasingly global context of international trade unionism. The number of organisations affiliated to the ICFTU had grown rapidly from 67 organisations in 51 countries in 1949 to 135 organisations in over 100 countries by 1961.[27] This growth was partly explained by the membership of newly independent states. In Africa, for instance, the number of affiliates had increased from 3 in 1949 to 20 by 1961.[28]

The discussion of 'fair labour standards' was revived at International Labour Conference in June 1971 and by the late 1970s, the idea had been incorporated within the ICFTU Development Charter. The Charter stated that: 'The trade union movement would be failing in its historic mission if it were purely concerned about economic objectives and material well-being'.[29] It outlined the importance of unions to the prospects of future equitable development stating that: 'The encouragement of the growth of independent and representative trade union organisations is an essential pre-requisite for a fair distribution of income and wealth in society and for sustained economic and social development.'[30] Drawing heavily on the ILO, the ICFTU defined 'fair labour standards' as 'those provisions which assure the work force of reasonable protection and income maintenance through fair wages, unemployment benefit, safety, workmen's compensation, etc.'.[31]

The 1970s: The limits of international trade unionism

The emergence of the Fair Trade movement in Britain from the early 1970s coincided with the peak of the TUC's standing both in terms of membership and political recognition. However, while a growing civil society coalition of NGOs and voluntary organisations called for international labour solidarity in support of a New International Economic Order (NIEO), the TUC seemed constrained by a narrow policy framework. In its interactions with counterparts in the global South and civil society organisations in Britain, the TUC leadership showed limited 'moral imagination' and an inability to move beyond traditional, nationally focused, labour politics.[32]

The plight of Sri Lankan tea workers

As shown in earlier chapters, media coverage of tea production on plantations in India and Sri Lanka was a significant factor in uniting the early Fair Trade movement in campaigns for fair pay and working conditions. The TUC was also drawn into this controversy, through its membership of the ICFTU. For some trade union representatives, Sri Lanka represented an opportunity for the TUC to demonstrate its commitment to international labour solidarity and engage in debates about the growing power and influence of MNCs across global supply chains. But, as will be explored, the TUC's failure to act in support of Sri Lankan workers instead damaged their credibility among some sections of the NGO community and highlighted limitations of the TUC's international development agenda.

The plight of the Sri Lankan tea workers was first raised in an international trade union setting at the ICFTU working party on MNCs in Tokyo, October 1973. At this meeting the General Secretary of the Ceylon Workers' Congress (CWC) appealed for solidarity with his union's struggle, in particular with multinational British-owned tea companies.[33] The CWC looked to the TUC to challenge the power of multinational corporations and take action by lobbying the British government and mobilising consumers in support of tea workers. For some within the trade union movement, the Sri Lankan tea plantations took on a wider significance. Carl Wilms-Wright, an official at the ICFTU, argued that: 'Helping workers in Sri Lanka fight against the abuses of multinational capital is not merely an abstract act of charity towards the Third World. It is a test case for evolving an effective world-wide countervailing trade union strategy.'[34] Wilms-Wright argued that this action was also in the interests of British trade unionists: 'Tomorrow it may be necessary to call upon the same international labour solidarity to defend the interests of the British worker against the manipulations of multinational companies.'[35] But this strategy did not appear to gain traction within the TUC as they continued to resist calls for a co-ordinated campaign in support of Sri Lankan workers.

In explaining its lacklustre response, the TUC argued that it was, 'placed in a difficult situation where it is being asked to provide support when it has no substantive evidence of what the CWC, in particular, has done.'[36] In an attempt to salvage its own reputation, the TUC pointed instead to the limited communications and conflicts over policy within the international trade union movement. The TUC argued that 'there appears to have been no co-ordinated strategy carried out by the ICFTU, IFPAAW [International Federation of Plantation, Agricultural and Allied Workers] and the CWC in Sri Lanka itself to develop the collective bargaining strength of workers on tea plantations.'[37] No doubt many of the communications between the various organisations were incomplete, but was this sufficient justification for the TUC's inaction? An ICFTU report concluded that: 'The TUC kept wanting more information, even though it was difficult to obtain, even though time was pressing, and even though it was clear to everyone that the workers were in a bad way.'[38]

War on Want: 'An Account of Trade Union Imperialism'

One of the first NGOs to highlight the plight of the Sri Lankan tea workers was War on Want.[39] Initially as news broke, War on Want looked to trade union solidarity in order to confront and resolve the issue of labour exploitation. In 1974, War on Want published a report titled, *The State of Tea*, in which they stated that, 'it is the responsibility of the British Trade Unionists to ensure that co-workers employed by the same companies receive fair wages and are not exploited'.[40] At the beginning of the decade, War on Want still believed that the trade union movement had the potential to be a 'countervailing force' to the exploitation of Third World poor by multinational companies. But growing frustration over the TUC's failure to act, led War on Want to publish a highly critical assessment of the international trade union movement in 1978 titled, *Where Were You, Brother? An Account of Trade Union Imperialism*.[41]

War on Want held the TUC responsible for allowing British companies to avoid the issue of compensation payments to Sri Lankan tea workers for the human and environmental costs of tea production. They stated that, 'according to the Ceylon Workers Congress, the job in hand following nationalisation of the estates was pressure on the British government on the issue of compensation. Only the TUC had the necessary muscle to push this through.'[42] War on Want asked, 'Why is it left up to charities and newspapers to expose British company maltreatment of

Third World labour when, through the ICFTU, we're meant to have a global exchange of worker information?'[43] They contrasted the limited role played by the TUC with the extensive campaigns organised by the TUC's counterparts in Holland and Belgium. War on Want believed that the TUC should have tried to 'encourage shop floor interest and get action going against multinational Third World exploitation at the place where it would count – at factory floor level in the home base of these companies'.[44]

The critique of international trade unions developed in *Where Were You, Brother?* was not limited to a critical assessment of dealings with Sri Lanka. War on Want went as far as to claim that 'TUC concern about the Third World is almost non-existent'.[45] In justifying this accusation, they highlighted the fact that Allan Hargreaves, TUC International Secretary, in his 58-page report to the 1977 TUC conference included only 'five paragraphs on ICFTU work in Latin America, one paragraph on Asian work and nothing at all about Africa'.[46] War on Want was left with an overall impression that, 'international exchange between worker movements is pitifully small and in most cases non-existent. When this combined with a lack of information from the leadership the effect is to drive labour movements into dangerous isolation making them vulnerable to outside manipulation.'[47] This stinging indictment of international trade unionism was all the more telling since War on Want had always identified itself as 'the only charity that openly allies itself with the labour movement and has twelve national trade unions affiliated to it'.[48]

TUCICD: A partnership for development education

War on Want was not the only NGO during this period to consider the TUC as a potential ally in promoting Third World development. Formed in 1976, the Trade Union Committee for International Co-operation and Development (TUCICD) aimed to encourage international trade union networks, particularly between the North and the South. TUCICD was the brainchild of Mike Brown, trade union liaison officer for the World Development Movement (WDM).[49] The TUCICD argued that 'the existing economic order which is based on profit must be replaced with one based on social control and planning in the interests of all peoples and nations and on an equitable distribution of wealth'.[50] The TUCICD's main objective was to encourage British trade unionists to 'increase their international trade union contacts and to increase the solidarity of all workers in support of the objectives of a New International Economic Order (NIEO)'.[51]

In April 1978, the TUCICD wrote to the TUC requesting formal recognition and enquiring about the possibility of TUCICD assisting the TUC in its development and education work. The TUCICD's focus on development education was partly driven by new government funding opportunities that could potentially free up WDM from covering TUCICD's annual running costs (approximately £10,000).[52] But primarily the TUCICD's aim was to build links beyond supportive NGOs and campaigners in order to promote the ideas of a New International Economic Order to the general public more widely.

The response from the TUC demonstrated an institutional rigidity that made it difficult to work with newly formed NGOs: 'The TUC does not formally recognise outside bodies and has its own policies on international trade, co-operation and development. It would broadly support the objectives of TUCICD except that they are rather more radical, particularly in respect of the rather rigid TUCICD approach to the New International Economic Order, and language it uses to describe its objectives is also rather emotive.'[53] The Fair Trade movement evolved as a 'network of networks', shaped by civil society organisations promoting issues of international development and trade justice. In contrast, the TUC's focus on bolstering its influence within official corridors of power seemed out of step with the dynamics of these new partnerships evolving among NGOs and voluntary organisations working on alternative – or fair – trade.

Ministry of Overseas Development: Trade Union Foundation

In 1975, the Labour Government's white paper on international development demonstrated a 'new emphasis' whereby priority would be given to 'helping the poorest people in the poorest countries'.[54] As part of this new strategy, the Ministry for Overseas Development (ODM) undertook a re-evaluation of how they worked with NGOs. One of the recommendations was that the ODM should seek to capitalise on the TUC's ability to contribute to Britain's international development efforts. John Grant, Parliamentary Under-Secretary at the ODM commented that, 'it is my view that the Trades Unions likewise have much experience, albeit of a somewhat different kind, which could be of great value to the developing world if harnessed in a practical fashion'.[55] Further, he commented that, 'this is a view which I have also encountered in developing countries and which has been represented to me from our own voluntary societies'.[56]

In 1976, the Labour government made a grant available to the TUC to set up the Trade Union Foundation. The object of the Foundation was to promote 'trade union education and training and the participation of trade unions in social development in developing countries'.[57] This was the government's response to what it saw as a failure by the TUC and the ICFTU to prioritise Third World development. A report by Ministry of Overseas Development found that: 'In present circumstances protection of employment would seem to be the ICFTU's first priority. But what of protection for employment in the LDCs [Least Developed Countries]? There is a significant potential conflict here.'[58] The report concluded that, 'Much will depend on the extent to which the trade union movement in the developed world can provide increased training opportunities and financial assistance to the Third World trade union movement. Up to now there is not much evidence that this process has really been put in hand. However, in this connection the ODM grant to the TUC of £75,000 a year aims at stimulating precisely this kind of effort.'[59]

Funding for the Trade Union Foundation began modestly at £75,000 annually and rose to £186,000 by 1979–1980. Grants were primarily used for trade union training and conferences. Even funding at these relatively modest levels was attracting 'parliamentary interest' and led the ODM to question whether conference dinners were appropriate activities for the TUC to be spending Trade Union Foundation grants on.[60] Some officials at the ODM were clearly disappointed with the TUC's level of commitment to the Foundation, stating that, 'they may have written us a few letters but don't let them kid you that they're really concerned about the Third World'.[61]

From the early 1980s, with Margaret Thatcher set on reducing the international aid budget and limiting the power of trade unions, the future of the Trade Union Foundation seemed precarious. In 1980, the funding for the Foundation was cut back to £75,000, and in 1981, there were further cuts which left the grant at £50,000 a year. By August 1982, there was speculation that both the development grant and the education grant could be cut, which would leave the TUC without Government funds of any kind. *The Financial Times* reported that, 'Mr Marten is under pressure from Conservative backbenchers to save the money, on the grounds that education of union officials in developing countries is not an appropriate object of development aid.'[62] But the Trade Union Foundation survived international aid budget cuts and, although the Conservatives did little to develop the Foundation, it continued to receive a grant of £50,000.

The 1980s: a New International Economic Order?

For Oxfam, and its supporters, the Brandt Report and proposals for a New International Economic Order (NIEO) demonstrated the possibility of 'a jointly managed world economy in the interests of the working population of both north and south'.[63] They looked to the TUC to join with them in educating their membership about the key terms of these reports and in stimulating a wider discussion of the proposals. But for the TUC, the 1980s was a period of steep decline and crisis – membership had fallen by 2.9 million and politically the TUC was sidelined by the Thatcher administration.[64] This meant that domestic concerns took priority and initiatives, such as the ICFTU Development Charter, struggled to balance concerns for international development and the protection of jobs for British workers.

The Brandt report: ICFTU Development Charter

The *Report of the Independent Commission on International Development Issues*, known as the Brandt report, was presented to the Secretary-General of the United Nations on 12 February 1980 and published in March 1980.[65] The Commission's terms of reference specified three main areas of study: the past record of development in the Third World; the prospects for the world economy; and the creation of a new economic order.[66] The Brandt report's main recommendations highlighted the need to increase aid, reduce debt burdens of Third World countries and to work towards fairer international trade. The report was seen as particularly timely by many NGOs, coming as it did only weeks after the Conservative government's announcement that it intended to give greater weight to 'political, industrial and commercial considerations' when allocating Britain's aid expenditure.[67] British development NGOs did not accept the Brandt report uncritically, but they recognised it as an opportunity to engage the public in a debate about Britain's role in international development.[68] The NGO community looked to the TUC to lobby government and ensure that international development was kept on the political agenda.

There was an expectation among the international development lobby that the TUC would be a strong advocate for the Brandt report. With Joe Morris, President-Emeritus of Canadian Labour Congress on the Commission, it seemed that trade union interests would be well represented. From 1977 to 1978, Morris was the Chairman of the ILO Governing Body and was Vice-President of the ICFTU from 1976 to 1978. This trade union presence was regarded as particularly significant by British NGOs since no international NGO representative had been invited to sit on the Commission.[69] But it seems that Morris was unable to convince the Commission that international trade unionism was a viable solution to Third World poverty. On reviewing the Brandt report the TUC recognised that: 'Throughout the report there are few references to the role of trade unions in Third World countries and the position of trade unions in promoting development.'[70]

Anthony Sampson, writing in *The Observer* in December 1980 about the political impact of the Brandt report, commented that, 'It is always interesting to observe the tides and winds of public opinion which force politicians to change their course. Something of the kind seems to be happening in the determination of Britain's attitudes to the Third World.'[71] Sampson questioned, 'what lies behind this undercurrent, and why should it be stronger in Britain than elsewhere in the West (except Holland)?'[72] He reflected on the diverse range of stakeholders, from development agencies and Christian groups to far-sighted industrialists and bankers, who were beginning to appreciate that the future prosperity of the North was interlocked with the South. But in concluding, he commented that, 'among the groups that have welcomed the Brandt report the most notable absentees have been the trade unionists, who regard imports from Korea or the Philippines as a direct threat to their livelihood'.[73]

The ICFTU responded to Sampson's criticism on behalf of the TUC:

> As I am sure you are aware, newspaper coverage of trade union affairs is somewhat selective and it is not entirely surprising that work of the ICFTU, TUAC,[74] TUC and others on the Brandt report is not widely known. The TUC is the largest affiliate and has participated fully, indeed has been instrumental, in the ICFTU's work on the Brandt report and its follow-up.[75]

But the TUC maintained that the Brandt report should have given specific approval, at least in principle, to the trade union proposal of a social clause. They stated that: 'The commission's unwillingness to give open support to the social clause idea is further confirmation of their insufficient grasp of the totality of issues concerning adjustment policy.'[76]

The fact that the report did not specifically refer to the ICFTU Development Charter reflected the Brandt Commission's concern that the social clause could act as a protectionist measure at the expense of developing countries. The TUC's response to the Brandt report would seem to confirm the Commission's reservations about the motivations behind the Development Charter. Although the TUC welcomed 'increasing industrialization in Third World countries both for its own sake and for the resultant increases in North-South trade it will bring';[77] it also criticised the Brandt report's failure to realise the 'importance of temporary protective action in the North to ease the transitional problems caused by structural adaptation'.[78]

Despite the TUC's lukewarm response to the Brandt report, few NGOs were openly critical; instead they looked to win the TUC's backing for future campaigns. Oxfam, for instance wrote to Len Murray, General Secretary of the TUC, enquiring whether, 'the TUC and individual British unions may be prepared to join with us in stimulating wider discussion of the proposals in the report in the period leading up to the Summit Conference in Mexico City in June of this year'.[79] War on Want also declared its intention to, 'build a firm and constructive relationship with the trade union movement over the coming years'. [80] Terry Lacey, the General Secretary of War on Want, argued that: 'It will not be possible, therefore, to interest ordinary working people in the problems of the Third World except upon the basis of understanding the economic and social realities here in Britain.'[81]

GLC and TWIN Trading: An alternative trade network

In 1984, the Greater London Council (GLC) established a Third World project within its Industry and Employment branch. This initiative led Margaret Thatcher to remark, 'So Ken [Livingstone, the then GLC leader] proposes to have a foreign policy now, does he?'[82] But Livingstone and the GLC responded that, 'to attempt to solve the problems of London at the expense of the Third World would be inconsistent and wrong'.[83] This philosophy led the GLC to establish Twin and Twin Trading in 1985, a networking organisation and an alternative trading venture.[84] Twin Trading represented a new approach to Fair Trade and its objectives were based on the ideals of international trade unionism and labour solidarity, rather than charity or international development.

Twin Trading's Statement of Principles declared that, 'Trade Unions in First and Third World countries should seek opportunities for meeting together to draw up a code of labour for manufacturing industries in order to universalise best practices, such as the ILO Code.'[85] Ken Livingstone, opening Twin Trading's inaugural conference, stated that, 'London workers have a proud tradition of solidarity. They welcomed Garibaldi, and the Paris Commune. They founded with Marx the First International. They refused to load arms to supply the enemies of the Russian revolution.'[86] Livingstone argued that there was a need to revive international labour solidarity if unions were to counter the influence of multinational companies. He stated, 'Our problems are the same. We both suffer from unaccountable activities of the giant transnational companies. We are both seeking to find an alternative framework for international economic links and we know there is a great unexplored potential for trade and exchange between us.'[87] For some delegates, such as Horacio Listo, from Mozambique, the suggestion that London and the Third World were in the 'same boat' was a fallacy.[88] But beyond the bold language, delegates agreed on the need to put into practice a viable alternative trade network drawing on international trade unionism. Olivier Le Brun, Twin Trading's first Director, stated that: 'We regard ourselves as part of the movement which is today behind the GLC. The labour and trade union movement has a key role to play in transferring technology to working in the Third World.'[89]

By the time Twin Trading was established in February 1985, the GLC's days were clearly numbered. Thatcher had returned to office in June 1983 and intended to fulfil the Conservative's manifesto pledge of abolishing the GLC. This meant that in the short term the GLC's finances were placed under increased scrutiny. From July 1984, the Conservative government insisted that all new GLC contracts over £100,000 required ministerial consent and from March 1985 the GLC was prevented from entering into any contracts worth more than £15,000 prior to abolition.[90] But the most controversial aspect of GLC finances was so-called 'tombstone' funding. At the beginning of 1986, there were reports that the GLC intended to transfer £70 million to a range of voluntary organisations to ensure the future funding of schemes they felt were under threat. On 7 February, Anthony Scrivener, QC, stated that the 'GLC has no power to make a will'.[91] The Conservative-controlled London boroughs, led by Westminster, moved to block tombstone funding and were granted a temporary injunction on 12 February 1986.[92] Despite this injunction, the GLC still succeeded in allocating a lump sum of £690,247 to be held in a trust which could be used to make payments to cover Twin Trading's expenditure for its first four years.[93]

Twin Trading's immediate survival had been secured, but its future progress would depend on its ability to develop links with like-minded groups and organisations. The first real test of Twin Trading's networking capacity came in 1989, after the collapse of the International Coffee Agreement. Twin proposed to develop and market a mainstream fairly traded coffee that would appeal to a wider cross-section of consumers. This ambitious goal was beyond the reach of Twin's own limited resources, but in partnership with Equal Exchange, Traidcraft and

Oxfam, Twin successfully launched Cafédirect in 1991. What was particularly revealing about this new venture was that despite Twin's original links to the labour movement, it was actually the ATO and NGO community that gave their backing to idea of Cafédirect, not the trade unions. The experience of building these networks would also influence more broadly the model of alternative trade that Twin Trading championed in its partnerships with producers in the global South.

During the 1990s, handcrafts also continued to be seen as an important project for Twin Trading with crafts imported from Vietnam, Peru and Columbia to be sold in their shop in north London. In addition to authentic crafts, Twin sourced gold for wedding rings bearing the anti-apartheid symbol, cigars from Nicaragua and metals and textiles from Cuba.[94] Twin targeted its support for artisans in isolated regions for whom the income generated through crafts was an important means of survival. In common with other ATOs, Twin Trading's buying strategy also considered the organisational structure of producer groups: 'We buy mainly from producers organised in groups, co-operatives or producer associations who can guarantee a regular supply of good quality crafts for export and at the same time benefit the artisans favouring a process of self-reliance and self-determination.'[95]

Through its innovative work launching and developing Cafédirect (1991), Divine Chocolate (1998) and Liberation Foods CIC (2007), Twin Trading has helped shape mainstream understanding and engagement with the idea of Fair Trade. With all three companies Twin Trading worked directly with producer co-operatives and also encouraged models of producer ownership: at Cafédirect, following the 2004 share issue, producers received 5% of the group equity and two places on the board for producer representatives; Divine Chocolate is part owned by Kuapa Kokoo and they have a 45% stake in the business; Liberation is 42% owned by a co-operative of 11 farmers' groups from 8 countries in Africa, Asia and Latin America. When it was first established Twin Trading represented an opportunity for a deeper level of trade union engagement with Fair Trade, but before long it was the co-operative model of partnership among small farmers that proved to be a 'stickier idea' than collective bargaining by trade union workers in factories and plantations.

The 1990s and early 2000s: Fairtrade certification and hired labour standards

The Fair Trade movement witnessed rapid expansion in awareness and sales during the late 1990s and early 2000s, but as it looked to capitalise further on its success in mainstream markets it faced some tough decisions. Sandra Kruger and Andries du Toit have defined this moment as one in which FLO's 'own interpretative and ideological narratives were in crisis, and many otherwise settled issues were up for contestation'.[96] Central to these discussions was the question of how (and if) Fair Trade could successfully be expanded to include a larger number of plantation workers without undermining the principles of the movement.[97] Was Fair Trade's expansion in danger of undermining the benefits it had brought to small-holder farmers, while at the same time presenting a risk to freedom of association?

In a detailed study of Fair Trade bananas, Henry Frundt explores the meaning and identity of fairness and looks at the impacts of Fairtrade certification on small farms and plantation production.[98] Frundt argues that the certification programme developed by FLO was set up without sufficient Southern input and there was soon difficulty in monitoring whether workers had formed their own organization and if workers were involved in democratically reviewing how the Fairtrade Premium was spent.[99] In particular, unions objected that FLO-CERT was accepting joint labour-management committees, or Joint Bodies', as meeting the requirement for democratic representation, which would not assure true independence.[100] Frundt argues that the lack of a joint understanding on cooperative leadership and worker empowerment was the result of, 'antiunion attitudes, inspector ambivalence, and failed complaints procedures'.[101] Despite these challenges, opportunities for united identities and networks are explored and Frundt distinguishes the Fairtrade Foundation and Oxfam as being 'more scrupulous than many other organizations about respecting bona fide unionization as a measure of free association'.[102]

The plantation vs. smallholder farmer debate

When the Fairtrade label was first launched in the United Kingdom in 1994, certification of plantations was limited to those products that were not traditionally produced by smallholder farmers.[103] In practice, up until 2003, this meant that tea was the only plantation crop that could gain Fairtrade certification. Although the United Kingdom has traditionally been one of the largest markets for tea, sales of Fairtrade tea have been relatively modest. In 1998, tea sales accounted for £2 million or 12% of UK Fairtrade market.[104] In comparison, Fairtrade coffee sales in 1998 reached £13.7 million, 82% of total UK Fairtrade sales. By 2003, sales of Fairtrade tea had reached £9.5 million, but this was still only 10% of total UK Fairtrade sales. Overall, this meant that commodities traditionally grown by smallholder producers, which included: coffee, chocolate and honey, accounted for between 80 and 90% of UK Fairtrade sales during this period.

From 2003, there was increasing pressure for Fairtrade International to make Fairtrade certification available to coffee plantations. It was argued that this would open up the benefits of Fairtrade to a larger number of workers. But it was not the international trade union movement that was calling for this change, but Italian coffee company Illy.[105] Illy, whose blends contain Brazilian plantation coffee, argued that they could not change the sourcing of the blends it had taken years to develop and that it would only adopt the Fairtrade label if it could maintain its previous suppliers. Smallholder producers were concerned by the revelations that they could be facing competition from large plantations and argued that this would jeopardise their livelihood. With the backing of ATOs such as Equal Exchange, the smallholder producers won assurances from FLO that coffee, cocoa, cotton and honey would only be sourced from smallholder producers. The Latin American and Caribbean Network of Small Fair Trade Producers (CLAC) argued that the plantation owners, not the workers, would be the main beneficiaries of Fairtrade certification and that only if plantations were converted to worker-owned collectives could real worker benefits be assured.[106]

It was the case of South African fruit producers that finally provided FLO with an example of how plantations could be included in the Fair Trade system in a way that maintained the political objectives of changing power relations.[107] The number of FLO certified producers in South Africa rapidly expanded from 2003 to 2005 and by May 2005, of the 42 producers certified, only three were small farmer co-operatives.[108] There was growing criticism that too many of these plantations were large commercial, white-owned farms. It was argued that Fairtrade certification of these farms could undermine the objectives of the Broad-Based Black Economic Empowerment Act 2003. During the second-half of 2004, FLO engaged South African producers and NGOs in a consultation process; the result of which was a set of Fairtrade standards specific to South Africa, which importantly included a 25% minimum interest of workers in the agricultural enterprise.[109] As the debates about worker representation on plantations intensified, there was an opportunity for the TUC to reimagine its role within the Fair Trade movement and make the case for unionisation throughout Fairtrade supply chains. But despite the fact this consultation process was focused on worker rights and participation, the international trade union movement did not engage.[110]

With increased awareness of Fair Trade among consumers and campaigners in Europe, United States and Canada, the supply chain activities of suppliers, retailers and multinational brands have faced greater scrutiny. Scholars and union leaders have highlighted the tension that exists whereby some companies are publicly supporting Fair Trade, and buying Fairtrade certified products, yet in their operations in the global North pursue an anti-union stance towards their employees. Gavin Fridell in an exploratory study of Fair Trade networks in the North, compares the approach and experience of Planet Bean, a worker-owned co-operative, and Starbucks Coffee.[111] While Starbucks employees are paid above the minimum wage, the majority are still low-paid, precarious workers without an effective voice in labour relations. Detailing the long-running dispute between the union representatives in Vancouver, British Columbia (CAW 3000)[112] and Starbucks, Fridell concludes that Starbucks is 'interested more in its ability to *sell* its CSR image than with the needs and demands of its stakeholders'.[113]

The continued challenge of anti-union employment practices raises the question of whether new Fairtrade Standards are needed for Northern licensees in order to cover ethical labour practices, including a unionized workforce.[114] Fairtrade International does not monitor ethical standards of Northern partners, except for where it relates directly to trading relations with Fairtrade certified producers. In the United Kingdom, working conditions in factories run by Fairtrade banana importers and ripeners made the news following allegations that Eastern European migrant workers were being exploited. In May 2007, a Polish worker at Pratt's Bananas in Luton, took the firm to an industrial tribunal with claims that she had miscarried after being denied rest and lighter duties.[115] The Fairtrade Foundation, reacting to the press coverage, stated that the real issue was working conditions in the United Kingdom, not Fairtrade itself.[116] And without the power to directly intervene it was unclear how the Foundation could respond. A year later, following extensive negotiations, the Pratt's management finally agreed to recognise the GMB union's right to represent the site's workers.[117]

Conclusions

The Fairtrade Foundation has stated that: 'The onward momentum of the Fairtrade movement will require increased engagement with hired labour and that in turn will need improved co-operation with trade unions to ensure continued success'.[118] But historical accounts of the limits of labour solidarity have cast a shadow over the international work of the TUC in this area. There has been a tension between the ideals of international trade unionism, which articulated a philosophy consistent with the main principles of Fair Trade, and the limits of an international programme that prioritised the job security of TUC members at the expense of workers in the Third World. NGOs and Fair Trade campaigners, unfamiliar with the internal politics of the TUC, were surprised by the apparent reluctance of the British trade union movement to join campaigns supporting international labour rights. Where they had expected the TUC to show leadership in campaigning on behalf of workers in the Third World they were left disappointed and frustrated.[119]

In the early years of the ICFTU its membership and governance structure was arguably not conducive to a progressive international agenda or the formation of an alternative trade network. Although the ICFTU, by 1959, represented 56.5 million members in over one hundred countries, three organisations constituted 50% of the total ICFTU membership: the AFL-CIO (American Federation of Labor and Congress of Industrial Organizations), the TUC and the German DGB (Deutscher Gewerkschaftsbund).[120] In total, Third World affiliates only accounted for 24.8% of ICFTU members: Asia (11.2%), Latin America (11.3%) and Africa (2.3%).[121] Financially the ICFTU was also restricted and almost completely dependent on North American and European affiliates that provided 95% of the ICFTU's income.[122]

During the 1970s and 1980s, with the membership of the ICFTU expanding and becoming more diverse, hopes of a 'new labour internationalism' were revived.[123] As the Fair Trade movement developed there were opportunities for trade unions to engage with civil society organisations and 'reimagine' their role in a global society.[124] Instead, the leadership of TUC directed attention towards national concerns and politics. The domestic political pressures that faced the TUC during this period were significant; even so, the judgement of campaigners in the global South was that the TUC had relinquished its international responsibilities too readily. A defensive response by the TUC to the global challenges of labour mobility, capital and the environment, reflected a disjointed 'moral imagination' that reinforced political and economic barriers to a progressive international agenda on trade and workers' rights.

Closer to home, there was also apprehension about European moves to legislate for workers' right to participate in the management of companies. The Bullock Report, published in 1977, put forward the British case for co-determination and outlined the opportunities for increased worker participation and control.[125] But the TUC was unable to counter suspicion that works councils could become rival channels of representation that would undermine union collective bargaining strength.[126] Without the committed support of the wider labour movement the Report's recommendations were soon forgotten and Britain saw the renewal of unrestrained free collective bargaining and strike action that would culminate in the 1978–1979 'Winter of Discontent'.[127] Peter Ackers, Professor of Industrial Relations & Labour History, described Bullock as: 'Very much a historical "road not taken" – as British society went off in much more free market, individualist approach to managing people at work'.[128] When Fairtrade International subsequently developed its Hired Labour Standards for plantation workers, it was the German model of co-determination that was the established reference point for worker representation on Joint Bodies.[129]

By the late 1990s, the TUC's agenda for addressing workers' rights throughout international supply chains was focused on its involvement with the Ethical Trading Initiative (ETI). The policy direction taken by Fairtrade, as a development model, meant that for many trade unionists it was seen as primarily interested in working with co-operatives and therefore only a niche response to the issues of worker representation and labour rights. Tony Young, former President of the TUC, argued that the ETI was, 'much more ambitious than Fair Trade. Fair Trade is only looking at one section of what's on the supermarket shelf. Great stuff, but we know that as a market percentage, it's tiny. Here we are trying to look at everything on the supermarket shelf.'[130] However, despite the ambitions of the ETI, impact studies have shown that its record in promoting worker representation and membership of trade unions has been disappointing.[131]

The TUC has argued that:

> Trade union support for the Fair Trade movement would undoubtedly be even greater if all processing of Fair Trade products (including that which takes place in the industrialised countries in which Fair Trade products find their main market) were to take place in unionised workplaces. It is hard for trade unions to encourage members to purchase Fairtrade products made in non-union workplaces, rather than non-Fairtrade products made in large enterprises by their own members.[132]

While this stance is understandable, the historical reluctance of the TUC to engage with workers in the global South, and civil society groups in Britain, also contributed to the sidelining of trade union interests within the Fairtrade certification scheme. In recent years, Fairtrade International has revised its strategy to 'better support and empower workers'.[133] And the new Hired Labour Standards for the first time specify a 'right to unionise guarantee'.[134] There are also new requirements for progress towards a living wage and greater recognition of the opinions and needs of migrant labourers. Smallholder farmers and co-operatives remain central to the Fairtrade system, and deeply embedded in the Fairtrade Foundation's Theory of Change, but there are signs of a new understanding and approach to workers' rights and renewed willingness to work more closely with established trade unions.[135]

5
Ethical Consumerism: 'Shopping for a Better World'

The Fair Trade Mark Steering group met for the first time in August 1989 and had soon defined the main objectives of the project: 'The Fair Trade Mark is an ambition to engage UK consumer power on a significant scale, to give a fairer deal to Third World producers of basic commodities.'[1] By the early 1990s the idea of 'ethical consumerism' was starting to gain attention among the mainstream media and business commentators as an exciting innovation focused on marketing the social and environmental values of consumer products. Strategically this was an opportunity for Fairtrade to position its approach to trade and development in a way that resonated with the dominant language and belief system of a consumer society.[2] The previous decade had seen the emergence of the 'green consumer' and the success of market-focused campaigns backed by the environmental movement.[3] The green consumer quickly became established as a 'sticky idea' that connected with retailers and shoppers – for the Fair Trade movement it seemed that the 'ethical consumer' held similar potential. It looked as if this might be the moment when positive consumption, or 'buycotting', would finally take centre stage. By voting with their wallets, consumer demand for 'green' and ethical products would send a clear signal to the markets that would lead to improvements in conditions for those at the end of the supply chain.

The anxieties and ambitions of the 'ethical consumer' soon became closely entwined with the aims and objectives of Fair Trade. However, the economic significance of consumer demand for ethical products was only part of the story. Utilising this broad framing concept enabled Fairtrade to find common ground, and a shared language, with which to engage multiple stakeholders on issues of trade and development. At a time when the Fairtrade Foundation was looking to establish its legitimacy as a labelling initiative, and representative voice of Fair Trade more broadly, the 'ethical consumer' offered an opportunity to build consensus. At one level, there was a need to overcome some of the introspection that had characterised alternative trade organisations' (ATOs) ambitions to operate a 'socially ideal' trade system. Opening up Fair Trade to established mainstream brands would be part of this move to widen the outlook of the movement and to build commercial scale. There was also a need to maintain a connection with the past and to build on the goodwill and practical experience of established ATOs. This meant that it was crucial that trusted ATOs remained part of the Fair Trade story and were supportive of the new labelling initiative.

The first Fair Trade label was launched in the Netherlands in 1988. The Max Havelaar label was designed to allow consumers to easily identify 'fair trade' coffee in Dutch supermarkets. Max Havelaar was the title of a controversial nineteenth-century novel critical of a Dutch colonial trading system that provided cheap coffee to the Netherlands, but profited at the expense of coffee farmers in Indonesia.[4] The modern initiative prompted consumers to consider the parallels with trading practices and conditions that many assumed had long been consigned to history. The Max Havelaar label was launched as a joint programme between the ecumenical development agency, Solidaridad, and UCIRI (Union de Comunidades Indigenas de la Region del Istmo), a coffee producer cooperative in Mexico. Encouraged by the success of eco labels, in particular the German 'Blue Angel', the Max Havelaar label was envisaged as way raising awareness of social and development issues in the coffee industry and offering consumers a way of supporting small-scale coffee farmers through their shopping choices.[5]

From the outset commercial roasters were involved in an attempt to divest the coffee of its 'alternative' image.[6] In only two years, the sales of Max Havelaar labelled products had increased the market for 'ethical coffee' from 0.2% to 2.2% of the Dutch coffee market.[7] The goal was for Max Havelaar coffee to be available to all consumers at their regular supermarket store. Max Havelaar argued that, 'in practice Alterative Trade can only be a real alternative when the products are available in every supermarket, in every grocery store, at every street corner, there where the average consumer usually is doing her or his shopping, and not just in special Third World shops'.[8] By 1990, following a successful media campaign about the benefits of Fair Trade, 89% of all supermarkets in the Netherlands had introduced Max Havelaar certified coffee.[9]

In the United Kingdom, the newly formed Fairtrade Foundation recognised that, with limited resources, building scale and market presence would require a network of strategic partnerships with ATOs, campaign groups and big business. It is within this wider social and political context that an understanding of the 'ethical consumer' should be considered. A challenge for academics and commentators is that Fair Trade's positioning as 'in and against the market' has, in practice, relied on a range of sub-frames in order to contextualise its key policies and objectives. Hudson et al. identified three key frames: warm glow, fair exchange and decommodification. They note that the Fair Trade movement was competing with wider social economic messages to maintain credibility and the political and economic context inevitably influenced the strategies chosen by the Fair Trade movement.[10] However, the response to changing circumstances was not set or predetermined – as one door opened another door closed.[11] This chapter will explore how the Fairtrade Foundation managed the opportunities presented in its interactions with potential licensees and social entrepreneurs (Typhoo Tea and Green & Blacks), its partnerships with 100% Fairtrade companies (Cafédirect and Divine Chocolate), and its negotiations with major brands (Nestlé). Understanding how the Fairtrade Foundation pursued these parallel, and seemingly conflicting, strategies offers an important insight into the expansion of Fairtrade in mainstream markets.

Fair Trade 'in and against the market'

The Fair Trade movement's expansion beyond an 'alternative' niche and entrance into mainstream markets has been celebrated and criticised in almost equal measure. Whichever side of the debate academics find themselves on, consumer agency provides the framework for the existing narrative. Alex Nicholls and Charlotte Opal have been among the most optimistic about the benefits brought through widening market access to Fair Trade.[12] They define Fair Trade's transformation in generally positive terms, stating that, 'Fair Trade has moved from being purely an activist-led advocacy and empowerment model towards being a market-led commercial success story.'[13] Fair Trade is characterised as a 'unique solution to the market failures in the global trading system' and as a 'consumer choice movement' outside the scope of government regulation or trade policies.[14]

In contrast, Raynolds et al. have questioned whether the introduction by supermarkets of Fairtrade certified own brand products provided an opportunity to integrate Fair Trade values with the market or whether 'it is instead leading to the co-opting of Fair Trade by the same agrofood system it was set up to oppose'.[15] By buying into Fair Trade without demonstrating a significant commitment, it is claimed that MNCs have effectively undermined the 100% Fair Trade companies. Stephanie Barrientos and Sally Smith have argued that one of the most significant impacts of supermarket involvement has been that they are 'driving a shift from producer-led to consumer-led Fair Trade'.[16] This suggests a fundamental shift in the dynamics of Fair Trade and a repositioning of consumers as the definitive stakeholder group.

While the framing of Fairtrade as a consumer-led market response has resonance with a broader understanding of how market values have seemingly permeated throughout society,[17] the empirical evidence from Fair Trade stakeholders demonstrates a more strategic and instrumental approach to ethical consumerism. There was criticism from some world shops that Fairtrade certification and the use of mainstream marketing was simply a 'bid for quick growth'.[18] However, this normative critique was tempered by those ATOs[19] that saw the concept of ethical consumerism as consistent with their existing objectives of 'seeking conventional commercial markets for producers'.[20] Oxfam, reflecting on the new messaging, explained to craft producers that, 'We at OXFAM Trading are increasingly trying to market the products you make in terms of "shopping for a fairer world".'[21] For Fair Trade retailers and campaigners 'the ethical consumer' represented a positive theory of change that defined the individual as the key moral agent; but was this stance compatible with campaigns for trade justice that challenged the market fundamentals of the dominant economic system?

From an academic perspective, this internal tension about the role of the consumer has not been reflected in critical discussions. Instead the focus has been on interpreting the public discourse that is predominantly framed around the role of 'ethical consumption'. However, a reassessment of the empirical evidence supports the case for a more nuanced approach that recognises the influence of political (and commercial) decision-making, and begins to move beyond a narrow economic discussion of Fair Trade.[22] As part of this reassessment, the work of campaigners and commercial intermediaries (both in the global South and the North) should be brought to the foreground, so that agency is no longer identified primarily in the activities of ethical consumers. An understanding of Fair Trade's success as a 'consumer movement for change' needs, therefore, to be recognised as highly contingent on its connection to wider social and commercial networks.

This chapter aims to contribute to this analysis by exploring the Fairtrade Foundation's involvement in building these networks and investigating the conceptual framing of ethical consumerism as a strategy and tool for managing stakeholder relationships. The second part of this chapter looks in more detail at how a stakeholder identification and salience model can be applied to Fairtrade and provides five case studies that investigate how this strategy was implemented. Before exploring the empirical data it is useful to understand how the concept of ethical consumerism was defined and how it achieved credibility and resonance. As mentioned in the introduction, 'green consumerism' set an important precedent in establishing a wider 'political' role for consumers. The following section explores the history of green consumerism and looks at how conceptual tensions were negotiated in order to present a consistent narrative. We then turn attention to the concept of ethical consumerism and explore how this framing was constructed and employed by the Fairtrade Foundation. In contrast to green consumerism, increasingly it was questions of ownership that would become the dividing line for supporters and critics of Fairtrade labelling. These conflicts and negotiations heightened the challenge for the newly established Fairtrade Foundation in managing stakeholder relations and establishing 'who or what really counts?'.[23] As predicted by Mitchell et al.'s stakeholder salience theory, the Fairtrade Foundation's response was driven by its assessment of stakeholders' attributes in relation to power, legitimacy and urgency.[24] Essentially this was a dynamic relationship that transitioned over time. As a membership organisation, the Fairtrade Foundation's own legitimacy and power was also fundamentally determined (and constrained) by the changing ambitions and competing claims of its diverse stakeholders.

Green consumerism: 'environmentally friendly'

The idea of the 'green consumer' set an important precedent that Fair Trade was quick to capitalise on. The market success of 'green' products showed that it was possible to constructively engage the interests of business and civil society stakeholders. But at what cost? For Fair Trade there were potential lessons to be learnt from better understanding the tensions and compromises involved in attempting to align environmental protection and mass consumerism. Early consumer guides, such as Friends of the Earth (FoE), *The Consumers' Guide to the Protection of the Environment* (1971) attempted to tackle questions of 'how much is enough?'[25] In a passage that parallels recent discussions about collective consumption, FoE offered this challenge: 'The first question is do you need it? Do you really need an electric can-opener, electric hedge trimmer or power lawn mower ... Can you share it? Not everyone needs to have exclusive ownership of everything.'[26] However, the assumption was that a well-informed consumer could successfully navigate these conflicts. FoE argued for good consumer information, rather than simply corporate communications (described by FoE as 'eco-pornography').[27] Despite the implied challenge to mass consumerism, this was not a radical critique of a market society. The tension was framed as a question of personal priorities and the decision about 'need' was ultimately left to individual consumers.

It was during the late 1980s that momentum behind green consumerism really started to build – reinforced by a language of consumer choice.[28] John Elkington was one of the leading advocates for the potential of green consumerism. He argued that, 'consumer power is one lever among many, but as yet an under-exploited one. We make consumer choices much more often than we vote or lobby or demonstrate, so the potential for increased pressure on industry and government could be considerable.'[29] Published in 1989, John Elkington's and Julia Hailes', *The Green Consumer's Supermarket Shopping Guide* soon became a handbook for the well-informed (and well-off) green consumer. *The Guide,* aimed to 'put into everybody's hands direct information about the social and ethical policies of the companies who make and sell a large part of the products they buy regularly'.[30]

Covering everything from 'shampoo to champagne', questions about over-consumption and its implied critique of luxury goods had been largely sidelined.[31] Central to this new form of green consumerism was an approach that favoured 'positive engagement' with mainstream business, and supermarkets in particular. Supermarkets had expanded rapidly in the United Kingdom since 1964 (when minimum resale price maintenance was abolished), and by 1989 the big five supermarkets controlled over 60% of all grocery spending.[32] Elinkington and Hailes recognised that supermarkets had been responsible for significant environmental destruction, but they argued that it was possible to change them from within. They stated that: 'The potential impact of the supermarkets in the greening of industry is increasingly clear. From the point of view of the Green Consumer the supermarket is the place where we can exert our power most effectively.'[33] Green Consumerism had set a precedent of positive engagement with supermarkets – a model that Fairtrade would look to replicate and develop.

Ethical consumerism: 'people friendly'

By the early 1990s there was a growing enthusiasm among British ATOs about the possibility of harnessing the power of the 'green consumer'.

Oxfam Trading's Press Officer, Caroline Lucas, citing the success of the Body Shop highlighted that, 'at this time of unprecedented consumer power and awareness, alternative trading organisations must seize the opportunity to broaden the debate: we need to demonstrate that for a product to be environmentally friendly alone is still not enough. It must be people and development friendly too'.[34] Oxfam Trading, as a founding member of the Fairtrade Foundation, was particularly important in reinforcing the idea that by purchasing Fair Trade products consumers could become agents of change. Oxfam's credibility as a principled and pragmatic 'thought leader' was significant in engaging the development agencies and building a broad consensus around the role of the 'ethical consumer'.

Perhaps the most vocal proponent for 'ethical consumerism', among the Foundation's membership was a small research organisation called New Consumer. Established in February 1989, by Richard Adams, New Consumer advocated a new approach to consumer politics that would begin to define the public profile of the Fairtrade Foundation. Adams believed that green, or ethical consumerism, heralded the way for a 'radical rethink about consumer power'.[35] The opportunity that ethical consumerism represented was illustrated by a simple comparison between consumer spending and levels of charitable giving. In 1988, the British public gave about £1.5 billion to charity and in the same year spent £280 billion on consumer goods and services. This meant that for every six pence given to charity, £10 was spent on consumer goods.[36] At one level this was an attempt to reconnect with earlier debates about trade not aid, but the context and questions of agency had shifted from government trade policy to individual shopping choices.

Following the lead of Elkington and Hailes, New Consumer published its own shopping guide – *Shopping for a Better World: A Quick and Easy Guide to Socially Responsible Shopping*. The message was that, 'the everyday shopper needn't be a "problem" but can be part of the solution'.[37] Reaching this newly informed 'ethical consumer' would not rely solely on alternative outlets and world shops. Adams believed that the supermarket take-up of 'environmentally friendly' products could be extended without too much difficulty to 'people-friendly' products. Adams argued that: 'When it comes to much of mainstream business I believe that we don't need to start a fight with people who can be won over'.[38] Adams and New Consumer believed that the stage was now set for an ambitious programme of Fairtrade consumer growth.

Fairtrade seemed to be well-positioned to capitalise and build on the momentum that was driving the growth of 'green' products. For Oxfam

Trading this trend was beginning to look like the start of tipping point: 'The idea that we can use our everyday consumer decisions to influence the world we live in is not new – but the degree to which the Green Consumer is pushing industry in more environmentally-acceptable directions is.'[39] And there was evidence that changes within the grocery sector were already underway. In 1991, the Institute of Grocery Distribution (IGD) set up the new Policy Issues Council – a think-tank tasked to investigate and report on the strategic challenges facing the food and consumer goods industry. John Beaumont, Chief Executive of the IGD, cautioned ignoring the vocal consumer, he stated that: 'The mass of consumers are becoming more aware, more confident, more assertive and ultimately reflect their opinions more forcefully through their purchasing patterns'.[40] Beaumont warned unprepared retailers: 'It has happened with the "greening" of a range of alternatives. It will happen with the Third World.'[41]

Despite these moves, some commentators remained cynical about the motivation behind this retail response and saw 'more than a little opportunism involved'.[42] Among those critical voices was the Ethical Consumer Research Association (ECRA). Founded in June 1987, as a worker co-operative, the ECRA's main publication *Ethical Consumer* positioned itself as 'a magazine dedicated to the promotion of the ideals behind "ethical consumption"'.[43] The first issue described *Ethical Consumer* as 'the alternative WHICH? guide'.[44] But by the second issue, following pressure from the Consumers' Association, the direct reference to *Which?* had been dropped and in its place the new strap-line read 'the alternative shoppers' guide'.[45] The ECRA's stance was highly critical of MNCs, arguing that they helped to defend the 'dominant economic theory that maintains that economics and ethics do not mix'.[46] ECRA openly criticised many corporate ethical initiatives as simply 'tokenism' or 'niche-marketing' with little connection to, or impact on, their main operations.[47]

Fairtrade products now regularly feature in *Ethical Consumer* as 'Best Buys', but in December 1991 (Issue 17), ECRA directly challenged the 'product specific' approach being advocated by New Consumer and the Fairtrade Foundation. In four pages of critical review articles and editorial the ECRA dissected and challenged the two consumer guides published by New Consumer (*The Global Consumer* and *Shopping for a Better World*). However, this was more than just competition between rival publications. What was at stake was the economic basis and core narrative that underpinned the concept of 'ethical consumption'. It was the ECRA's belief that consumers could only exert influence if they knew about both the products and the companies behind them. They argued that a product-specific approach did not address key questions about ownership and therefore 'disempowers consumers because it perpetuates the idea that there is nothing to be gained from understanding the companies behind the brand names'.[48] ECRA argued that product certification offered limited incentive for companies to drive improvements throughout their supply chain; instead new ethical products could be launched to cater specifically for the demands of a niche market.

This critique was not only limited to negative book reviews, but also directly challenged New Consumer's involvement in building support for the Fairtrade Mark. The editorial of the *Ethical Consumer* argued that, 'the support of a number of the same UK Third World charities and development groups for "The Global Consumer", and a related "Fair Trade Mark" project, appears to be a very worrying shift on their part to the political right.'[49] This forthright political critique of Fair Trade seemed to come as a surprise to New Consumer and the newly established Fairtrade Foundation – they had not expected their promotion of 'ethical consumption' to be so controversial. Ultimately this challenge did little to alter the product-focused consumer positioning within the Foundation. The ECRA's insistence that 'ownership mattered' seemed to be out of step with the political and economic thinking of the time. But it was still an important lesson for the Fairtrade Foundation – it demonstrated that a politics of consumption would not be uncontested and that to build resilient networks they would need to engage with stakeholders that represented a diverse range of perspectives.

Stakeholder identification and salience: Fair Trade and strategic management

The idea of a growing consumer base engaged and motivated by ethical consumption was commercially important for the Fairtrade Foundation as they looked to drive mainstream adoption of the FAIRTRADE Mark. Likewise, the broad acceptance and political elasticity of what could be termed the 'consumer agenda' offered opportunities to strategically engage with a range of stakeholders. The Fairtrade Foundation had ambitions of entering the mainstream and recognised that this meant working with big established brands. However, the Foundation also knew that its legitimacy depended on the continued support of its member organisations that represented ATOs, development agencies and campaign groups. Crucial to the mainstream growth of Fair Trade in the United Kingdom has been the Fairtrade Foundation's ability to balance these competing interests in order to build power and establish its institutional legitimacy.

Conceptually, this chapter looks to empirically test Mitchell et al.'s theory of stakeholder salience and provide a historical assessment of the key stakeholder relationships as Fairtrade entered the mainstream.[50] The stakeholder identification and salience model was developed as a dynamic management tool designed to encourage greater strategic consideration of a company's stakeholders. However the stakeholder attributes of Civil Society Organisations (CSO), such as the Fairtrade Foundation, suggest an additional multidimensional aspect of stakeholder networks and partnerships, whereby transitions in power, legitimacy and urgency present specific challenges and have an institutional relevance not usually prioritised by commercial organisations. In the following case studies (Typhoo Tea, Cafédirect, Green & Black's, Divine Chocolate and Nestlé) this chapter investigates the strategies adopted as the Fairtrade Foundation entered into negotiations with its first commercial licensees and built networks with its NGO partners.

Engaging social intrapreneurs: Typhoo Tea

For the Fairtrade Foundation the most likely root to supermarket listing was winning the support of a major brand. In 1992 it looked as though Typhoo could be this brand. On 26 June 1992, the Fairtrade Foundation's Richard Adams met with Philip Mumby, Technical and Quality Director for Premier Teas. In his notes, Richard Adams revealed his positive reflections on this first meeting: 'In some respects this is our dream ticket. A high profile, national brand which has been modified to meet FT [Fair Trade] criteria and also a range of own label products covering a large part of the main grocery market.'[51] As well as their main tea brands, Premier Teas also supplied teas for a number of own labels including Tesco, Iceland, Waitrose and M&S. Although the popularity of tea had been in decline since the late 1960s, the UK tea market in 1991 was still valued at £731 million and Premier Teas accounted for 14% of UK sales.[52] Premier Teas' position as a major player within the tea industry made it a powerful stakeholder in a sector that the Fairtrade Foundation hoped to target in order to build consumer recognition and establish a market for ethical tea.

Premier Teas was quickly identified as a legitimate stakeholder and potential commercial partner. In part this was based on the company's technical expertise; but equally significant was the commitment of Philip Mumby as a Fair Trade supporter and 'social intrapreneur'. Premier Teas was already ahead of the Fairtrade Foundation in drawing up a criteria and pricing structure for Fair Trade on tea plantations. Richard Adams recognised that, 'Premier Teas is already doing expertly much of the work we see as necessary to set Fair Trade standards and checking tea estates against them.'[53] Rather than focus marketing and sales resources on creating a new ethical brand, Philip Mumby's proposal was the full conversion of Premier Teas' leading brand – Typhoo Tea. This would be a major commitment and move into unchartered territory. The concept of a Fair Trade Mark was untested in the United Kingdom and Premier Teas executives still needed to be won-over to the value of third-party certification. For its part the Foundation recognised that there was a risk that 'the public may perceive the Mark as belonging to Premier Teas and therefore not independent.'[54] However, the Fairtrade Foundation Executive Group was assured that there was no fundamental conflict of interest and that Premier Teas' role in establishing a mechanism for assessment should be 'appropriately acknowledged'.[55]

Philip Mumby brought an expert knowledge of the tea supply chains and the challenges of direct sourcing. As a former Traidcraft representative and New Consumer subscriber, Mumby was recognised as an 'insider' within the Fair Trade movement and his personal commitment to reforming the tea business was never in doubt.[56] Mumby's role in this initiative convinced the Fairtrade Foundation that the motivation was more than simply 'greenwash'. Premier Teas had developed a close relationship with suppliers in India, Kenya, Bangladesh and Indonesia and this meant that the company only purchased a very small percentage (2–3%) of their tea requirement at auction.[57] This contrasted with the challenges faced by Oxfam Trading, whereby the majority of its tea was coming from auctions.[58] However, despite the positive opening to talks it soon became apparent that within Premier Teas (in the view of Richard Adams) there was 'a suspicion about any agency-led initiative or even the use of the term "Fair Trade"'.[59] Adams was clear that this was the result of the fair tea campaigns of the 1970s. When Adams visited Premier Teas' Kenyan tea estates in August 1992, he was again faced with issues of mistrust regarding NGOs. Adams reported that:

> There is a need to build trust and to assure estate managers that the Fairtrade Foundation are not intent on gaining access to estates in order to expose poor conditions in campaigns. Without this trust, there is no question of gaining access to estates for spot checks, and the scheme would fail on rather poor grounds.[60]

As seen in Chapter 2, the 'battery tea workers' campaign and newspaper advert launched by Christian Aid was blamed for undermining trust between the two parties and effectively ending negotiations. However, there were also commercial and strategic factors that influenced Premier Teas' decision. The proposed license fee was thought to be uncompetitive and there was some scepticism about the role of third-party auditing and certification. While Philip Mumby may have been convinced of the benefits of Fairtrade certification, and personally demonstrated the characteristics and drive of a 'social intrapreneur', the commercial pressures and conservatism of the Board at Premier Teas proved resistant to change.[61] The Fairtrade Foundation had perhaps relied too heavily on the goodwill of Mumby as a proxy for the support and legitimacy of the wider company. Following the restructuring of the Board at Premier Teas, Fairtrade certification dropped off the agenda and the urgency soon faded. Premier Teas later launched its own brand of ethical teas but chose not to pursue independent third-party certification.

Partnering ATOs and campaign networks: Cafédirect

Today, Cafédirect is established as the fifth largest coffee brand in the United Kingdom and is frequently highlighted for its efforts to innovate a business model that goes beyond minimum Fairtrade standards. Launched in 1991, Cafédirect represented the first joint initiative by leading British ATOs to create and market a Fair Trade product. Cafédirect was marketed as both 'people-friendly' and 'environment-friendly'.[62] Backed by Oxfam, Traidcraft, Equal Exchange and Twin Trading – Cafédirect represented a new concept for 'alternative' coffee and a new approach to engaging with consumers. With the change of government in Nicaragua and an independent South Africa on the horizon, solidarity markets were no longer seen as a consumer priority. The message behind Cafédirect was 'towards people and away from "origin/cause" profile'.[63] This framing was designed to position Cafédirect as a response to the collapse of the International Coffee Agreement in 1989 and subsequent crisis in the coffee industry. For the Fairtrade Foundation, Cafédirect represented an important strategic challenge about how to engage with ATOs in order to manage the transition from alternative to mainstream markets. The legitimacy of Cafédirect as a Fair Trade stakeholder was not in doubt, but its salience fluctuated as its other key attributes of power and urgency were put to the test.

Despite its 'alternative' roots, Cafédirect had ambitions to become a mainstream consumer brand. This meant moving beyond established ATO networks of world shops and church stalls, and approaching high street chains – including supermarkets. To begin with the team at Cafédirect was enthusiastic about the potential of capitalising on the growth of 'green' or 'ethical' consumer markets. However, some of this initial optimism was tempered following their first meetings with the major supermarkets. Richard Pugh, technical manager for Tesco (and previously responsible for the introduction of organic-produce and free-range eggs), was distinctly cautious about promoting Fair Trade. Pugh's response at the time was that, 'Fair Trade sounds more like a question of moral judgement'.[64] And he insisted that he needed 'the weight of scientific opinion to adopt a new idea with confidence.'[65] There were doubts about whether commercial markets would embrace an unknown brand, particularly if it meant consumers paying a higher price for their coffee.

In November 1991, the Fairtrade Foundation opened discussions with Cafédirect about Fairtrade certification. The Fairtrade Foundation was seeking to secure an agreement in principle that Cafédirect would apply for the FAIRTRADE Mark once it was officially launched. But Cafédirect had serious reservations about the potential loss of mainstream sales due to the higher retail price required to cover the Fairtrade minimum price for coffee beans. Up until this point, Cafédirect had set its own purchase price for buying coffee. For 1992 it had agreed to pay coffee producers $0.92 per pound. Although this was 53% above the market price of $0.60 per pound, it was significantly below the Fairtrade minimum, set at the time at $1.20 per pound.[66] Cafédirect justified their decision due to supermarket buyers' intention to retail Cafédirect at £1.39 not the £1.70 proposed by the consortium. Cafédirect argued that in their experience 'there was no evidence of an acceptance that the Fair Trade concept commanded a price premium'.[67] This appears to contradict the campaign messaging and the NOP/Omnibus poll findings that Christian Aid were using, at the time, as part of their *Trade for Change* campaign.[68] In public the Fair Trade messaging showed a consistently optimistic outlook for the growth and support of the ethical consumer, but privately there were serious doubts as to whether this would translate into sales.[69]

As plans for the launch of the FAIRTRADE Mark progressed it became apparent that Cafédirect's lack of urgency could prove a stumbling block. By January 1994, there was increasing pressure on Oxfam Trading and Traidcraft to review their position in relation to Cafédirect. The dynamic and multidimensional nature of this relationship was recognised by managers at the Fairtrade Foundation. Mike Drury argued that if new products were launched by Cafédirect carrying the agencies' names as verification of Fair Trade, instead of carrying the FAIRTRADE Mark it would make it less likely that mainstream traders would license the Mark. Drury believed that NGO involvement with the Fairtrade

Foundation and Cafédirect was 'very confusing for the public and put the two organisations in commercial conflict with each other'.[70] Even among its closest stakeholders, its member organisations, there was uncertainty about the salience and commercial applicability of the concept of a FAIRTRADE Mark. It was not until March 1994 that Cafédirect eventually agreed to revise its purchasing criteria and apply for the FAIRTRADE Mark.

These extended negotiations meant that Cafédirect would not be ready for the official public launch of the FAIRTRADE Mark. However, despite these delays the Fairtrade Foundation realised that successfully integrating the existing ATO networks was crucial for the public recognition and trust in the FAIRTRADE Mark. It was ATOs such as Oxfam Trading, Traidcraft, Equal Exchange and Twin Trading that had established the concept of fair or alternative trade and it was these organisations that had built consumer awareness and support. ATOs represented a direct link to the past, and a connection to the international campaigns for fair prices and fair wages that had engaged CSOs and periodically received wider public attention from the early 1960s onwards. For the newly formed Fairtrade Foundation to establish its institutional legitimacy, it was vital that all of its member organisations were seen to give their full backing to a market-led approach and engage constructively with plans for product certification.

Working with organic and green entrepreneurs: Green & Black's

Following the breakdown of negotiations with Typhoo, and frustrations about the ongoing discussions with Cafédirect, there were real concerns about the timing and launch of the FAIRTRADE Mark. The prospect of launching without the backing of a high street brand or supermarket distribution was a serious setback to the mainstream ambitions of the Fairtrade Foundation and dominated management discussions.

On 3 December 1993, Mike Drury, Managing Director of the Fairtrade Foundation, attended a press conference organised by Cafédirect to promote the work that they were doing with coffee farmers and to raise awareness of the benefits Fair Trade.[71] It was at this event that Drury met Craig Sams, the co-founder of Green & Black's. On learning about Green & Black's sourcing programme in Belize, Drury suggested to Sams that Green & Black's might qualify for the FAIRTRADE Mark. Launched only a few years earlier, Green & Black's had already established its brand within the expanding organic and whole foods market. With major supermarkets competing to be recognised for their organic credentials, Green & Black's was well-placed to grow the ethical chocolate market.[72]

Green & Black's position as a legitimate stakeholder was based primarily on Craig Sams' green credentials. Sams had been running Whole Earth, a successful organic business, since 1967 and was an active member of the organic movement throughout the 1960s and 1970s. For Sams, organic represented a concrete, credible theory of change that could help farmers and their families. Where Green & Black's and Fairtrade shared a common goal was in their support and recognition of the importance of smallholder farmers in global cocoa production.[73] The contract that Green & Black's offered the Toledo Cacao Growers Association (TCGA) in November 1993 aimed to ensure that the new Maya Gold chocolate would be produced under mutually beneficial terms of trade.[74] The main features of the contract were:

1. A five-year rolling contract, paying $1.25 per pound of fermented, dried cocoa beans.
2. Help in obtaining organic certification.
3. A $US20,000 cash advance to guarantee 'spot cash' rather than receipt vouchers for the farm members.
4. Training for key co-op members in management accounting, correct fermentation and quality control to ensure the best quality of cacao.
5. An additional 5c/lb premium for farmers who planted mahogany, cedar and cohune palm as shade trees.

At the beginning of January 1994, Mike Drury from the Fairtrade Foundation and Bill Yates from Oxfam flew out to visit Green & Black's new cocoa farm in Belize. The reaction was positive, and both Oxfam and the Fairtrade Foundation seemed impressed with the progress that had been made. Sams recalls with some satisfaction Drury's response that 'it embodies everything we were led to expect, and more'.[75] The purchasing criteria established by Green & Black's was already in line with the Fairtrade requirements and, because a premium was already included, the price was also very close to the Fairtrade level.[76] With the first successful product certification complete, plans for the official launch of the FAIRTRADE Mark gained pace. Only a few months later, on 7 March 1994, Green & Black's Maya Gold was launched on the Oxfam stand at the BBC Good Food Show in London. Sainsbury's was the first to stock the Fairtrade certified Maya Gold chocolate bar, and although they had been offered a six-month exclusivity deal by Green & Black's, they waived this right – therefore allowing Tesco, Waitrose, Safeway to quickly follow suit in stocking Maya Gold. Sams described how, 'overnight the Fairtrade Mark became a supermarket shelf reality ... until then it had been a worthy idea but had yet to appear on any actual products'.[77]

Despite the positive reception surrounding the launch of Maya Gold, it appeared that there was a lack of urgency and even resistance from Green & Black's about proposals to convert the rest of their chocolate range to Fairtrade.[78] In Sams' own words Green & Black's relationship with the Fairtrade Foundation was 'pretty complicated, and has had its ups and downs'.[79] Despite Green & Black's pioneering role as the first certified product, this did not guarantee its position within the wider Fair Trade movement. From Green & Black's perspective they had commercial concerns about the license fee, charged at 2% of product turnover, (in comparison ATOs, such as Cafédirect, only paid 1% and organic fees to the Soil Association were only 0.3%).[80] Green & Black's also seemed to be caught in the middle of a dispute between the competing European Fair Trade schemes. The Fairtrade Foundation, Max Havelaar and Transfair began as separate initiatives and were keen to defend their national consumer market. This led to complaints to the Fairtrade Foundation and calls for Green & Black's to refrain from selling Maya Gold in Scandinavia, Holland and Germany, or pay a license fee to the national labelling initiatives.[81] The conflict intensified in October 1994 when Martin Kunz of Transfair Germany told the Fairtrade Foundation that they would not be willing to have the Transfair mark on Maya Gold at all as the sugar was not Fair Trade.[82] Many of these practical certification issues were addressed with the formation of FLO (Fairtrade Labelling Organisation) in 1997, but while these strategic differences remained unresolved, Green & Black's was wary of extending the FAIRTRADE Mark to other products.

It was not only the uncertainty around certification that caused Green & Black's to hold back from Fairtrade – at a more fundamental level, Sams believed that organic certification made the biggest difference to farming practices and community investment. For Green & Black's operations, the quality of the cocoa was key and their success was seen to be directly related to the fact that it was produced by independent smallholders using organic farming methods.[83] Sams argued that, 'being organic nearly always brings fair trade practice in its wake', and if Green & Black's had to choose a single ethical mark, 'it would probably be a 100 per cent organic-based system'.[84] For Sams, the NGO backing and membership of the Fairtrade Foundation was also problematic. Green & Black's had direct experience of picking up the pieces after the failed attempt by USAID (United States Agency for International Development) to revitalise the cocoa industry in Belize.[85]

Sams' conclusion was that, as a company, it was more effective for them to invest in their suppliers directly rather than partner with aid and development programmes. Gregor Hargrove, Green & Black's project manager, was more direct in his criticism: 'Fairtrade guarantees a better deal for third-world producers, and a hell of a deal for first-world bureaucrats.'[86] While these criticisms only received limited press coverage, within the Fairtrade Foundation they raised questions about the legitimacy of Green & Black's position as a 'definitive stakeholder' and underlined the strategic importance of partnering with ATOs and the 100% Fairtrade companies.

Innovating through social enterprise: Divine Chocolate

By the mid-1990s the Fairtrade Foundation was beginning to consider alternative routes into the UK confectionary and chocolate market. It seemed unlikely that Green & Black's would extend Fairtrade certification beyond Maya Gold, and the major chocolate brands had yet to show any real interest. In 1998, a new 100% Fair Trade chocolate company was launched with an innovative ownership model that brought together UK development agencies, social enterprise and cocoa producers. Divine Chocolate represented a new way of doing business and new type of Fair Trade stakeholder.[87] Comparisons with Green & Black's were perhaps unavoidable. And while Green & Black's appeared somewhat dysfunctional in its role as Fairtrade pioneer – Divine consciously positioned itself within the core of Fair Trade, both commercially and as a supporter of community campaigns such as Fairtrade towns. As the Fairtrade Foundation's commercial ambitions expanded, Divine's approach of 'radical mainstreaming' would become the baseline by which Fair Trade campaigners and supporters would judge new entrants into the Fairtrade system.

Divine Chocolate's ownership model has been described as an experiment in 'social justice'.[88] Its original structure brought together Christian Aid, Body Shop, Twin Trading and Kuapa Kokoo as member-owners of the brand.[89] For Fair Trade campaigners and supportive retailers it was Divine's story that was central to its legitimacy and salience as a pioneering Fair Trade company. The close relationship with Kuapa Kokoo gave Divine an authenticity that other brands lacked and, in part, also provided a response to criticisms about Fairtrade's limited consideration of structural issues of power and ownership.[90] Divine was established as a mission-driven company focused on improving the lives and opportunities of small-scale cocoa farmers in West Africa. From the outset the goal was to develop a dynamic, branded Fairtrade chocolate that would enable them to achieve the following objectives:

- To take a quality and affordable range of Fairtrade chocolate bars into the mainstream market.
- To raise awareness of Fairtrade issues among UK retailers and consumers of all age groups.
- To be highly visible and vocal in the chocolate sector and thereby act as a catalyst for change.
- To pay a Fairtrade price for all the cocoa used in products.[91]

Divine's commercial success was founded on a competitive advantage established through 'social resources'.[92] For many Fair Trade supporters, Divine also represented a revival of the 'social ideals' of the Fair Trade movement.[93] Divine's work in building and nurturing these networks showed both a normative recognition of the intrinsic value of stakeholder engagement and a more instrumental understanding of the commercial value of an active supporter base. Divine was quick to identify strategic partnerships, and in November 1999 launched a campaign with Christian Aid which involved a special feature in their campaign mailing and a Divine coupon that could be redeemed at Sainsbury's stores. This initiative resulted in an unusually high coupon redemption rate and by January 2000 succeeded in persuading Sainsbury's to increase the distribution of Divine from 70 stores to 343 stores.[94]

Securing sound financial backing was crucial to Divine's plans to launch a new mainstream brand and while this presented challenges there was also an opportunity to reach out to new stakeholders. With the Labour Government's strategic repositioning of UK international aid and development, Divine recognised that there was potential to partner with the newly formed Department for International Development (DFID). In 2000, DFID guaranteed a bank loan from NatWest for £400,000 to Divine as part of its poverty alleviation programme in Ghana. This was the first time this financial instrument had been used and was recognised as significant innovation by policymakers at DFID. Through this strategic partnership the dynamics of the stakeholder landscape began to shift towards a more favourable environment for Fair Trade investment. For DFID, it was an opportunity to test the viability of small-scale farmers owning shares, through co-operative structures, in a company engaged in the UK market. For Divine, the provision of the guarantee meant that the bulk of its start-up funds could come in the form of borrowing rather than investment and this enabled Kuapa Kokoo to own a 33% share in the UK company.[95] The real achievement was the creation of a company in which it was possible for the farmers to own a significant share although they did not have the capital to launch it.[96]

The commercial impact and significance of Divine's innovative approach to Fair Trade went well beyond its own operations. David Croft, Head of Co-op Brand & Technical Affairs at Co-operative Retail Group (CRG), recognised that without Divine, 'the CRG Fairtrade chocolate communications strategy would have been more piecemeal and more disparate, the partnership has resulted in greater Co-op brand equity. This has been achieved through a strong relationship with DCC and its amazing "story"'.[97] As a business with mainstream ambitions the wider expansion of the Fairtrade market was initially welcomed by Divine. However, as major supermarkets began to pursue own-brand Fairtrade chocolate, the operating environment became increasingly challenging. Divine was licensed to produce some retailers' own-brand chocolate, but this did not necessarily offset the loss of existing sales.[98] While this was partly a question of marketing strategy, it also highlighted the unequal power relationship within supermarket supply chains.[99]

Divine Chocolate showed that it was possible to reimagine Fairtrade in way that went beyond compliance with minimum standards. But this innovation represented a challenge both to conventional businesses and the Fairtrade Foundation. Divine's experience of the realities of market competition led to calls for the Fairtrade Foundation to apply Fairtrade standards for behaviour by UK licensees. It was argued that practices such as market cannibalisation had the potential to be particularly damaging to the 100% Fair Trade companies that had invested so much in building consumer support for Fair Trade.[100] However, this placed the Fairtrade Foundation in a difficult situation – it was not set up to regulate UK retailers and was further limited by competition laws designed to prevent price-fixing. Constrained by a conservative economic and legal environment, questions began to be asked about whether the Fairtrade brand could continue to successfully represent what was beginning to look like a two-tier certification system.[101]

Auditing and certifying MNCs: Nestlé's Partners' Blend

In October 2005, Nestlé announced that they would be launching a Fairtrade certified coffee – 'Nescafé Partners' Blend'. Alastair Sykes, CEO of Nestlé, UK and Ireland, said: 'Increasingly our consumers expect us to bring this commitment to social responsibility alive in our brands and show them how farmers can be helped to have a better life ... We are therefore delighted to offer consumers a product carrying the approved FAIRTRADE Mark.'[102] This was the first time that one of the major coffee multinationals had applied for Fairtrade certification. Eleven years after the launch of the Fairtrade labelling scheme, the Fair Trade movement now had a foothold in mainstream markets, but at what cost?

Press reports claimed that Nestlé's involvement was 'the most serious threat the Fairtrade movement has faced'.[103] This was underlined by the response of civil society groups such as Baby Milk Action. They argued that: 'If Nestlé really cared about suppliers in developing countries it could change its lobbying and oppressive business practices which have helped cause the crisis for coffee farmers. Perhaps refusing the mark until there was progress could have helped far more farmers in the long run.'[104] The certification of 'Partners' Blend' also prompted criticism from within the membership of the Fairtrade Foundation. The World Development Movement, in defiance of the official line, declared that, 'the launch of Nestlé Partners' Blend coffee is more likely to be an attempt to cash in on a growing market or a cynical marketing exercise than represent the beginning of a fundamental shift in Nestlé's business model'.[105] Academic studies reinforced some of these concerns and highlighted that with Partners' Blend only represented 0.02% of Nestlé's overall coffee purchasing and therefore reflected a superficial involvement with Fairtrade principles.[106] It appeared that strategically, Nestlé may have intended to use Fairtrade certification to advertise its own code of conduct, rather than extend its commitment to Fairtrade.[107]

The Fairtrade Foundation responded somewhat defensively stating that:

> The FAIRTRADE Mark is only given to individual products and not to companies. The Mark indicates that Nestlé's Partners' Blend has complied with the internationally agreed standards for Fairtrade certification. It does not refer to any other product marketed by the company. This product has undergone exactly the same certification process as all other Fairtrade products whether marketed by multinationals or smaller companies.[108]

Had the Fairtrade Foundation underestimated potential stakeholder objections of associating the FAIRTRADE Mark with a commercial partner with significant market power, but a perceived legitimacy problem?[109] It was left to Twin Trading to highlight the potential benefits of Nestlé's involvement:

> We are delighted that Nestlé's senior management, after many years of attacking Fair Trade, have responded to the wishes of consumers and to the wider development movement to change their trading practises. Since Nestlé accounts for one sixth of the world's international coffee trade, they have the power to help make poverty history.[110]

As the largest buyer of coffee beans in the world, why did Nestlé change its position when historically it had been a vocal critic of Fairtrade certification? For some commentators this change of heart looked like a case of 'corporate greenwash'. Hilary Parsons, Head of the Partners' Blend Project at Nestlé UK, recognised that, 'One of the realities we face is that there's a great deal cynicism in the UK. We don't want consumers perceiving us at not being serious about helping out the farmers.'[111] The roots of the Partners' Blend concept were identified as dating back to the late 1990s, when Nestlé began developing a traceable and transparent supply chain for smallholder farmers in Ethiopia and El Salvador. The objective of the project was to launch a soluble instant coffee for the expanding 'ethical' coffee segment in the United Kingdom.[112] Strategically Nestlé's motivation for developing this new approach was explained by three market drivers:

- The ethical coffee segment was attractive as it had grown at a compound annual growth rate (CAGR) of 75% since 2001.
- Nearly all growth was in the roast and ground market, leaving the door open for a major player to enter with an ethical soluble product.
- Nestlé had received feedback both on formal consumer panel testing and through letters to the company requesting a product in the ethical category.[113]

Nestlé's marketing department had been conducting consumer research on ethical consumer trends since the late 1990s. The resulting market segmentation identified three consumer stances relating to the ethical product category: the 'Global Watchdogs', the 'Conscientious Consumers' and 'Do What I Cans'. The Nescafé Partners' Blend brand was aimed at the 'Do What I Cans' – thought to represent the bulk of consumers. Market research suggested that these individuals were not active campaigners, but took actions to be responsible whenever they could. Success in this category would require a high-quality coffee comparable in taste to the Nescafé Gold product line. Originally, the plan was for Partners' Blend to be sold in Nescafé's signature shaped glass jar. But feedback from top Nestlé executives suggested that the product take on a more rustic and distinctive look.[114] So instead Partners' Blend was launched in recyclable can wrapped in brown paper with black and white pictures of El Salvadorian and Ethiopian farmers. Partners' Blend would be priced at £2.69 per 100 grams at retail, the exact same price point as the market leader Cafédirect.[115]

With plans for the new product well underway, Nestlé and the Fairtrade Foundation met in February 2005 to discuss the possibility of launching Nescafé Partners' Blend with the FAIRTRADE Mark. It proved an important meeting for both sides. One Nestlé executive stated:

> The biggest decision in all of this was when we agreed to meet with Fairtrade to talk about this face to face ... They presented what they were doing and it was very clear that they had moved on from just the fixed price idea ... they were now talking about sustainability and diversification. This was exactly the same stuff we were doing.[116]

Harriet Lamb, Executive Director of the Fairtrade Foundation, was also optimistic stating that:

> This is a turning point for Fairtrade in the UK – the first time that one of the four major coffee roasters has taken its first step in response to rapidly growing consumer demand for products independently certified by the Fairtrade Mark ... We expect the addition of NESCAFE Partners' Blend to bring a new wave of coffee drinkers to Fairtrade, bringing more opportunities to more farmers in more countries.[117]

However, the Fairtrade Foundation's goal to increase the percentage of Nestlé's certified coffee was not achieved.[118] A study of Nestlé's Partners' Blend commercial strategy showed that in the 5 years following Fairtrade certification neither the market share nor the number of markets had shown any significant increase since the product's launch.[119] Marianne Pemberton argued that Nestlé was taking 'a clever, but passive, approach' and that this passivity in creating demand for its certified products revealed its true ambivalence towards the label itself.[120]

Conclusions

The Fairtrade Foundation set out with a clear objective – to engage consumers and to provide a fairer deal for producers. Less well defined were the mechanisms by which this would be pursued. In the Netherlands, the Max Havelaar scheme offered a model of how product certification could achieve mainstream commercial recognition and deliver benefits for producer communities. In consumer markets, retail sales soon became the most tangible marker of success, and in turn this reinforced the idea of Fairtrade as 'a market-led commercial success story'.[121] Strategically, by defining Fairtrade as a consumer choice movement, the Fairtrade Foundation was able to actively engage and partner with stakeholders which otherwise may have been antagonistic towards the idea of 'alternative trade'. It seemed that consumer choice was a concept that almost no one could object to. But with Fair Trade no longer positioned as an alternative movement, was the FAIRTRADE Mark reinforcing and embedding the values of free market capitalism?

The Fairtrade Foundation's strategy of constructive corporate engagement was largely based on the experience and apparent success of the environmental campaigns during the previous decade. However, a reassessment of the outcomes of these campaigns suggests that many of the gains were short-lived and probably did little to achieve pro-environmental behaviour change.[122] In recent years, there has been a more critical reassessment of the role of the consumer in environmental campaigning. Increasingly organisations such as WWF (World Wildlife Fund) are placing greater emphasis on the importance of values and culture as drivers of behaviour change. Tom Crompton, Change Strategist at WWF-UK, argues that: 'Green consumerism is a cul-de-sac. As a strategy for responding to environmental challenges it risks reinforcing all those values that underpin apathy about environmental problems, and resistance to tackling them.'[123] This presents a challenge for business; but Crompton argues that: 'business plays a crucial role in shaping cultural values – for example, through culture in the workplace, pay structures, and its marketing and advertising activities'.[124] In this context, the role of NGOs, such as WWF and the Fairtrade Foundation, is to act as 'critical friends' and work with those businesses taking action to address their wider social, cultural and environmental responsibilities.

Recent research on the Fair Trade movement has begun to explore the role of frames and values and analyse how these reference points have shaped the public understanding and meaning of Fair Trade.[125] Based on an international study of ten years of print and radio coverage of the Fair Trade movement, Hudson et al. investigated whether there was evidence of a dominant framing strategy.[126] The research findings showed that Fair Trade was framed in many different ways by movement participants and was likely to become more divergent than convergent.[127] However, some patterns did emerge from the sample. Overall, the dominant category was 'fair exchange' (representing 41% of comments), this was followed quite closely by decommodification (34% of comments) and 'warm glow' comprising just over 12%.[128] This runs counter to what some social movement theorists might predict about the need to resonate with the predominant consumer culture. But despite this apparent resilience, there was still little evidence of messages or frames that directly challenged neoliberalism – anti-capitalist framing accounted for only 1% of comments.[129] However, as Fairtrade International works to develop its 'Theory of Change', there may be an opportunity to articulate a more nuanced understanding of the ethical consumer – one that better represents the complexities of the market reality and provides new frames to challenge and explore meanings of Trade Justice.[130]

Conclusion: A New Direction for Consumer Politics

Reflecting on 20 years of the FAIRTRADE Mark in the United Kingdom, Barbara Crowther, Director of Policy and Public Affairs at the Fairtrade Foundation, commented that: 'When the first products with the FAIRTRADE Mark appeared twenty years ago, industry commentators predicted a temporary fad that wouldn't last or become mainstream. Today Fairtrade is part of the fabric of British society and the leading ethical label in the UK and the world.'[1] As the Fairtrade Foundation reaches this milestone there are significant achievements to recognise including benefits to more than 1.3 million farmers and workers, retail sales of £1.78 billion and the FAIRTRADE Mark now being recognised by 78% of the UK public. It is also an opportunity to reflect on the future direction of the movement and the challenges that remain.

Balancing the interests of civil society organisations, producers and 100% Fair Trade companies, against those of major brands and supermarkets remains the key strategic challenge for Fairtrade. Historically the conversion of major brands has been vital to the expansion of Fairtrade sales. However, this mainstream commercial presence also raised the threat of corporate co-option and dilution of standards.[2] Increasingly the Fairtrade Foundation is pressing companies to 'Go Further'.[3] Backed by the Fairtrade Towns movement, the Foundation has been making the case for smallholder farmers and encouraging supermarkets to actively source from co-operatives rather than plantations. This move is an attempt to realign corporate engagement with Fairtrade so that companies go beyond compliance and recognise Fairtrade as a new way of doing business – one that actively seeks to build value for producers and suppliers.

This concluding chapter outlines five main themes that bring together the key findings of this book and highlights promising areas for future research. First, we consider the concept of global citizenship and how it relates to consumer politics and Fair Trade. Secondly, we explore the identity of Fair Trade as a social movement. Thirdly, we investigate the elements involved in building support for Fair Trade – both the practical and philosophical drivers for change. Fourthly, we assess the British case within a global context; while recognising that the shortage of national case studies limits direct international comparisons, some promising directions for further research are identified. Finally, we revisit the consumer/producer relations at the heart of the Fair Trade movement and look at whether there is an opportunity to re-evaluate how we conceptualise these distinctions and what implications this might have for Fair Trade.

'Global Citizenship' or 'Globally Minded Citizens'?

Campaigns such as Make Poverty History and Enough Food for Everyone IF have called on international governments to tackle global issues of land rights, taxation, transparency, aid and development. The Fair Trade movement has been seen as an important coordinator and mobiliser for these campaigns, but to what extent does this activity represent the ideals of global citizenship and what are the lessons for Fair Trade?

In an approach they have defined as 'cosmopolitan democracy', Daniele Archibuigi and David Held have explored whether there is scope for individuals to have some voice in deciding on issues affecting the world as a whole.[4] Despite their ambitious proposals for the reform of the UN Assembly, in practice there remains an absence of institutional channels to define and enforce the legal and political rights of global citizenship.[5] These limitations have led April Carter to respond that 'global citizenship expresses an aspiration, not a reality'.[6] While highlighting tensions present in national politics Carter still contends, somewhat frustratingly that, 'in some circumstances it is nevertheless possible for an individual to identify as a member of a national community and to claim simultaneously to be a global citizen'. By not defining what these circumstances might be it seems that Carter deliberately sidesteps this crucial issue.

Peter Singer, in contrast, argues that individuals identify themselves as citizens of the world and therefore actively recognise cosmopolitan moral obligations to other individuals. Singer, writing in 1972, argued that, 'from the moral point of view, the development of the world into a "global village" has made an important, though still unrecognized, difference to our moral situation'.[7] Writing in the context of the refugee crisis in East Bengal, Singer dismissed arguments about distance and lack of personal knowledge and made an uncompromising argument for individual responsibility for tackling famine and poverty in other parts of the world. He stated that:

> Expert observers and supervisors, sent out by famine relief organizations or permanently stationed in famine-prone areas, can direct our aid to a refugee in Bengal almost as effectively as we could get it to someone in our own block. There would seem, therefore, to be no possible justification for discriminating on geographical grounds.[8]

One of the clearest routes for identifying Fair Trade with citizenship (and potentially global citizenship) is seemingly in the concept of the citizen-consumer. Tim Lang and Yiannis Gabriel have argued that 'ethical-consumerism maps one clear path for consumers, a route for translating consumerism into citizenship, consumer/citizen being one conventional ideological contrast'.[9] But this optimistic sounding endorsement is followed by the caveat that, 'much as we would like consumers to take the "high" road, evidence suggests that there are powerful forces pushing and pulling consumers in different [directions] and "low" roads too'.[10]

The clarity offered by the citizen-consumer route may in fact be illusory. Corianne Gendron argues that 'it is not the consumer who takes the place of the citizen, but rather the citizen who stands behind the consumer, with the limits and the potential that this status offers'.[11] For Michele Micheletti and Andreas Follesdal there are obvious problems with 'the sole reliance on voluntary consumer choice and using personal money and private capital to solve human rights problems by shopping them away'.[12] They contend that 'shopping is not and cannot be a sufficient agent of human rights'.[13] This is a position that is echoed by many within the Fair Trade movement. Tomy Mathew, outspoken founder of Fair Trade Alliance of Kerala, has commented that 'the larger battle for trade justice cannot be won with shopping bag politics'.[14]

So where does this leave Fair Trade and notions of global citizenship? Brett Bowden, a political scientist based at the Australian National University, Canberra, has argued that 'the notion of a global citizen or citizen of the world is not a viable one'.[15] But Bowden proposed that this need not be at odds with what he calls 'globally minded citizens'.[16] There are some clear parallels between the aims of the Fair Trade movement and Bowden's concept of 'globally minded citizens'. Bowden offers a broad definition of what being a globally minded citizen means in practice, and argues that it involves 'being aware that actions taken in one part of the world can have an effect on people/nations beyond one's borders'.[17] Specific activities that are singled out for attention include: 'atmospheric polluting and other environmentally detrimental action' and 'unfair trade and/or unethical investment'.[18]

If the global dimensions of citizenship are problematic, within a national context the existence of the Fair Trade movement is consistent with a particular sense of 'British citizenship' that is defined by membership of voluntary associations and community groups rather than political parties. Ivor Crewe and Donald Searing have argued that from a British perspective, 'citizenship is involvement in social networks, in the groups, organisations and voluntary associations that connect citizens with the life of their communities'.[19] By amalgamating elements of these latter concepts we arrive at a definition that can be aligned with the Fair Trade movement, at least within a British context. So rather than a new form of global citizenship, Fair Trade is perhaps more accurately defined as a social movement of globally minded citizens – whereby participation is publicly demonstrated by engagement in prescribed activities including: campaigning, volunteering and 'conscious consumption'.

A grassroots social movement

From the early 1970s Fair Trade represented a new and distinctly modern approach to campaigning that resonated with individuals and organisations looking to influence debates about how Britain should conduct international trade and development.[20] Although building on the politics of the past, the messages and organisational structure of Fair Trade identified it as more closely aligned with the 'new social movements' than traditional labour or consumer politics. In 2003, *The Guardian* described Fairtrade as 'one of Britain's most active grassroots social movements'.[21]

Donatella Della Porta, has identified three key elements of a social movement: they are involved in conflictual relations with clearly identified opponents, they are linked by dense informal networks, and they share a distinct collective identity.[22] Della Porta argues that the networks of organisations involved with Fair Trade are characteristic of a social movement: 'The spread of fair-trade practices is facilitated by the existence of extended networks of co-operatives and small retail operators in the West, who try somehow to reach a balance between ethic-driven public action and market requirement.'[23]

This book has looked to extend the assessment of Fair Trade as a social movement beyond an understanding of 'co-operatives and small retailers', to include consumers, religious groups, NGOs and trade unions.[24] By widening the field of investigation what becomes apparent is the sheer breadth of ideas that Fair Trade has encapsulated. For different groups, and at different times in its history, Fair Trade has been defined in relation to: internationalism, charity, social justice, solidarity, social enterprise, consumer activism, and moral duty. This book has explored how groups motivated by these differing and sometimes conflicting objectives were able to unite under the banner of Fair Trade. In the following sections the main driving forces behind the formation of these Fair Trade networks are discussed in turn.

Building a movement

In order to build a picture of how the Fair Trade social movement developed, it is important to understand what provided the main organising themes during different moments of the movement's history, and why different groups identified with Fair Trade. The factors that encouraged the formation of Fair Trade networks can be divided into two groups. Firstly, 'practical drivers' – most notably the role of charismatic leaders and the influence of the media. Secondly, 'philosophical drivers' – such as the positioning of Fair Trade in relation to Christian ethics and voluntarism, the pioneering of an 'alternative' approach to trade and development, and the promotion of political consumption and consumer activism.

Practical drivers: Charismatic leaders

Fair Trade has been described as one of the fastest growing grassroots social movements across Europe and the significance of NGOs and campaign groups in shaping the growth Fair Trade has increasingly been recognised in academic studies.[25] Clarke, Barnett et al. have argued convincingly that, 'agency needs to be located not in the activities of consumers but in the articulation of intermediary organisations, social networks, and every day practices of social reproduction'.[26] But while recognising the contribution of activists and campaigners to the growth of Fair Trade, I argue that the history and governance of the movement cannot be fully understood without also referring to the leadership of a relatively small number of key individuals.

In the formative years of Fair Trade's development (during the 1970s and 1980s) there were several prominent individuals who proved important in shaping the future direction of the movement in Britain.

Among them were managers and directors from a range of established organisations and newly formed Fair Trade companies. They saw in Fair Trade a practical way of driving forward a new agenda on international trade and development. This group included: Roy Scott (Oxfam 'Bridge' and One Village); Richard Adams (Tear Craft, Traidcraft, New Consumer, Fairtrade Foundation and Out of This World); Michael Barratt Brown (TWIN Trading); Hedley Whitehead (the Co-operative).[27]

Within the business management literature the role of leadership is well documented, particularly during times of structural change.[28] The concept of 'charismatic leadership' is defined by David Nadler and Michael Tusman as referring to a special quality that 'enables the leader to mobilize and sustain activity within an organization through specific personal actions combined with perceived personal characteristics'.[29] The importance of leadership has received less attention in the new social movement literature; here the focus tends to be on understanding the dynamics of grassroots activist networks.[30] Michael Barratt Brown, speaking about the importance of social networks at the 1988 Conference on Development, Trade and Co-operation, stated that, 'they don't happen spontaneously. There have to be networkers.'[31] It seems that this is an issue that is too often overlooked in studies of Fair Trade.

What is required is an academic approach that accurately reflects the specific nature of Fair Trade as it straddles both the business world and social activism. In recent years, there has been an increased interest in studies of social entrepreneurship, with a particular focus on business administration and microeconomics. There has been a growing awareness and recognition of this field since Muhammad Yunus, founder of the Grameen Bank, won the Nobel Peace Prize in 2006.[32] Although the term 'social entrepreneur' was not in common use during the 1970s, the concept can still be drawn on to better understand the role of Fair Trade leaders and their approach to business innovation, aimed at delivering greater social and economic benefits from international trade.

While definitions of a social entrepreneur often vary from country to country and author to author; one of the most widely cited definitions in the academic literature is the one devised by Gregory Dees, Jed Emerson and Peter Economy. They define a social entrepreneur as a change agent who:

> Adopts a mission to create and sustain social values; recognizes and relentlessly pursues new opportunities to serve that mission; engages in a process of continuous innovation, adaptation, and learning; acts

> boldly without being limited by resources currently at hand; exhibits heightened accountability to the constituencies served and the outcomes created.[33]

The further significance of applying the definition of social entrepreneur to these Fair Trade pioneers is that it challenges the 'lingering associations with hippy lifestyles'.[34]

The gender imbalance in the above list of early pioneers is striking, particularly since Fair Trade has frequently been identified with a feminist political theory. It is not hard to find echoes of 'the personal is political' within the campaign literature of the Fair Trade movement.[35] Harriet Lamb, speaking on the tenth anniversary of the launch of the FAIRTRADE Mark declared that, 'now with globalization has come a way to make political changes through your personal choices'.[36] In recent years initiatives such as the Triodos Women in Ethical Business Awards have highlighted the role of female social entrepreneurs such as: Safia Minney (People Tree), Sophi Tranchell (Divine Chocolate), Penny Newman (Cafédirect) and Harriet Lamb (Fairtrade Foundation). Commentators have asked: 'Why are so many ethical businesses run by women?'[37] Predominantly the answer provided is that, 'money is not enough to persuade women into business ... women crave an extra factor to complete the picture'.[38] But are these simply the traits of an entrepreneur? This is an interesting field that would benefit from further research into the management practices of Fair Trade companies. Can female leadership be seen as part of Fair Trade's modern social agenda or are these developments consistent with wider social trends in employment and business management over the last 20 years?

There is a growing literature on Fair Trade and issues of gender inequality but to date the focus has been on studying the relative impact on female producers in less developed countries.[39] There has yet to be a detailed study of the role gender played within the Fair Trade movement as it gained support in the Global North. The National Federation of Women's Institutes (NFWI) would seem to offer a potential avenue for studying the specific contribution made by women in building the Fair Trade movement.[40] Some commentators have identified the WI's involvement with Fair Trade campaigns as further evidence of the 'edgy new world of the Women's Institute'.[41] It is perhaps surprising that recent WI publications and reports offer few details about their involvement with Fair Trade beyond the stereotypical references to the 'WI Fairtrade Chocolate Cake'.[42] A review of the WI's recent campaigning activities also shows that there has been no resolution passed on Fair Trade by the

WI AGM since 2002.[43] There is still more work to be done to understand the role women have played in developing Fair Trade through their membership of community groups and voluntary organisations, as social entrepreneurs and as consumers. A study of this type has been beyond the scope of this book, but with Soroptomists of Great Britain and Ireland becoming the fifteenth member of the Fairtrade Foundation in 2007, there are further grounds for pursuing this research agenda.[44]

Practical drivers: The media

In recent years, there has been greater academic attention on how the media is used by NGOs in anti-poverty campaigns, and this work has been developed and applied to studies of Fair Trade campaigns and marketing.[45] The majority of studies have focused either on the marketing of Fairtrade products by companies such as Cafédirect or they have looked at high profile media campaigns such as Make Poverty History or Live 8. But as this book has shown, links with the media have been an important practical driver in building support for the Fair Trade Movement since the 1970s and the dynamics of this relationship merit further consideration. An historically informed debate may also provide useful context for some of the contemporary discussions about how Fair Trade positions its media profile.

Mike Goodman, drawing on the work of Arjun Appadurai, questions 'Can the media ever be turned to the interests of the poor?'[46] Goodman explores the use of celebrities in Fair Trade and anti-poverty campaigns such as Make Trade Fair and Live 8. He argues that, 'this growing *celebritisation* of environment and development has reached an almost fever pitch in the UK's Fair Trade movement. Here, the newest Fair Trade campaigns are less about trouble-making than they are about *market-making* through the judicious use of celebrity and marketing wherewithal.'[47] Returning to his opening question, Goodman concludes that the media has been turned to the interests of the poor but in a particularly spectacular and potentially ambiguous way.

An area that has received less academic attention to date is the role played by investigative reporting in raising awareness of the general public about the links between everyday consumer choices and conditions for producers in developing countries. This represents the less spectacular side of Fair Trade's interactions with the media, but the impact that investigative journalism has had, both on television and in print, should not be overlooked. One of the first Fair Trade campaigns to benefit from access to a mass television audience was the Campaign for Fair Tea Prices (1973–1977).[48] As discussed in proceeding chapters, World in Action's

'Cost of a Cup of Tea', first broadcast in September 1973, played a vital role in raising consumer awareness of the conditions on tea plantations. These images prompted widespread debate and led to a Parliamentary Select Committee enquiry. Most British consumers had little knowledge of how these 'exotic' products were produced and up to this point had accepted an idealised picture of plantation life, as portrayed in corporate marketing that had changed little since the 1930s. In this context, the comical picture of the British public being fooled by Panorama's 'spaghetti trees' perhaps reveals a darker side about post-war consumer ignorance of goods produced beyond British shores.[49]

While it is sometimes assumed that television programmes popularised by NGO campaigns have in some way been commissioned by those NGOs; with 'Cost of a Cup of Tea' this was not the case. It was filmed and produced largely in secret (in order to avoid a backlash from the tea companies or the Sri Lankan government) and without direct input of any NGO campaign groups.[50] The motivation for filming came from colleagues working on *Disappearing World* (an anthropological series) who had been filming in Sri Lanka early in 1973. On hearing shocking reports about the conditions on tea estates, the World in Action team decided to travel to Sri Lanka to investigate further. Their cover story was that they were making a children's television programme about tea. This meant that they could get general footage on the estates and auctions during daytime. At night, with the support of the local tea workers union, they conducted an undercover investigation and filmed a doctor assessing the appalling condition of tea workers and their families.

What does this case study reveal about the interaction between the Fair Trade movement and the media and how this relationship has developed over time? Does it reinforce Goodman's contention that in recent years there has been a shift away from the 'once vaunted transparency of Fair Trade'?[51] Certainly the Fair Trade movement, and the Fairtrade Foundation in particular, have become more media savvy and Goodman is probably right to question the *celebritisation* of public communications. But I would argue that there is still room for thought-provoking investigative reporting that has the potential to challenge both consumers and the Fair Trade movement to look beyond the marketing hype.[52]

Philosophical drivers: Christian ethics and voluntarism

Although it may be tempting to argue that churches were 'natural allies' of the Fair Trade movement, this would underestimate the amount of work involved in encouraging some churches to support Fair Trade.[53] As argued by Barnett, Clarke, Cloke and Malpasss, 'it should not be assumed that the fair-trade movement has a natural home in church-based networks'.[54] Rather than focusing on church institutions themselves as a driver for change, Barnett et al. identify 'a shared discourse of faith' as a strategic option open to Fair Trade campaigners.[55] It is this abstract concept of 'a shared discourse of faith', or what I have defined as 'Christian ethics and voluntarism' that played an important role in uniting the Fair Trade movement, particularly during the 1970s and 1980s. As already noted in Chapter 2, identifying Christian ethics and voluntarism as important philosophical drivers for the growth of Fair Trade provides an interesting dimension, (and an additional complexity), to the secularisation debate, particularly in relation to Callum Brown's assertion of the 'Death of Christian Britain'.[56] But any assertion that support for Fair Trade and the Christian development agencies represented a broader revival of Christian values of charity and justice, needs to be prefaced with a caveat that, for much of this period, politically international development remained a relatively minor issue – as reflected in the modest budgets allocated to the Government department responsible.[57]

International development, and Fair Trade in particular, still represented an important opportunity for Christian groups (not necessarily the Church) to demonstrate the relevance of Christian teachings during a period when they had been seen to no longer provide 'a compelling explanation for the ills of society'.[58] In contrast to many of the recent revisionist studies on religion in Britain, Fair Trade does not lend itself to local studies.[59] Although Fair Trade campaigns may have been networked at a local level through discussion groups, Traidcraft stalls and Church meetings; the focus was on influencing the media, national supermarket chains and government policymakers. Fair Trade campaigns can therefore provide an interesting, and new approach to important questions such as: 'Why the churches – as supposedly declining institutions – should have achieved in the 1980s and 1990s such a persistently high public profile ... By what authority and in whose name have the churches intervened in public debate?'[60]

Grace Davie in her influential and challenging work identifies a mismatch between 'Believing and Belonging'.[61] Davie argues that 'the sacred does not disappear – indeed in many ways it is becoming more rather than less prevalent in contemporary society'.[62] But her assessment of the 1970s as a period of religious revival is based on the emergence of the 'New Age' phenomenon rather than Christianity. Fair Trade allowed the Christian Church, through the work of the main agencies, Christian Aid, CAFOD and Tearfund, to demonstrate a united approach to international development.[63] This was in notable contrast to the denominational rifts that divided the Churches over matters of individual morality. Fair Trade demonstrated a practical role for the Church and was seen as a positive direction among the UK public that were largely supportive of the Church's involvement with issues of 'Third World' aid and development.[64]

The Fairtrade Foundation increasingly talks about 'a vibrant network of faith communities' rather than singling out Christian support for Fairtrade.[65] Recent publications by Islamic Relief Worldwide have provided an Islamic perspective on Fair Trade. Ajaz Ahmed Khan and Laura Thaut have shown that there is 'a rich heritage in Islam of high moral standards, ethics, values and norms of behaviour, which govern personal, professional and business life'.[66] They conclude that:

> 'The fair trade vision of a trade system based on just social relationships between producers and workers, as well as between buyers and sellers, coincides with the teachings in Islam that instruct people to defend and pursue just economic relationships. . . From an Islamic perspective, there are indeed strong and clear faith-based reasons to supporting fair trade initiatives'.[67]

While recognising that there are some positive moves towards an inter-faith dialogue, it should be noted that the Fairtrade Foundation remains a predominantly Christian organisation with 7 of its 15 member organisations having Christian allegiances and no other faith groups are represented.[68]

While Christian ethics have continued to motivate supporters they have not been integral to the modern identity of Fairtrade Foundation.[69] There remains a perception that openly Christian language could alienate the general public.[70] There is no evidence that the Christian members of the Fairtrade Foundation have been pushing for a stronger Christian message within the Foundation's brand identity.What lessons from this study of Christian agencies and Fair Trade companies can be applied to the wider secularization debate? Jeremy Morris, has argued that, 'for the time being it is a strange sort of death that leaves churches still amongst the largest voluntary organisations in the country, and Christianity still notionally the conviction of a majority of the population'.[71] In relation to Fair Trade, Church leaders are vocal spokespersons for the movement and consistently receive mainstream media coverage when they speak on issues relating to international development and Trade Justice.[72] At a community level, church halls remain popular venues for talks and events each Fairtrade Fortnight; framing discussions of trade, economics and development within a distinctly Christian landscape.

Philosophical drivers: An alternative approach

Earlier chapters have explored how Fair Trade developed as an alternative approach in the 1970s that filled the vacuum left not only by government and business reluctance to engage consumers on issues of international trade and development, but also the reluctance of the traditional consumer movement, in the form of the Co-operative, and the labour movement, as seen with the TUC.

Up until the early 1990s the term 'alternative trade' was preferred by the majority of campaigners and organisations involved. Carol Wills, former executive director of IFAT,[73] commented that, 'alternative was rather a good word, because it was alternative in all kinds of ways: cutting out the middleman, trading directly . . . ; alternative distribution channels; alternative work force, volunteers in many cases, and so on and so forth'.[74] The concept of an alternative approach developed in parallel with Christian ethics and voluntarism as a defining theme of Fair Trade from the mid-1970s. In general, there was little real tension between these approaches, despite the idea of 'an alternative' opening up opportunities for more overtly political campaigns than may have been possible in debates framed by Christian ethics.[75]

The politics of alternative trade were often expressed initially through solidarity campaigns with countries such as Nicaragua and Tanzania that were seen to have politically progressive regimes. For many supporters of Fair Trade in the 1970s and 1980s, one of the major motivations was the belief that they had to respond to the growth in multinational corporations (MNCs), because they were seen to be setting back any attempts to implement international development programmes.[76] An alternative approach meant finding new supply chains outside the control of big business. Roy Scott envisaged a marketing structure that 'avoids the conventional chain of profit-seeking employers, middlemen, agents, exporters, importers, wholesalers and through the economies of direct marketing is able to pay producers better'.[77]

An alternative approach also represented a move away from charity. Roy Scott stated that Bridge has 'nothing to do with charity or paternalism; it provides security and Fair Trade basis producers need for development; and it satisfies the need for products to be sold on their merit'.[78] But most supporters of Fair Trade were sufficiently pragmatic to realise the benefits of registration with the Charity Commission and did not shun the various grants available or the opportunity to receive tax relief. Central to the success of the Fair Trade movement has been its ability to balance the often conflicting, requirements of charity, campaigning and commercial enterprise. Despite the initial resistance of the Charity Commission and the ambivalence of some within the movement, in February 1995 the Fairtrade Foundation gained charitable status, after prolonged negotiations and a year after the launch of the FAIRTRADE Mark.[79]

Although Fair Trade continued to be described as 'an alternative approach' in the movement's agreed definition up until 2009, public messages had quickly moved away from this terminology by the early 1990s.[80] Carol Wills has acknowledged that alternative ideas quickly went out of fashion; in the public's mindset they were too closely associated with, 'brown rice, sandals and beards'.[81] The formation of the Fairtrade Foundation, in 1992, was a direct attempt to engage with mainstream markets and it was argued that the 'alternative' label would have to be dropped. In its place was a stated ambition to 'engage UK consumer power on a significant scale'.[82]

Philosophical drivers: Consumer activism

In much of the Fair Trade literature the importance of consumer demand and consumer choice have been highlighted as the main drivers of change.[83] At one level this provides a logical explanation for the increasing value of Fairtrade retail sales in Britain; but this account offers only a limited insight into the dynamics of the social movement behind the label. One consequence of an overly narrow focus on consumer demand has been to underplay the role of activist groups which could, with some justification, be considered 'the fundamental vanguard fostering Fair Trade markets'.[84] While recognising a role for consumer politics as part of the development of Fair Trade, there is a need to consider a more nuanced narrative that does not define Fair Trade as 'entirely a consumer choice model'.[85]

The politically neutral figure of the consumer proved a valuable tool in allowing NGOs to move beyond the social, cultural or religious affiliations of their core supporters and attempt to influence the general public in a way that few had succeeded in doing previously. This language of consumer activism has remained a prominent feature of many Fair Trade messages. But this campaign literature should not be accepted uncritically, rather it needs to be understood within a wider political the context that also takes into account outside influences such as: the charity commission, government and mainstream business.

If we look beyond the campaign material and marketing messages to study the strategies adopted by the Fairtrade Foundation; what is revealed is a significantly more complex picture, whereby a discourse of consumer choice is negotiated through a framework of corporate compliance and public procurement contracts. The evidence suggests that the Fairtrade Foundation has in fact adopted a strategy of, to use Tim Lang's phrase, 'choice editing'.[86] Lang argues that consumers can't be relied on to do the right thing and calls for a move away from consumer power. Lang states that: 'Individual action is not enough. It requires choice editing, not personal choice'.[87] This means removing ethical hazards before a product reaches the consumer. The 2006 Sustainable Consumption Roundtable report, 'Looking Forward Looking Back', endorses Lang's assessment, stating that: 'The evidence suggests that, historically, the green consumer has not been the tipping point in driving innovation. Instead, choice editing for quality and sustainability by Government and business has been the critical driver in the majority of cases.'[88]

It is perhaps not surprising that the Fairtrade Foundation has shied away from a critique of individual action and consumer choice; it would probably not play well in the boardrooms of Starbucks or Tesco. But 'choice editing' through public procurement has been an important focus for Fair Trade ever since the Greater London Council established TWIN Trading in 1985, and has been revived as part of the five goals for achieving Fairtrade Town status. Olivier Le Brun, Director of TWIN Trading was clear about where attention should be focused, and it was not individual consumers:

> If we want to develop more direct and permanent trading links between the south and the north we have to open new opportunities for the distribution of Third World products. We have to explore the social market: the supply departments of local authorities, their purchasing associations and civic catering, universities, polytechnics, schools, social services, hospitals, trade unions, labour clubs etc.[89]

There also seems to be a reluctance to leave the fate of Fairtrade to the whims of consumer choice when it comes to dealings with big business. Harriet Lamb in a public statement recognising the commitment by Cadbury to achieve Fairtrade certification for Cadbury Dairy Milk, said that: 'The Fairtrade Foundation set out an ambitious strategy last year to double its positive impact for producers by 2012 ... It is precisely this kind of big commitment by a major player such as Cadbury that could make it possible to achieve these goals.'[90] So while the Fairtrade Foundation objectives have been 'to *empower consumers* to take responsibility for the role they play when they buy products from the third world';[91] in practice, the Foundation's role has more often been about *shepherding consumers* and lobbying local councils (and MNCs) in order to promote a choice architecture (and retail landscape) conducive to responsible and ethical consumption.

The British case in a global context

The Fairtrade retail market in the United Kingdom is among largest in the world and arguably the most advanced, with the widest range of Fairtrade products available to mainstream consumers.[92] The UK market has also been a test ground for major multinational brands expanding their presence in the ethical sector. In 2009, Starbucks committed to serving only Fairtrade coffee in its UK stores.[93] This move was greeted with particular enthusiasm because it meant that in the United Kingdom Fairtrade would not have to compete with Starbucks's own sourcing initiative (C.A.F.E. Practices).[94] The British case has received considerable international attention from academics, Fair Trade companies and campaigners, interested in whether comparable market growth might be replicable in other national contexts.

Steve Ogden-Barnes, programme director at Monash University's Australian Centre for Retail Studies, commenting on Marks & Spencer's 'Look behind the Label' campaign, stated that it was significant because, 'generally once trends have taken hold in Europe and America, we see them arrive in Australia'.[95] Sarah Scarborough, from Scarborough Fair, one of the leading Australian Fairtrade brands, reinforced this position stating that:

> Trends that start in Britain do generally follow in Australia and getting Fairtrade to the mainstream makes it practical for the consumer. They no longer have to go to an Oxfam shop and pay $10 for a bag of coffee, they can go to the supermarket aisle and switch their brand of coffee.[96]

While the general trend, seen in Britain, of a move away from NGO-backed charity shops towards a greater uptake by mainstream retailers seems to fit with the experiences of other national Fairtrade labels, it is not clear how far these similarities can be extended. For a start, it seems that the speed and extent of these developments has varied significantly and is not necessarily a linear or predictable process.

In recent years this increased engagement with MNCs has led to further questioning about the direction of Fair Trade and its ability to influence corporate behaviour. The Fairtrade Foundation has managed this development more successfully than some national labelling initiatives, notably TransFair USA/Fair Trade USA.[97] In 2004, five small 100% Fair Trade coffee roasters, part of the Co-operative Coffees Network, withdrew from the TransFair USA certification. They claimed that the original vision of a better model was being watered down by corporate engagement.[98] The initial response by Paul Rice, President and CEO of TransFair USA, was somewhat dismissive of these moves: 'If a corporate giant roasts a million pounds of fair-trade coffee in one year they are still doing far more than some smaller 100% roasters will in their entire history.'[99] In 2006 there were briefly signs of an attempt by TransFair to try to mitigate the damage done to its reputation and standing within the movement:

> TransFair USA acknowledges and values the vital role of NGOs, advocacy groups and producers in growing the Fair Trade market and movement ... At times, in our efforts to extend the benefits of Fair Trade to farmers and farm workers rapidly, we have failed to adequately engage the broader Fair Trade community effectively.[100]

This undercurrent of tension within the movement became a very visible split as the US labelling initiative, Fair Trade USA (formerly TransFair USA), broke off from the international umbrella organisation Fairtrade International on 1 January 2012.[101] While the technicalities of the split were about certification standards and the expansion of plantation-grown products into commodities such as coffee, it also 'reflected profound differences in the visions for fair trade's future'.[102] For Hudson et al., it was economic democracy that was at the crux of the split. They argue that, 'under FTUSA's new, more conservative standards the transformation-orientated, non-capitalist commitment of the fair trade label for coffee has been dropped'.[103] Their research findings suggest that the Fair Trade USA/FLO split will lead to a greater divergence within the movement about how Fair Trade is framed and envisaged by different actors.[104] This has implications for the identity and positioning of Fair Trade.

These controversies have led to a growing critique about the robustness of the governance frameworks within the national labelling initiatives.

There is an opportunity for historical research to better inform these contemporary debates; however, to date, historical accounts remain largely anecdotal and written by former staff of Fair Trade organisations.[105] Bob Thomson, Managing Director of TransFair Canada, has provided one of the most intriguing accounts of the development of the European Fair Trade movement, from what he describes as 'an outsider' perspective.[106] Thomson characterises the process as,

> even more complex than just national politics. It involves personalities, national cultural traits, 'ideologies' and turf battle for market share. If forced to put it very simply, I could say that it amounts to groups of people arguing about who has the most angels on the head of their pin. It can't be put simply however![107]

Thomson describes how Max Havelaar Netherlands left a vacuum by initially not wanting to expand beyond coffee and not providing an alternative pan-European structure or forum to EFTA. According to Thomson, the result was that, 'when TransFair Germany got started in 1992, there was already a history of personality clashes, resentments and probably some elements of turf battles for influence on new national label initiatives'.[108]

While providing many interesting anecdotes, Thomson's account, in common with other histories of Fair Trade, mainly draws from personal experience rather than documented archive records and as such is difficult to verify. There is a call for academic research into both the European and international Fair Trade movements that draws on interviews with practitioners and is reinforced by archive research. Initial research has pointed to some potentially significant differences that may have impacted on the structure, governance and approach adopted by different national Fair Trade movements. Unfortunately there is not yet sufficient detail at a national level to undertake a global comparative study, although this has the potential for an exciting future collaborative research project.[109]

A new direction for consumer politics?

This book has argued that consumer demand offers only a partial explanation for the growth of Fair Trade and that consumer choice was not the main driver of change within the Fair Trade movement. But this is not to suggest that Fair Trade campaigners should discard consumer activism; conversely there may be real value in widening definitions of consumer politics in order to address the question of living standards of Fair Trade producers in the global South from a new perspective. It is clear however, that this approach may run counter to the arguments of some global justice activists. Vandana Shiva speaking at the second World Social Forum in 2002 argued that:

> The philosophical and ethical bankruptcy of globalization was based on reducing every aspect of our lives to commodities and reducing our identities to merely that of consumer on the global market place. Our capacities as producers, our identity as members of communities, our role as custodians of our natural and cultural heritage were all to disappear or be destroyed.[110]

Speeches such as this have had a lasting impact on the direction of the global justice movement. In response Fair Trade has largely remained on the fringes of these global gatherings – a consumerist approach being seen as too closely aligned with corporate interests. Fair Trade set out to 'bridge' the gap between consumer and producer, but as the movement developed there were few signs that this was happening, instead the distinctions seemed to sharpen. With the recent development of Fairtrade consumer labels in the global South, (Mexico, South Africa, Kenya, India and Brazil), there is now an opportunity for the Fair Trade movement to rethink how it addresses the dynamics of consumer/producer relations.[111]

Additionally, Consumers International (CI), the world federation of consumer groups, has also shown a greater interest in understanding the impact of Fair Trade. Its report on coffee posed several important questions: 'When a consumer chooses to buy certified coffee what effects ripple along the commodity chain, from retailer to grower? What are the factors that prompt consumers to buy certified coffee – and equally, what are factors that keep them from such a purchase?'[112] There is potential to develop these links in a new direction, if the Fairtrade Foundation is willing engage with CI and explore how the dynamics of consumer activism have adapted to reflect the increased representation from consumer organisations based in the global South. From an organisation predominantly concerned with product testing in Europe and the United States, CI has evolved into an influential lobbyist demanding rights to basic necessities for all – including the world's poorest consumers.[113]

Throughout Fair Trade's history, how the movement has defined issues of fairness has been the result of a process of negotiation and compromise. For some academics this represents an ideological inconsistency that threatens the authenticity of the movement.[114] But this ability to adapt and evolve has also been one Fair Trade's strengths and has contributed to its resilience and relevance. The recent development of consumer labels in the global South, has the potential to open up a new set of possibilities about how the Fair Trade movement frames debates over pricing and living wages. In responding to this challenge there is an opportunity for the Fairtrade Foundation to consider more holistically how it addresses questions of impact, empowerment and development. The consumer agenda has the potential to be a dynamic and creative force within Fair Trade, but only if this is matched with the moral imagination to continually challenge concepts of fairness and to question the progress made towards a 'socially ideal' model of trade.[115]

Appendix

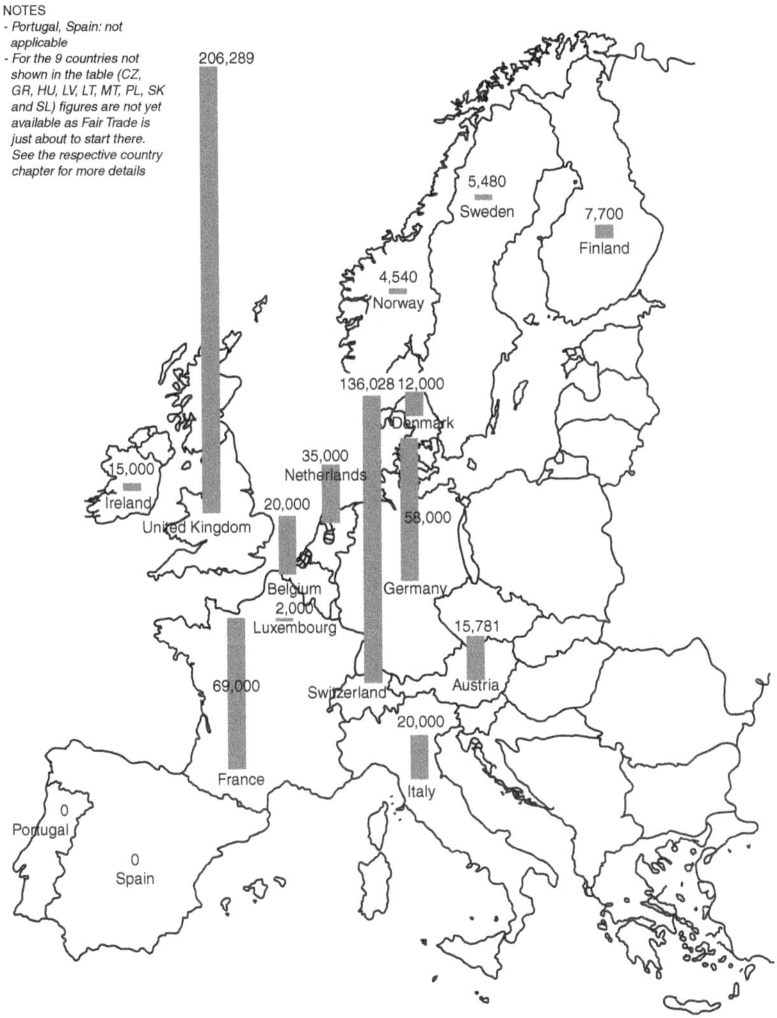

Figure A.1 Retail value of European Fair Trade labelling organisations (2005)
Source: EFTA – European Fair Trade Association – Fair Trade in Europe 2005. http://www.european-fair-trade-association.org/efta/Doc/FT-E-2006.pdf

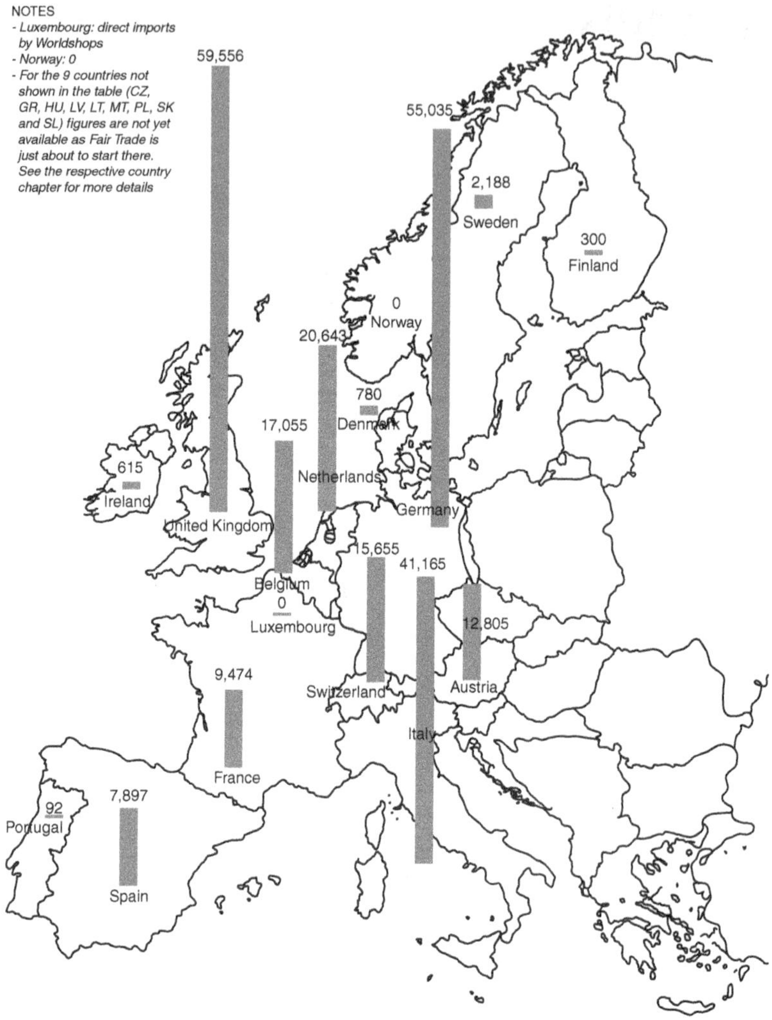

Figure A.2 Turnover of Fair Trade importing organisations (2005)
Source: EFTA – European Fair Trade Association – Fair Trade in Europe 2005. http://www.european-fair-trade-association.org/efta/Doc/FT-E-2006.pdf

Figure A.3 Turnover of European Fair Trade importing organisations in 000 € (July 2000)

Source: EFTA – European Fair Trade Association – Fair Trade in Europe 2001. http://www.european-fair-trade-association.org/efta/Doc/FT-E-2001.pdf

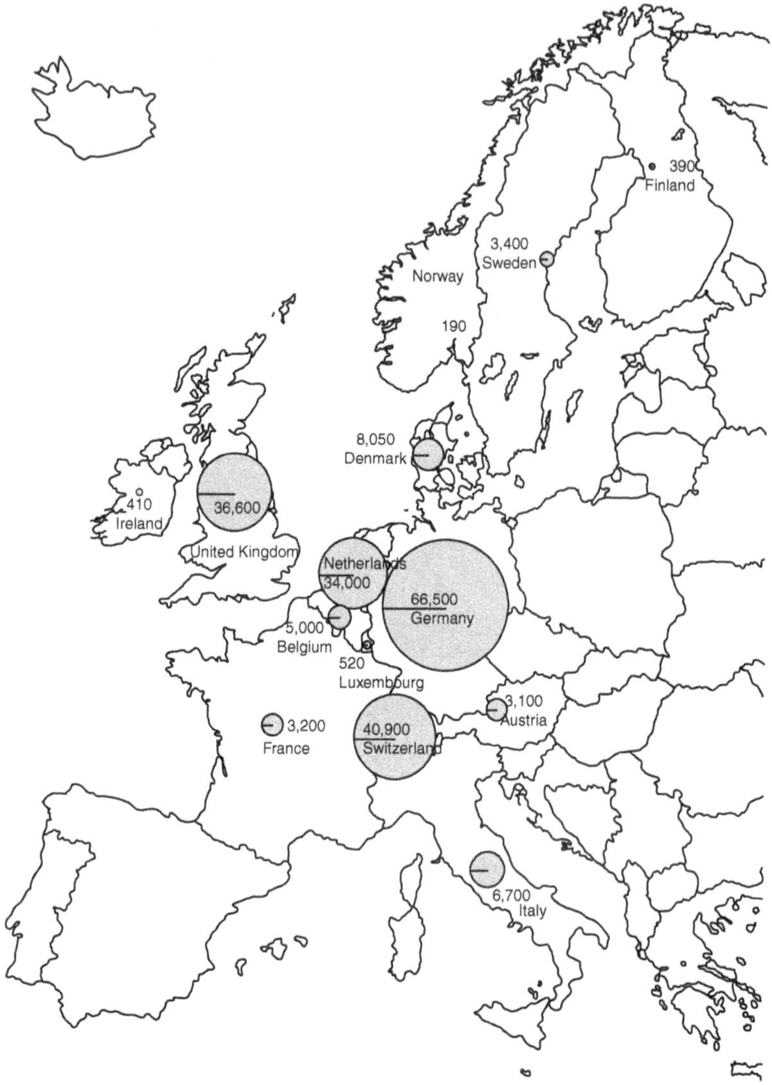

Figure A.4 Turnover of European Fair Trade labelling organisations in 000 € (July 2000)

Source: EFTA – European Fair Trade Association – Fair Trade in Europe 2001. http://www.european-fair-trade-association.org/efta/Doc/FT-E-2001.pdf

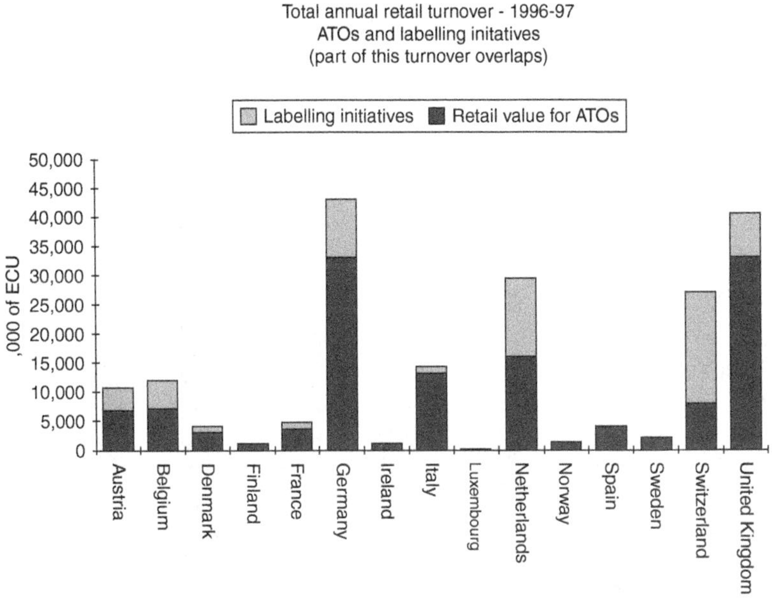

Tabel with summarised information of the 16 European countries in the study (numbers are rounded off):

Importing organisations:	70+
Selling points:	70,000
Including	
World Shops	3,000
Commercial shops (incl. supermarkets)	33,000
Chains of supermarkets:	50
Employees (equivalent full-time positions):	1,500
Volunteers:	100,000
Labelling initiatives:	Max Havelaar, TransFair, Fairtrade Mark
Budgets for education & public relations:	8 million ECU
Retail turnover:	200 million ECU
Market share of fair trade coffee:	1.7% (European average)

Figure A.5 Total annual retail turnover 1996–1997, ATOs and labelling initiatives
Source: EFTA – European Fair Trade Association – Fair Trade in Europe 1998. http://www.european-fair-trade-association.org/efta/Doc/FT-E-1998.pdf

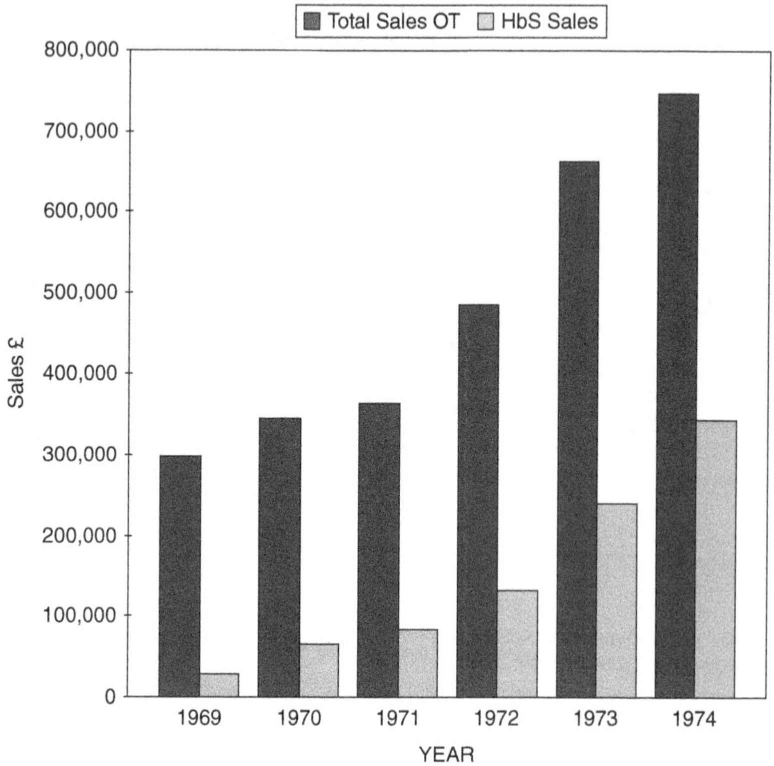

Figure A.6 Helping by Selling sales in relation to total Oxfam Trading sales, 1969–1974

Source: OXFAM: Guy Stringer, Director's Report to the Executive Committee (February 1974).

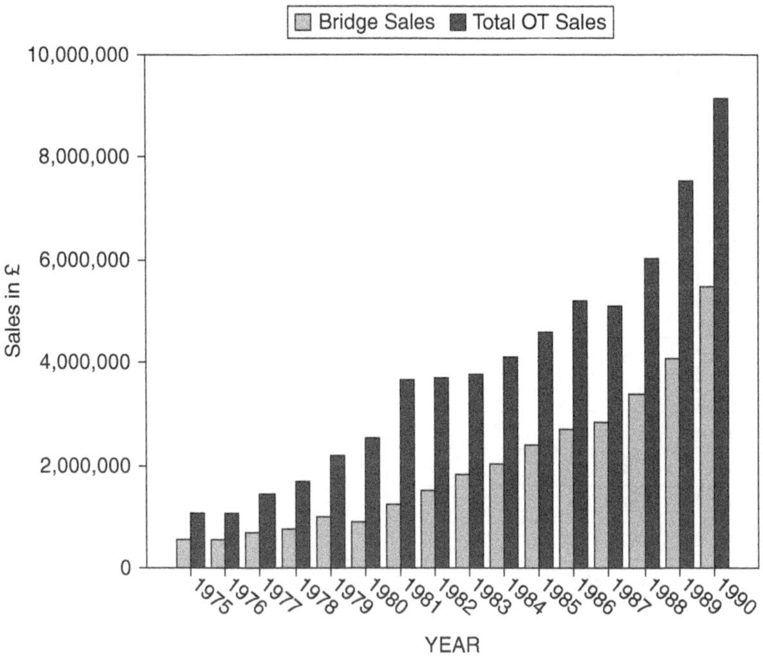

Figure A.7 Bridge sales in relation to total Oxfam Trading sales 1975–1990
Source: OXFAM, BRIDGE COM: *Analysis of Bridge imports* (1990).

Year	OT sales (£)	Bridge sales (£)	Bridge as % of OT sales	Net profit
1975	1,054,274	532,871	51.0%	81,296
1976	1,050,199	540,474	51.0%	–
1977	1,439,077	687,814	47.8%	–
1978	1,664,930	757,055	45.5%	–24,000
1979	2,183,707	989,581	45.3%	30,611
1980	2,543,868	902,818	35.5%	8,280
1981	3,564,191	1,224,368	34.4%	65,367
1982	3,695,634	1,503,677	40.7%	51,238
1983	3,776,229	1,812 399	48.0%	73,206
1984	4,124,279	2,011,740	48.8%	75,509
1985	4,584,856	2,384,126	52.0%	102,863
1986	5,193,103	2,689,744	51.2%	119,386
1987	5,109,245	2,825,519	55.3%	197,000
1988	6,026,043	3,378,620	56.1%	197,000
1989	7,530,845	4,073,670	54.1%	66,000
1990	9,133,866	5,494,105	60.2%	188,000

Figure A.8 Bridge sales as percentage of overall Oxfam Trading sales 1975–1990
Source: OXFAM, BRIDGE COM: *Analysis of Bridge imports* (1990).

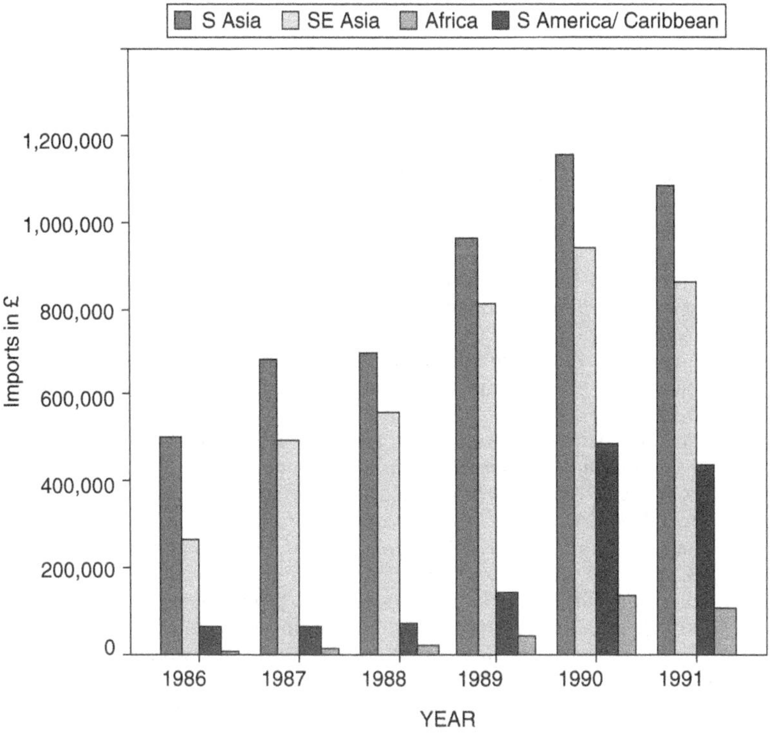

Figure A.9 Analysis of Bridge imports by region 1986–1991
Source: OXFAM, BRIDGE COM: *Analysis of Bridge imports (FOB value) by country* (1990).

Notes

Introduction: A New International 'Moral Economy'?

1. Mintel, *Attitudes Towards Ethical Foods, Market Intelligence* (August 2006).
2. The Fairtrade Foundation, 'Annual Report and Financial Statements for the year ended 31 December 2013'. Available http://www.fairtrade.org.uk/en/what-is-fairtrade/social-and-annual-reports
3. See Appendix Figure A.1 and Figure A.2.
4. L. Jones, 'How Fair Trade hit the mainstream', *BBC News* (2 March 2004).
5. T. Macalister, 'How consumer power sparked a Fairtrade revolution on our high streets', *The Guardian* (8 March 2006).
6. A. Nicholls, 'Strategic options in Fair Trade retailing', *International Journal of Retail & Distribution Management,* 30.1 (2002), pp. 6–17.
7. The Co-operative Bank, *The Ethical Consumerism Report* (2007).
8. Mintel, *Attitudes Towards Ethical Foods.*
9. D. Jaffee, *Brewing Justice: Fair Trade Coffee, Sustainability, and Survival* (Berkley: University of California Press, 2007); L. Raynolds, D. Murray and J. Wilkinson, *Fair Trade: The Challenges of Transforming Globalization* (London: Routledge, 2007); L. Raynolds, 'Fairtrade, certification, and labor: Global and local tensions in improving conditions for agricultural workers', *Agriculture and Human Values,* 31.3 (2014), pp. 499–511; C. Cramer, D. Johnston, C. Oya and J. Sender, 'Fairtrade, employment and poverty reduction in Ethiopia and Uganda', Final Report to DFID (April 2014).
10. C. Heath and D. Heath, *Made to Stick: Why Some Ideas Take Hold and Others Come Unstuck* (London: Arrow Books, 2008).
11. M. Gladwell, *The Tipping Point: How Little Things Can Make a Big Difference* (London: Abacus, 2000).
12. F. Trentmann, *Free Trade Nation: Commerce, Consumption, and Civil Society in Modern Britain* (Oxford: Oxford University Press, 2008).
13. Social Intrapreneurs are defined as corporate changemakers that work inside big business, to innovate and deliver market solutions to social and environmental challenges. SustainAbility (2008) 'The social Intrapreneur: A field guide for corporate changemakers'. Available: http://www.sustainability.com/library
14. A note on terminology: 'Fair Trade movement' refers to the collection of civil society groups, producer organisations, certification bodies and consumers that work on, or participate in, Fair Trade initiatives involving agricultural products and also non-food items including handicrafts. 'Fairtrade' or 'FAIRTRADE Mark' relates specifically to the Fairtrade Foundation (the certifying body in the United Kingdom and member of Fairtrade International).
15. World Fair Trade Organization and Fairtrade Labelling Organizations International, 'A charter of Fair Trade principles' (January 2009). Available http: http://www.fairtrade.net/fileadmin/user_upload/content/2009/about_us/documents/Fair_Trade_Charter.pdf
16. Ibid.

17. I. Bretman, Vice-Chair of the FLO Board, 'The charter of Fair Trade Principles – the shared values of a diverse movement' (November 2009). Available http://www.fairtrade.net/fileadmin/user_upload/content/2009/about_us/documents/2009-09_board-letter_ft-principles.pdf
18. Fairtrade International (FLO) is a non-profit, multi-stakeholder association involving 23 Labelling initiatives (including the Fairtrade Foundation). Set up in 1997, FLO develops and reviews Fairtrade Standards and provide support to Fairtrade Certified Producers. FLO-CERT GMBH is responsible for the inspection and certification of producer organisations. Available http://www.fairtrade.net/home.html.
19. The World Fair Trade Organization (WFTO) is the global representative body of over 450 members committed to 100% Fair Trade. Previously called the International Federation for Alternative Trade (1989–2003) and International Fair Trade Association (2003–2004).
20. World Fair Trade Organization and Fairtrade Labelling Organizations International, 'A charter of Fair Trade Principles' (January 2009).
21. M. Anderson, P. Booth and S. Mohan. 'Crossfire: "Does Fairtrade have more impact than conventional trade or trade certified by other sustainability standards?",' *Food Chain,* 4.1 (2014), pp. 7–13.
22. C. Cramer, D. Johnston, C. Oya and J. Sender, *Fairtrade, Employment and Poverty Reduction in Ethiopia and Uganda: Final Report to DFID* (London: SOAS, University of London, 2013).
23. P. Hoebink, R. Ruben, W. Elbers and B. van Rijsbergen, *The Impact of Coffee Certification on Smallholder Farmers in Kenya, Uganda and Ethiopia. The Netherlands: Centre for International Development Issues Nijmegen (CIDIN)* (Radboud University Nijmegen, 2014).
24. V. Nelson and A. Martin, 'Exploring issues of rigour and utility in Fairtrade impact assessment'. *Food Chain,* 4.1 (2014), pp. 14–33.
25. V. Nelson and A. Martin, *Final Technical Report: Assessing the Poverty Impact of Sustainability Standards* (Greenwich, UK: Natural Resources Institute, University of Greenwich, 2013); A. Le Mare, 'The impact of Fair Trade on social and economic development: A review of the literature', *Geography Compass,* 2.6 (2008), pp. 1922–1942.
26. Green & Black's Maya Gold chocolate was the first product to receive the FAIRTRADE Mark, in March 1994. The certification of Cafédirect coffee and Clipper Tea followed shortly.
27. Fairtrade Foundation, *Introducing Fairtrade: A Guide to the Fairtrade Mark and the Fairtrade Foundation* (London, 2000).
28. Ibid.
29. New Consumer was a charitable, consumer research organisation established by Richard Adams in February 1989. It has no direct links with the current New Consumer magazine. For more details see Chapter 5.
30. A report by Consumers International provided a detail review of the different certification schemes for coffee. In addition to Fairtrade, these included: Organic, Rainforest Alliance, Bird Friendly and UTZ Kapeh. Consumers International, *From Bean to Cup: How Consumer Choice Impacts on Coffee Producers and the Environment* (London: CI, December 2005).
31. Father Shay Cullen, 'Fair Trade logos and marks must benefit the poor and not the rich' (2006). Available http://www.preda.org/archives/2006/r06032901.html.

32. Ibid.
33. PREDA (People's Recovery, Empowerment and Development Assistance Foundation), is a Fair Trade organisation based in the Philippines. PREDA was set up in the 1970s as a charitable organisation with the aim of tackling the diverse social problems that troubled Olangapo City. From the mid-1970s PREDA began exporting handcrafts and dried mangoes to Europe.
34. Father Shay Cullen, 'Fair Trade logos and marks must benefit the poor and not the rich' (2006). Available http://www.preda.org/archives/2006/r06032901.html.
35. M. Anderson, 'Fairtrade: Partners in development? A reassessment of trading partnerships within the Fairtrade model', in J. Dine and B. Granville (eds.), *The Processes and Practices of Fair Trade* (London: Routledge, 2012), pp. 79–95.
36. Fairtrade International, 'Producer ownership of Fairtrade moves to new level' (14 October 2011). Available http: http://www.fairtrade.net/new.html.
37. WFTO, 'WFTO Response to Fair Trade US – FLO split' (2011). Available http: www.wfto.com/index.php?option=com_content&task=view&id=1574&Itemid=314.
38. P. Griffiths, 'Ethical objections to Fairtrade'. *Journal of Business Ethics* (July 2011). (DOI) 10.1007/s10551-011-0972-0.
39. A. Nicholls and C. Opal, *Fair Trade: Market Driven Ethical Consumption* (London: Sage Publications, 2004), p. 13.
40. Ibid., p. 31.
41. C. Barnett, N. Clarke, P. Cloke and A. Malpass, 'The political ethics of consumerism', *Consumer Policy Review,* 15.2 (2005), p. 50.
42. C. Barnett, N. Clarke, P. Cloke and A. Malpass, 'The political rationalities of Fair-Trade consumption in the United Kingdom', *Politics and Society*, 35.4 (2007), p. 602.
43. D. Miller (ed.) *Acknowledging Consumption* (London: Routledge, 1995), p. 1.
44. Ibid., p. 48.
45. Y. Gabriel and T. Lang, *The Unmanageable Consumer: Contemporary Consumption and its Fragmentation* (London: Sage, 1995).
46. Ibid.
47. M. Hilton, *Consumerism in 20-Century Britain* (Cambridge: Cambridge University Press, 2003), p. 23.
48. F. Trentmann, *Free Trade Nation: Commerce, Consumption, and Civil Society in Modern Britain* (Oxford: Oxford University Press, 2008), p. 359.
49. Ibid.
50. F. Trentmann, 'Before "Fair Trade": Empire, free trade and the moral economics of food in the modern world', *Environment and Planning D: Society and Space,* 25 (2007), p. 1086.
51. Trentmann, *Free Trade Nation,* p. 234.
52. Ibid., p. 359.
53. Trentmann, 'Before Fair Trade', p. 1080.
54. E. P. Thompson, 'The moral economy of the English crowd in the Eighteenth Century', *Past and Present,* 50 (February, 1971).
55. Ibid., p. 78.
56. G. Fridell, *Fair Trade Coffee: The Prospects and Pitfalls of Market Driven Social Justice* (Toronto: University of Toronto Press, 2007), p. 285.
57. Ibid.

58. J. Ruskin, *Unto This Last: Four Essays on the First Principles of Political Economy* (London, 1862), p. 165.
59. Ibid., p. 116.
60. P. Gurney, 'The battle of the consumer in Postwar Britain', *Journal of Modern History*, 77 (2005), p. 960.
61. Thompson, 'The moral economy', p. 136.
62. S. Yeo (ed.), *New Views on Consumer Co-operation* (London: Routledge, 1988), p. 7.
63. T. Lang and Y. Gabriel, 'A brief history of consumer activism', in R. Harrison and D. Shaw et al. (ed.), *The Ethical Consumer* (London: Sage Publications Ltd, 2005), p. 51.
64. A. Nicholls and C. Opal, *Fair Trade: Market-Driven Ethical Consumption* (London: Sage, 2005). p. 20.
65. These themes are addressed in Chapter 3: *The Co-operative Difference: Co-operation Among Co-operatives?*
66. C. Barnett, N. Clarke, P. Cloke and A. Malpass, 'The political ethics of consumerism', *Consumer Policy Review,* 15.2 (2005).
67. M. Kaye, *1807–2007: Over Two Hundred Years of Campaigning against Slavery* (London: Anti-Slavery International, 2005).
68. Ibid.
69. J. Walvin, *Black Ivory: Slavery in the British Empire* (Wiley-Blackwell, 2nd Edition, 2001); J. Walvin, *The Trader, the Owner, the Slave: Parallel Lives in the Age of Slavery* (London: Random House, 2008); A. Hochschild, *Bury the Chains: The British Struggle to Abolish Slavery* (Pan, 2006).
70. Memorandum submitted by the TUC, House of Commons International Development Committee, Fair Trade and Development (14 June 2007), Ev. 127.
71. J. Vincent, 'The moral expertise of the British consumer, c.1900: A debate between the Christian Social Union and the Webbs', in A. Chatriot, M. Chessel and M. Hilton (eds.), *The Expert Consumer: Associations and Professionals in Consumer Society* (Aldershot: Ashgate, 2006), pp. 37–51.
72. Multatuli (Douwes-Dekker) *Max Havelaar: Or the Coffee Auctions of a Dutch Trading Company,* first published 1860 (London: Penguin Classics, 1986).
73. The novel is considered to be semi-autobiographical and closely based on Douwes-Dekker's own experiences as a Colonial administrator.
74. Multatuli (Douwes-Dekker) *Max Havelaar: Or the Coffee Auctions of a Dutch Trading Company,* first published 1860 (London: Penguin Classics, 1986), p. 12.
75. W. H. Frederick and R. L. Worden (eds.) *Indonesia: A Country Study* (Washington: GPO for the Library of Congress, 1993).
76. European Parliament, 'Report on Fair Trade and Development' (2005/2245(INI)) (Committee on Development, June 2006), p. 7.
77. T. Jackson, *Prosperity without Growth: Economics for a Finite Planet* (London: Earthscan, 2009), p. 5.
78. Ibid.
79. See for instance: The European Parliament Resolution on Fair Trade, OJ C 226/73 (20 July 1998); the Communication from the Commission to the Council on '*Fair Trade*', COM(1999) 619 final (29 November 1999); the Communication from the Commission to the Council, the European Parliament and the European Economic and Social Committee on '*Policy*

Coherence for Development – Accelerating progress towards attaining the Millennium Development Goals', COM(2005) 134 final (12 April 2005); Speech Pascal Lamy, EU Trade Commissioner (23 March 2004); Speech "The Fair Trade agenda" Peter Mandelson (22 June 2005).

80. G. Fridell, *Fair Trade Coffee: The Prospects and Pitfalls of Market Driven Social Justice* (Toronto: University of Toronto Press, 2007), p. 7.
81. Ibid., p. 47.
82. B. Huybrechts and D. Reed (2010) 'Introduction: Fair Trade in different national contexts', *Journal of Business Ethics*, 92, pp. 147–150.
83. A. Iriye, 'A century of NGOs', *Diplomatic History*, 23.3 (Summer 1999).
84. Practical Action, 'Our story', Available http://cdn1.practicalaction.org/i/n/4dd39fc0-9210-41d3-bd25-47671661b3dc.pdf
85. L. Pearson, *Partners in Development: Report of the Commission on International Development* (New York: Praeger Publishers, 1969), p. 77.
86. Ibid., p. 148.
87. Ibid.
88. Ibid., p. 18.
89. UN General Assembly Resolution 2626 (XXV), International Development Strategy for the Second United Nations Development Decade (24 October 1970).
90. C. Dankers and P. Liu, *Environmental and Social Standards, Certification and Labelling for Cash Crops* (Food and Agriculture Organization of the United Nations, 2003), p. 5.
91. Pearson, *Partners in Development,* p. 45.
92. Ibid.
93. Haslemere Committee, *The Haslemere Declaration* (London, 1969), p. 9.
94. In reality, few of the early projects identified as Fair Trade were designed to meet these broader objectives of community development. It was not until the early 1970s that ATOs, such as Oxfam Trading reviewed their terms of trade.
95. Fridell proposes greater attention should be paid to geopolitical actions of Southern states and provides a useful account of state intervention in the coffee market following the collapse of the International Coffee Agreements. However, while there are parallels with the objectives of Fair Trade, for the most part, government and state agencies were considered external stakeholders rather than part of the Fair Trade movement. See G. Fridell, 'Coffee Statecraft: Rethinking the global coffee crisis, 1998–2002', *New Political Economy,* 19.3 (2014), pp. 407–426.
96. Oxford, Bodleian Library, Oxfam archive (uncatalogued), Directorate correspondence, 'HS/5 Bridge', report by R. Scott, 'What, Why, How: Bridge summarized', 1973.
97. G. Rist, *The History of Development: From Western Origins to Global Faith,* Third Edition (London: Zed Books, 2008), p. 140.
98. Rist, *The History of Development,* p. 169.
99. 'The Brandt Report and After', *New Internationalist* (October 1981). Available http://newint.org/features/1981/10/01/keynote/
100. Ibid.
101. Rist, *The History of Development,* p. 143
102. UN General Assembly, Resolution 3201 (S-VI), May 1974.

103. Rist, *The History of Development,* p. 151.
104. Ibid., p. 153.
105. By the late 1970s the supposedly neutral term 'South' began to take over from 'Third World' with its political connotations. While this terminology has been widely adopted, its usage may reinforce the idea of homogenous blocs that are not consistent with geopolitical realities. Rist, p. 158.
106. New Internationalist, 'The Brandt Report And After', issue 104 (October 1981). Available http://newint.org/features/1981/10/01/keynote/
107. Now known as People and Planet.
108. R. Barnet and R Muller, *Global Reach: The Power of the Multinational Corporations* (New York: Touchstone 1974).
109. New Internationalist, 'The Brandt Report And After', issue 104 (October 1981). Available http://newint.org/features/1981/10/01/keynote/
110. Roy Scott, 'Bridge Co-operative' (1972); Gustavo Gutierrez, 'Theology of Liberation: History, Politics and Salvation' (1971); E. F. Schumacher, 'Small is Beautiful: Economics as if People Mattered' (1973).
111. Rist, *The History of Development,* p. 170.
112. Oxford, Bodleian Library, Oxfam archive (uncatalogued), Executive Committee minutes and papers, 'Letter by John Clark for key MPs taking part in the Debate on Famine and Debt', 27 Jun 1985.
113. Ibid.
114. Oxford, Bodleian Library, Oxfam archive (uncatalogued), Executive Committee minutes and papers, 'Director General's Report to Executive, Appendix II, Cuts in Government Aid Budget', 8 Jan 1981.
115. Ibid.
116. Ibid.
117. The Report of the Independent Commission on International Development Issues under the Chairmanship of Willy Brandt, *North-South: A Programme for Survival* (London: Pan Books, 1980).
118. MSS.292D931/7: TUC, 'The Brandt report' (12 March 1980).
119. New Internationalist, 'The Brandt Report And After', issue 104 (October 1981). Available http://newint.org/features/1981/10/01/keynote/
120. Rist, *The History of Development,* p. 161.
121. J. Curling, Does coffee need an artificial sweetener? Price drop puts a bomb under the Third World, *The Independent* (10 March 1990).
122. EFTA is an association of the ten largest importing organisations in Europe.
123. IFAT, now known as WFTO (World Fair Trade Organization) is a global network of over 450 members committed to improve the livelihoods of disadvantaged people through trade, and providing a forum for the exchange of information and ideas.
124. Rist, *The History of Development,* p. 197.
125. *The Challenge of the South: Report of the South Commission* (Oxford: Oxford University Press, 1990), p. 11.
126. *Ibid,* p. 82.
127. Rist, *The History of Development,* p. 204.
128. Ibid., p. 205.
129. Human Development Reports, UNDP, Available http://hdr.undp.org/en/reports/

130. G. H. Brundtland, *Are Common Future*, World Commission on Environment and Development (London; Fontana Books, 1988).
131. Rist, *The History of Development*, pp. 189–190.
132. C. Church and S. Young, The Future of Local Agenda 21 after the Local Government Act of 2000. EPRU Paper 1/00 (Manchester: University of Manchester, 2000).
133. T. Doyle, 'Sustainable development and agenda 21: The secular Bible of global free markets and pluralist democracy', *Third World Quarterly*, 19.4 (1998), pp. 771–786.
134. Jean-Marie Krier, *Fair Trade in Europe 2001: Facts and Figures on the Fair Trade Sector in 18 European Countries*, EFTA, January 2001.
135. Jean-Marie Krier, 'Fair Trade 2007: New facts and figures from an ongoing success story', Available http://www.european-fair-trade-association.org/efta/Doc/FT-E-2007.pdf
136. EFTA, 'Sixty Years of Fair Trade: A brief history of the Fair Trade movement' (November 2006) Available http://www.european-fair-trade-association.org/efta/Doc/History.pdf
137. Ibid.
138. Select Committee on International Development, 'The UK Government's Approach to Fair Trade' (June 2007) Available http://www.publications.parliament.uk/pa/cm200607/cmselect/cmintdev/356/35606.htm
139. The MDGs focused on combatting poverty, hunger, disease, illiteracy, environmental degradation and discrimination against women.
140. Fairtrade Foundation, 'Unlocking the Power of the Many: Fairtrade Foundation's 2013–15 strategy' Available http://www.fairtrade.org.uk/~/media/fairtradeuk/what%20is%20fairtrade/documents/unlocking%20the%20power%20of%20the%20many%20-%202013-2015%20strategy.ashx
141. S. Sununtar, *Can Ethical Trade Certification Contribute to the Attainment of the Millennium Development Goals? A Review of Organic and Fair-trade Certification*. ADBI Discussion Paper 115 (Tokyo: Asian Development Bank Institute, 2008). Available http://www.adbi.org/discussion-paper/2008/08/25/2675.organic.fairtrade.certification/
142. Fair Trade Advocacy Office, 'Post-2015 Development Agenda: Fair Trade Movement's position' (April 2013) Available http://www.fairtrade-advocacy.org/images/Final_FTAO_draft_Position_Paper_Post_2015_Agenda.pdf
143. Sununtar, *Can Ethical Trade Certification Contribute to the Attainment of the Millennium Development Goals?*
144. Ibid., p. 19.
145. A. Marwick. *The Sixties: Cultural revolution in Britain, France, Italy, and the United States, c. 1958–c. 1974* (A&C Black, 2011).
146. Nicholls and Opal, *Fair Trade*, p. 20.
147. R. Mitchell, B. Agle, and D. Wood, 'Toward a theory of stakeholder identification and salience: Defining the principle of who and what really counts', *Academy of Management Review*, 22.4 (1997), pp. 853–886.
148. Fairtrade International (December 2013). *Fairtrade Theory of Change*. Available http://www.fairtrade.net/fileadmin/user_upload/content/2009/resources/140112_Theory_of_Change_and_Indicators_Public.pdf.

1 Oxfam 'Helping by Selling': Charity, Trade and Advocacy

1. Fairtrade International (FLO) 'Making the difference: A new global strategy for Fairtrade', *Fairtrade Labelling's Strategic Review*, March 2009.
2. Guy Stringer joined Oxfam in 1969 in the specially created post of Commercial Director and from 1971 he was also Deputy Director. In 1983, he was appointed Director of Oxfam, holding the post until retirement in 1985. Available online: http://www.guardian.co.uk/global/2009/jul/27/obituary-guy-stringer.
3. Oxford, Bodleian Library, Oxfam archive (uncatalogued), Directorate correspondence, 'HS/5 Bridge', G. Stringer & R. Scott, 'The improvement and development of HbS: a wider vision', Nov 1973.
4. Oxford, Bodleian Library, Oxfam archive (uncatalogued), Directorate correspondence, 'HS/5 Bridge', report by R. Scott, 'What, Why, How: Bridge Summarized' 1973.
5. In 1996 Oxfam's international trading initiative 'Bridge', was renamed the 'Oxfam Fair Trade Company'. The Oxfam Fair Trade Company continued trading up until 2002 when Oxfam took the decision to focus on its campaigning and advocacy work.
6. Oxford, Bodleian Library, Oxfam archive (uncatalogued), *Bridge News*, Issue 6, Feb 1990, 'Oxfam Trading Celebrates its 25th Anniversary'.
7. Ibid.
8. W. Low and E. Davenport, 'Postcards from the edge: Maintaining the "Alternative" character of Fair Trade', *Sustainable Development*, 13 (2005), pp. 143–153.
9. House of Commons International Development Committee, 'Fair trade and development' (14 June 2007).
10. A. Nicholls and C. Opal, *Fair Trade: Market-Driven Ethical Consumption* (London: Sage, 2005), p. 19.
11. Fridell, *Fair Trade Coffee*, p. 40.
12. W. Low and E. Davenport, 'Postcards from the edge: Maintaining the "Alternative" character of Fair Trade', *Sustainable Development*, 13 (2005) pp. 143–153.
13. T. Buchanan, 'Human Rights campaigns in Modern Britain', in M. Hilton, N. Crowson and J. McKay (eds.), *NGOs in Contemporary Britain: Non-state Actors in Society and Politics since 1945* (London: Palgrave, 2009), p. 113.
14. Ibid., p. 121.
15. Oxford, Bodleian Library, Oxfam archive (uncatalogued), Fair Trade reports, R. Wilshaw, 'Bridge in context: the history and development of the bridge concept and its implementation', Sep 1991.
16. Maggie Black, former editor of New Internationalist and ex-Oxfam staff, offers a more detailed account of events in: M. Black, *A Cause for Our Time: Oxfam the First 50 years* (Oxford: Oxfam 1992), pp. 99–100.
17. *Ottawa Citizen*, Friday 30 June 1961, Features Section p. 11.
18. Ibid.
19. Black, *A Cause for Our Time*, p. 99.
20. M. Andrews, *Lifetimes of Commitment: Ageing, Politics, Psychology* (Cambridge University Press, 1991), p. 84.
21. Black, *A Cause for Our Time*, p. 76.

22. Oxford, Bodleian Library, Oxfam archive (uncatalogued), Directorate correspondence, 'HS/5 Bridge', 'Oxfam as an importer: Why; How. An explanation for our customers', 1973.
23. A. Spandau, *Economic Boycott against South Africa* (Johannesburg: Juta & Co Ltd., 1979). R. Fieldhouse, *Anti-Apartheid: A History of the Movement in Britain* (London: The Merlin Press Ltd, 2005).
24. World Fair Trade Organization and Fairtrade Labelling Organizations International, 'A charter of Fair Trade principles' (January 2009). Available online: http://www.fairtrade.net/fileadmin/user_upload/content/2009/about_us/documents/Fair_Trade_Charter.pdf.
25. 'Few charities escaping tax on card sales', *The Guardian* (4 November 1966).
26. Ibid.
27. In addition to its growing network of shops, Oxfam also established innovative operations such as the Oxfam Wastesaver Centre in Huddersfield. Launched in 1975, this was the first comprehensive waste-recycling scheme in Britain. M. Black, *A Cause for Our Time: Oxfam the First 50 Years* (Oxford: Oxfam 1992), p. 207.
28. P. Burnell, *Charity Politics and the Third World* (London: Harvester Wheatsheaf 1991), p. 51.
29. Black, *A Cause for Our Time*, p. 165.
30. Directors report to the Executive (January 1970).
31. Oxford, Bodleian Library, Oxfam archive (uncatalogued), Executive Committee minutes and papers, 'Oxfam Charter for Public Relations', 1970.
32. Fridell, *Fair Trade Coffee*, p. 42.
33. Oxford, Bodleian Library, Oxfam archive (uncatalogued), Executive Committee minutes and papers, Directors report to the Executive, Jan 1970.
34. Oxford, Bodleian Library, Oxfam archive (uncatalogued), Executive Committee minutes and papers, Directors report to the Executive, Feb 1974.
35. Oxford, Bodleian Library, Oxfam archive (uncatalogued), Fair Trade reports, J. Stockland, 'Bridge – an Evaluation', 1986.
36. Oxford, Bodleian Library, Oxfam archive (uncatalogued), Directorate correspondence, 'HS/5 Bridge', report by R. Scott, 'What, Why, How: Bridge Summarized' 1973.
37. Ibid.
38. Darcy DiNucci is credited with popularising the term Web 2.0 as a way of describing the cumulative changes in how web pages are made and used. Web 2.0 represents a new version of the World Wide Web. D. DiNucci, 'Fragmented future', *Print*, 53.4 (1999), p. 32.
39. Oxford, Bodleian Library, Oxfam archive (uncatalogued), Directorate correspondence, 'HS/5 Bridge', R. Scott, 'Bridge Cooperative Europe – First full discussion meetings between Oxfam and SOS, Kerkrade, Netherlands, January 13–14, 1973'.
40. Oxford, Bodleian Library, Oxfam archive (uncatalogued), Directorate correspondence, 'HS/5 Bridge', report by R. Scott, 'What, Why, How: Bridge Summarized' 1973.
41. E. P. Thompson, 'The moral economy of the English crowd in the eighteenth century', *Past and Present*, 50 (1971), pp. 76–136.
42. Oxford, Bodleian Library, Oxfam archive (uncatalogued), Directorate correspondence, 'The development of the Oxfam handicraft operation', 1975.

43. Oxford, Bodleian Library, Oxfam archive (uncatalogued), Fair Trade reports, E. Stamp comments on 'Future of the Helping by Selling Project', 1 Aug 1972.
44. Under this proposal Bridge would only be an 'Oxfam programme' in the short term, then would operate entirely independent of Oxfam.
45. Oxford, Bodleian Library, Oxfam archive (uncatalogued), Directorate correspondence, 'HS/5 Bridge', R. Scott, 'How can international marketing be best organised to give maximum opportunities and benefits to the participants (producers & consumers)?', 24 Mar 1975.
46. Oxford, Bodleian Library, Oxfam archive (uncatalogued), Directorate correspondence, 'HS/5 Bridge', report, 'Oxfam as an importer: Why; How. An explanation for our customers', 1973.
47. Oxford, Bodleian Library, Oxfam archive (uncatalogued), Directorate correspondence, 'HS/5 Bridge', report by R. Scott, 'Bridge Co-operative', 1972.
48. Oxford, Bodleian Library, Oxfam archive (uncatalogued), Directorate correspondence, 'HS/5 Bridge', report by R. Scott, 'Agreed Joint Statement of Conclusions', Jan 1973.
49. Oxford, Bodleian Library, Oxfam archive (uncatalogued), Directorate correspondence, 'HS/5 Bridge', Bridge Dividend Distribution, 1973.
50. Oxford, Bodleian Library, Oxfam archive (uncatalogued), Directorate correspondence, 'HS/5 Bridge', report 'The purpose, principles and motivation of Bridge', Nov 1975.
51. Oxford, Bodleian Library, Oxfam archive (uncatalogued), Bridge Committee minutes and papers, Analysis of Bridge imports, 1990. See Appendix Figure A.7 and Figure A.8.
52. Oxford, Bodleian Library, Oxfam archive (uncatalogued), Executive Committee minutes and papers, 'Director's report to the Executive', 16 Sep 1976.
53. Oxford, Bodleian Library, Oxfam archive (uncatalogued), Oxfam Activities board meeting minutes and papers, Bridge Producer Dividend, Sep 1976.
54. E. Harriman, 'There's more to charity than faith and hope', *The Sunday Times* (31 October 1976).
55. R. Scott interview with author (14 September 2004).
56. Black, *A Cause for Our Time*, p. 85.
57. Ibid., p. 86.
58. Oxford, Bodleian Library, Oxfam archive (uncatalogued), Oxfam Activities board meeting minutes and papers, Bridge Producer Dividend, 17 Dec 1976.
59. Oxford, Bodleian Library, Oxfam archive (uncatalogued), Oxfam Activities board meeting minutes and papers, Oxfam Information Office, 'Making Leather Sandals and Belts – Palam Rural Centre, 11 Nov 1980.
60. Black, *A Cause for Our Time*, p. 89.
61. Oxford, Bodleian Library, Oxfam archive (uncatalogued), Directorate correspondence, 'HS/5 Bridge', 'Why you should shop at Bridge: an explanation for customers', 1975.
62. Trade Craft, No. 5, October–December 1978.
63. Trade Craft, 'Crafts are booming!' Issue 1, October 1977–January 1978.
64. See Chapter 3 for more details.
65. Oxford, Bodleian Library, Oxfam archive (uncatalogued), Executive Committee minutes and papers, Director General's Report to the Executive, 19 May 1977.

66. Oxford, Bodleian Library, Oxfam archive (uncatalogued), Executive Committee minutes and papers, Bridge Information, 'Withdrawal of Darjeeling, Nilgiri and Assam Teas from the OT range', 1989.
67. Ibid.
68. Ibid.
69. Oxford, Bodleian Library, Oxfam archive (uncatalogued), Bridge Committee minutes and papers, Analysis of Bridge imports (FOB value) by country, 1990.
70. Ibid.
71. There is no statutory definition of 'mainly'. However it is often argued that, if in a particular period the value of the sales of the donated goods exceeds the value of the sales of the bought-in goods, the premises are used 'mainly' for the sale of the donated goods, and thus for charitable purposes. Income from the sale or letting of donated goods must be separately identifiable in the charity's records from trading profits. http://www.charity-commission.gov.uk/publications/cc35d.aspx.
72. Oxford, Bodleian Library, Oxfam archive (uncatalogued), Fair Trade reports, J. Stockland, 'Bridge – an Evaluation', 1986.
73. Oxford, Bodleian Library, Oxfam archive (uncatalogued), Bridge Committee minutes and papers, C. Wills, 'Criteria for Selection of Producer Groups', Jul 1991.
74. Ibid.
75. Oxford, Bodleian Library, Oxfam archive (uncatalogued), Bridge Committee minutes and papers, J. Shaw, 'Report on a Tour by Jeremy Shaw of India and the Philippines', Jul 1983.
76. Oxford, Bodleian Library, Oxfam archive (uncatalogued), Executive Committee minutes and papers, R. Wilshaw, Talk given at South London Area Conference, 'Why Should Oxfam Trade', Feb 1989.
77. Ibid.
78. Oxford, Bodleian Library, Oxfam archive (uncatalogued), Bridge Committee minutes and papers, M. Zinkin, letter to Sir Geoffrey Wilson, 15 Jul 1980.
79. Oxford, Bodleian Library, Oxfam archive (uncatalogued), Bridge Committee minutes and papers, M. Zinkin, letter to John Pirie, 6 May 1983.
80. Oxford, Bodleian Library, Oxfam archive (uncatalogued), Fair Trade reports, J. Stockland, 'Bridge – an Evaluation', 1986.
81. Oxford, Bodleian Library, Oxfam archive (uncatalogued), Bridge Committee minutes and papers, E. Millard, 'Bridge in Africa', Dec 1989.
82. Oxford, Bodleian Library, Oxfam archive (uncatalogued), Bridge Committee minutes and papers, Analysis of Bridge imports (FOB value) by country, 1990.
83. Ibid.
84. See the Introduction to this volume p. 4.
85. Cafédirect and Divine Chocolate are not currently members of WFTO.
86. In 2003 The International Federation for Alternative Trade changed its name to International Fair Trade Association – although kept the same initials.
87. Oxford, Bodleian Library, Oxfam archive (uncatalogued), Bridge Committee minutes and papers, C. Wills and R. Wilshaw, memorandum to G. Rogers (Bridge Committee), 1 Jun 1989.
88. Oxford, Bodleian Library, Oxfam archive (uncatalogued), Bridge Committee minutes and papers, H. Smit, IFAT Secretariat, letter to Carol Wills, Bridge, 29 Jun 1990.

89. Oxford, Bodleian Library, Oxfam archive (uncatalogued), Bridge Committee minutes and papers, E. Millard, 'Bridge: Food Policy', 9 May 1990.
90. Oxford, Bodleian Library, Oxfam archive (uncatalogued), Bridge Committee minutes and papers, 'Food Products: Trade and Campaigns', 7 Nov 1990.
91. Oxford, Bodleian Library, Oxfam archive (uncatalogued), Bridge Committee minutes and papers, E. Millard, 'Fair Trade Mark: Update Report', 9 Apr 1991.
92. See Chapter 5 for more details on Cafédirect.
93. Oxford, Bodleian Library, Oxfam archive (uncatalogued), Bridge Committee minutes and papers, B.Yates, 'From the Margins to the Mainstream', Sep 1990.
94. Ibid.
95. R. Scott, interview with author (14 September 2004).
96. Oxford, Bodleian Library, Oxfam archive (uncatalogued), Bridge Committee minutes and papers, E. Millard, 'Fair Trade Mark: Update Report', 20 Mar 1991.
97. Oxford, Bodleian Library, Oxfam archive (uncatalogued), Bridge Committee minutes and papers, Feb 1993.
98. Ibid.
99. This focus on farmed products has only broadened gradually with the introduction of Fairtrade sports balls in 2004 and more recently gold (2011) and silver (2013).
100. Oxford, Bodleian Library, Oxfam archive (uncatalogued), Bridge Committee minutes and papers, B. Coote, 'Bridge in Africa', 6 Dec 1989.
101. It wasn't until 1992 that the supply of coffee from the highly-unstable Zaire (the present Congo) could be expanded to Tanzania and Uganda. Cited in '25 years of Fairtrade Max Havelaar from coffee till now'. (2013). Available online: http://s3-eu-west-1.amazonaws.com/maxhavelaar.nl/keplarcms/items/imagevalues/000/001/344/original/MH_JubileumBoek2_EN_A5_lowres.pdf?1398693380.
102. Oxford, Bodleian Library, Oxfam archive (uncatalogued), Bridge Committee minutes and papers, E. Millard, 'Fair Trade Mark: Update Report', 20 Mar 1991.
103. Jean-Marie Krier, *Fair Trade in Europe 2001 – Facts and Figures on the Fair Trade Sector in 18 European Countries* (EFTA, January 2001), p.13. Figures refer to turnover as quoted in annual accounts for 1999. Available online: http://www.european-fair-trade-association.org/efta/Doc/stats2001.pdf. Available http://www.european-fair-trade-association.org/efta/Doc/FT-E-2001.pdf.
104. Ibid.
105. M. Townsend, 'Oxfam bows to market and scraps Fairtrade brand', *The Observer* (19 January 2003).
106. Ibid.
107. Ibid.
108. Ibid.
109. *Bridge News*, 22 September 1996.
110. In contrast, Traidcraft's handcraft sales at this time only accounted for 20% of turnover. Jean-Marie Krier, *Fair Trade in Europe 2001 – Facts and Figures on the Fair Trade Sector in 18 European Countries* (EFTA, January 2001), p. 59.
111. R. Hopkins, *Oxfam Fair Trade Programme: Impact Assessment Study of Fair Trade*, (Oxford: Oxfam, 2000), p. 3.
112. Originally there had been two food producer groups involved, but one had to withdraw from the study.
113. Hopkins, *Oxfam Fair Trade Programme*, p. 41.

114. Ibid., p. vi.
115. Ibid.
116. Ibid., p. 36.
117. Oxfam International, 'Make Trade Fair' (December 2005) Available: http://web.archive.org/web/20060104033924/http://www.oxfam.org/en/programs/campaigns/maketradefair/index.htm.
118. Oxfam European buyers continued to import Fair Trade products.
119. Cafédirect, 'Committed to Our Gold Standard: Annual Review 2013', Available: http://www.cafedirect.co.uk/wp-content/uploads/2014/05/Cafedirect2013AnnualReviewandAccounts.pdf
120. Oxford, Bodleian Library, Oxfam archive (uncatalogued), Executive Committee minutes and papers, 'Oxfam Charter for Public Relations', 1970.
121. In October 2012, William Shawcross warned that he would step in to curb the political campaigning of charities if they 'overstepped the mark', and act as a 'policeman' if necessary. Available online: http://www.telegraph.co.uk/news/politics/9711825/Charities-warned-to-stop-interfering-in-politics-by-new-watchdog-chief.html.
122. Oxford, Bodleian Library, Oxfam archive (uncatalogued), Executive Committee minutes and papers, T. Fitzgerald, Charity Commission letter to Mr. Walker, Oxfam, 2 Aug 1979.
123. Ibid.
124. D. Green, *From Poverty to Power: How Active Citizens and Effective States Can Change the World* (Oxford: Oxfam International, 2008).
125. Ibid.
126. Duncan Green was Oxfam's Head of Research from 2004 to 2012.
127. Green, *From Poverty to Power*, p. 6.
128. Ibid., p.114.
129. Oxfam has attempted to move beyond the immediate symptoms of food poverty, such as, famine, or a bad harvest, and address the bigger issues within the global food system including: climate change, land grabs, food price spikes and intensive farming.
130. Launched in March 2013, the Behind the Brands Scorecard formed part of Oxfam's GROW campaign.
131. Oxfam, 'Behind the Brands', Available: http://www.behindthebrands.org/en-gb/about

2 Christian Ethics and Economics: Voluntary Organisations and Alternative Trade

1. Cited by Ed Mayo in R. Harrison, T. Hewholm and D. Shaw (eds.), *The Ethical Consumer* (London: Sage 2005). p. xvii.
2. In 1959, S.O.S. Wereldhandel was founded by a number of youth members of a Catholic political party in the Dutch town of Kerkrade. Available: http://www.web.net/~bthomson/fairtrade/fair645.html.
3. GEPA was originally established in the early 1970s as the German subsidiary of SOS Wereldhandel.
4. TradeWinds was originally called World Development Tea Cooperative (WDTC). In 1991, TradeWinds Tea and Coffee was incorporated and became the trading arm of WDTC which continued its educational role.

5. Trade Winds Archive, Letter to Michael Whiteley from Tom Whelan (10 April 1981).
6. In 1946 Edna Ruth Byler travelled to Puerto Rico and met women artisans. She purchased their needlework and sold it to her friends and neighbours in Central Pennsylvania. This became the Overseas Needlepoint and Crafts Project (renamed SELFHELP: Crafts of the World in 1968). In 1996, SELFHELP: Crafts of the World celebrated its 50th anniversary and changed its name to Ten Thousand Villages.
7. A. Gilbert, *Religion and Society in Industrial England: Church, Chapel and Social Change 1740–1914* (London: Longman, 1976), p. 129.
8. I. Kapoor, *Celebrity Humanitarianism: The Ideology of Global Charity* (London: Routledge, 2012), p. 4.
9. Tearfund, 'Why the church? Integral mission and theology', Available http://www.tearfund.org/en/about_us/how_we_work/why_the_church/
10. Charity Commission, 'The advancement of religion for the public benefit', Available http://www.charitycommission.gov.uk/detailed-guidance/charitable-purposes-and-public-benefit/charities-and-public-benefit/the-advancement-of-religion-for-the-public-benefit/#sthash.qOtuKRVd.dpuf
11. William Shawcross, Chair of the Charity Commission, 'ACEVO Annual Conference 2012: William Shawcross's speech', Available https://www.gov.uk/government/speeches/acevo-annual-conference-2012-william-shawcrosss-speech.
12. Kapoor, *Celebrity Humanitarianism*, p. 4.
13. F. Prochaska, *Christianity & Social Service in Modern Britain: The Disinherited Spirit* (Oxford: Oxford University Press, 2006), p. 25.
14. Ibid., p. 13.
15. Ibid., p. 149.
16. Ibid.
17. D. Barker, *The European Values Study 1981–1990* (Aberdeen: Gordon Cook Foundation, 1991). p. 47.
18. Ibid., p. 47.
19. In the United Kingdom, of the six original members of the Fairtrade Foundation, three had close links with the Christian Church (Christian Aid, CAFOD and Traidcraft Exchange). And as the membership expanded these organisations were joined by the Methodist Development Relief Fund, United Reformed Church, Scottish Catholic International Aid Fund and Tearfund.
20. Christian Aid, 'Our aims and values' Available http://www.christianaid.org.uk/aboutus/who/aims/our_aims.aspx
21. The main Churches in the BCC are Anglican, Presbyterian, Methodist, Baptist, United Reform and Church of Scotland. In 1985 the Methodist Relief and Development Fund was established as a separate agency, but the Methodist Church has remained committed to supporting Christian Aid.
22. P. J. Burnell, *Charity Politics and the Third World* (Hemel Hempstead: Harvester Wheatsheaf, 1991) p. 54.
23. Christian Aid's accounts for 2013/14, Available: http://www.charity commission.gov.uk
24. CAFOD 'Just one world: Our vision for change, our agenda for action' (July 2010).

25. *Catholic Herald*, 'Did you remember that fast day?' 11 March 1960. Available http://archive.catholicherald.co.uk/article/11th-march-1960/5/did-you-remember-that-fast-day-
26. CAFOD, 'Our History', Available: http://www.cafod.org.uk/About-Us/Our-History
27. Burnell, *Charity Politics and the Third World* p. 57.
28. CAFOD, 'Our History', Available: http://www.cafod.org.uk/About-Us/Our-History
29. CAFOD's accounts for 2013/14, Available: http://www.charitycommission.gov.uk
30. Tearfund became a member and charity shareholder of the Fairtrade Foundation in 2007. Traidcraft Exchange (Traidcraft's charity) traces its origins to Tearfund and was a founder member of the Fairtrade Foundation.
31. Tearfund, 'Our values', Available http://www.tearfund.org/en/about_you/jobs/our_values/
32. M. Endersbee, *They Can't Eat Prayer: The Story of Tear Fund* (London: Hodder & Stoughton, 1977).
33. The organisation is now referred to as Tearfund. In June 2007 Tearfund unveiled a new corporate logo featuring a cross to emphasise its Christian values.
34. Endersbee, *They Can't Eat Prayer*, p. 88.
35. Tearfund's accounts for 2013/14, Available: http://www.charitycommission.gov.uk
36. A. Nicholls and C. Opal, *Fair Trade: Market Driven Ethical Consumption* (London: Sage Publications, 2004), p. 4.
37. Ibid., p. 153.
38. Fairtrade Foundation, 'Who we are', Available http://www.fairtrade.org.uk/what_is_fairtrade/fairtrade_foundation.aspx
39. Fairtrade Foundation Board Minutes, 'The effect of the continuing charitable status debate on the prospects for FTF', R. Adams (10 November 1992).
40. Fairtrade Foundation Board Minutes, 'The structure and objectives of the Fairtrade Foundation' R. Adams (21 May 1992).
41. Fairtrade Foundation Minutes, Twentieth meeting (8 March 1995).
42. Oxford, Bodleian Library, Oxfam archive (uncatalogued), Fairtrade Foundation papers, 'R0716', 'P. White of the Charity Commission letter to M. Hayes at Shared Interest, re: The Fairtrade Foundation', 16 Mar 1992.
43. S. Sloane, R. Baillargeon and D. Premack, 'Do infants have a sense of fairness?', *Psychological Science*, 23 (2012), pp. 196–204.
44. Ibid.
45. P. K. Piff, D. M. Stancato, S. Côté, R. Mendoza-Denton, and D. Keltner, 'Higher social class predicts increased unethical behavior', *Proceedings of the National Academy of Sciences*, 109 (2012), pp. 4086–4091.
46. D. Hicks and M. Valeri (eds) *Global Neighbors: Christian Faith and Moral Obligation in Today's Economy*, (Grand Rapids: Wm. B. Eerdmans Publishing, 2008).
47. J. Berenguer, 'The effect of empathy in environmental moral reasoning', *Environment and Behavior* 42. 1 (January 2010), pp. 110–134; J. Farrell, 'Environmental activism and moral schemas: Cultural components of differential participation', *Environment and Behavior*, 45 (1 April 2013), pp. 399–423; 'Barack Obama and the empathy deficit', *The Guardian*, (4 January 2013).

48. The Lausanne Covenant (1974). Available http://www.lausanne.org/en/documents/lausanne-covenant.html.
49. D. Edgington, *Christians and the Third World* (Exeter: Paternoster Press, 1982), p. 123.
50. CA2/D/11 *The European Community and the Third World* letter to EC commissioners (25 April 1973).
51. Ibid.
52. Ibid.
53. CA/J/4 *A Look at Lifestyle from a Christian Viewpoint'* (1977).
54. Ibid.
55. P. K. Piff, D. M. Stancato, S. Côté, R. Mendoza-Denton, and D. Keltner, 'Higher social class predicts increased unethical behavior'.
56. CA/J/5 Christian Aid (1979) Hard Questions For Rich Christians: A Study and Action Guide for 'Rich Christians in an Age of Hunger'.
57. R. J. Sider, *Rich Christians in an Age of Hunger* (Sevenoaks: Hodder & Stoughton, 1978).
58. R. J. Sider, *Rich Christians in an Age of Hunger* (London: Paulist, 1977), p. 141.
59. T. Stafford, 'Ron Sider's unsettling crusade', *Christianity Today* (27 April 1992). Available http://www.christianitytoday.com/ct/2000/marchweb-only
60. R. Lee, A. Leyshon and C. Williams (eds.), *Alternative Economic Spaces* (London: Sage, 2003).
61. Christian Aid, *Partnership For Change: The Power to End Poverty* (March 2012). Available http://www.christianaid.org.uk/resources/corporate_reports/2012-plus-strategy.aspx
62. P. Clifford, *Theology from the Global South: Perspectives on Christian Aid's Work* (Christian Aid, April 2012).
63. For instance, from 1974, CAFOD began working with the Bartolomé de las Casas Institute an NGO set up by Gustavo Gutiérrez, in Lima, Peru.
64. *Towards a Church in Solidarity with the Poor* (WCC, Geneva, 1980) p. 17.
65. J. Nickoloff (ed.). *Gustavo Gutierrez Essential Writings* (Orbis Books, 1996). p. 5. This paper was later reworked into his influential book *Theology of Liberation: History, Politics and Salvation* (1971).
66. Ibid., p. 34.
67. Ibid.
68. SODEPAX, the Joint Committee on Society, Development and Peace, was set up in 1968 by the World Council of Churches (WCC) and the Roman Catholic Church.
69. D. Regan, *Why are They Poor? Helder Camara in Pastoral Perspective* (Münster|: LIT Verlag, 2003). p. 89.
70. Ibid., p. 5.
71. Ibid., p. 184.
72. The Lausanne Covenant (1974). Available http://www.lausanne.org/en/documents/lausanne-covenant.html.
73. See the introduction of this volume for a discussion of the definition and principles of Fair Trade.
74. D. Korten and R. Klauss, *People-Centered Development: Contributions Toward Theory and Planning Frameworks* (Boulder, Colorado: Kumarian Press, 1984).
75. M. Barratt Brown, *Fair Trade: Reform and Realities in the International Trading System* (London: ZED Books, 1993), p. 156.

76. R. Churchill. 'The man who gambled the Church's money: Yesterday the happy news – he has doubled its income', *Daily Mail* (20 October 1961).
77. Ibid.
78. A. Chandler, *The Church of England in the Twentieth Century: The Church Commissioners and the Politics of Reform, 1948–1998* (Woodbridge, Suffolk: Boydell Press, 2006), p. 157.
79. However, as Andrew Chandler highlights with the Church's money in investment trusts this official ban on breweries was difficult to implement.
80. Chandler, *The Church of England in the Twentieth Century*, p. 167.
81. Memorandum, 'Overseas investment and "banned categories", CC (69) 41, Board Papers, 11 December 1969, ser. 95083/32.
82. Overseas Development Institute, *A Third Force for the Third World: A Study of the Channels for Investment of Church Trust Funds in Economic Development.* (1972) CA2/D/14.
83. Ibid.
84. Ibid.
85. Ibid.
86. The World Council of Churches was formed in 1948 and now represents 286 member churches.
87. WCC, *World Council of Churches and Bank Loans to Apartheid* (Geneva, 1977), p. 11.
88. Ibid.
89. Ibid., p. 43.
90. Bodleian Library, 'Catalogue of the archive of End Loans to Southern Africa, 1974–95' Available http://www.bodley.ox.ac.uk/dept/scwmss/wmss/online/blcas/eltsa.html
91. CA2/D/24/4, Midland Bank Ltd A Great British Bank? (ELTSA 1975).
92. Ibid.
93. 'Christian leaders act against bank loans to apartheid', *Catholic Herald*, 16 January 1976. Available http://archive.catholicherald.co.uk/article/16th-january-1976/2/christian-leaders-act-against-bank-loans-to-aparth.
94. 'Anglicans oppose loans to S Africa', *Catholic Herald*, 27th February 1976 Available http://archive.catholicherald.co.uk/article/27th-february-1976/2/anglicans-oppose-loans-to-s-africa
95. WCC Bank Loans to Apartheid. 1977, p. 14.
96. 'Anglicans oppose loans to S Africa', *Catholic Herald*, 27th February 1976 Available http://archive.catholicherald.co.uk/article/27th-february-1976/2/anglicans-oppose-loans-to-s-africa
97. Shared Interest was established in 1990 and is and the world's only 100% Fair Trade lender.
98. T. Chester, *Awakening to a World of Need* (Nottingham: Inter Varsity Press, 1993).
99. M. Symonds, *Love in Action: Celebrating 25 Years of Tear Fund* (Guildford: Eagle 1993).
100. Chester, *Awakening to a World of Need*, p. 108.
101. Traidcraft, 'Policy and procedure: Purchasing policy' (May 2012) Available http://www.traidcraft.co.uk/media/8fc92970-2f77-4af3-80b0-9ac00aac4a64
102. By 1991 Tearcraft (now called Created) had an annual turnover of £1 million. In contrast, Traidcraft's annual sales at this time were £3.6 million (1987/88).

103. R. Adams, *Who Profits?* (Oxford: Lion Publishing, 1989), p. 155.
104. Ibid., p. 159.
105. Ibid., p. 90.
106. Ibid., p. 97.
107. CA/J/5 *Headline Magazine* (1984).
108. CA/J/5 Christian Aid, *Coffee, Grounds for Concern?* (1984).
109. 'Revolution or illusion? Nicaragua after 6 years', *Link* (Winter 1985).
110. Ibid.
111. CA8/C/179: Christian Aid, Asia Regional Grants.
112. This model would later be replicated by other Fair Trade companies such as Divine Chocolate.
113. In 1999 the Dutch based Ecumenical Development Cooperative Society was renamed Oikocredit.
114. S. Osborne, *Shared Interest: Investing in a Fairer World, 20th Anniversary* (Bristol: Tangent Books, 2010), pp. 19–20.
115. Ibid., p. 29.
116. The minimum shareholding had originally been set at £250; however in 1996 this was revised to £100.
117. Osborne, *Shared Interest,*, p. 128.
118. CA9/ER/1: External Relations Department, Development Education Grant DA 304: The Fairtrade Foundation (1996).
119. The Fairtrade Foundation – Grants/ Loans received from sponsoring agencies, MDD/7.9.94
120. CA/PUBS-CAN/3: 'Trade for change', *Christian Aid News*, No 77 (October/ December 1992).
121. Ibid.
122. Ibid.
123. Christian Aid advert, 'You have stopped using eggs from battery hens, but what about tea from battery tea workers', *The Times* (16 September 1992).
124. R. Adams letter to Nick Isles, *Christian Aid* (17 September 1992).
125. P. Johns, letter to Jenny Borden, *Christian Aid* (17 September 1992).
126. R. Adams letter to Nick Isles, *Christian Aid* (17 September 1992).
127. Christian Aid advert, 'You have stopped using eggs from battery hens, but what about tea from battery tea workers', *The Times* (16 September 1992).
128. R. Adams letter to Nick Isles, *Christian Aid* (17 September 1992).
129. CA/PUBS-CAN/3: 'Vouchers urge supermarkets to help poor farmers', *Christian Aid News*, No. 79 (April/June 1993).
130. 'Supermarkets move towards ethical trading', *Christian Aid News* (Winter 1998).
131. CAFOD, 'Fair deal update' (Summer 1997).
132. *Tear Times* (Autumn 1998).
133. Evangelical Alliance, 'Census: Is Britain still a Christian country?' Available http://www.eauk.org/current-affairs/news/census-is-britain-still-a-christian-country.cfm
134. C. Barnett, N. Clarke, P. Cloke and A. Malpass, 'Faith in ethical consumption,' Paper given at Countering Consumerism: Religious and Secular Responses (21 April 2006).
135. C. Barnett, N. Clarke, P. Cloke and A. Malpass, 'Fairtrade urbanism? The politics of place beyond place in the Bristol Fairtrade city campaign', *International Journal of Urban and Regional Research*, 31.3 (September 2007).

136. A. D. Gilbert (1976), *Religion and Society in Industrial England: Church, Chapel and Social Change 1740–1914* (London: Longman), p. xiv
137. Ibid., p. 54.
138. Ibid., p. 66.
139. Ibid., p. 15.
140. Ibid., p. 22.
141. Ibid., p. 129.
142. C. Brown, *The Death of Christian Britain: Understanding Secularisation 1800–2000* (London: Routledge, 2001), p. 3.
143. Ibid., pp. 3–4.
144. Ibid., p. 2.
145. J. Morris, 'The strange death of Christian Britain: Another look at the secularization debate', *The Historical Journal* 46.4 (2003), p. 976.
146. 'Ethical eating: how much do you swallow?' *The Guardian*, (26 February 2006) Available http://www.theguardian.com/lifeandstyle/2006/feb/26/foodanddrink.uk
147. H. McLeod, *Secularisation in Western Europe, 1848–1914* (London: Macmillan Press, 2000).
148. Ibid., p. 289.
149. D. Barker, *The European Values Study 1981–1990* (Aberdeen: Gordon Cook Foundation, 1991). p. 47.
150. Seven out of the sixteen member organisations of the Fairtrade Foundation have strong Christian allegiances (and no other faith groups are currently represented). CAFOD*, Christian Aid*, Methodist Relief and Development Fund, SCIAF, Tearfund, Traidcraft Exchange*, United Reformed Church. *Founder Member. Available http://www.fairtrade.org.uk/includes/documents/cm_docs/2008/a/annual_review.pdf.
151. BBC, 'Census shows rise in foreign-born' (December 2012). Available http://www.bbc.co.uk/news/uk-20675307.
152. Fairtrade Foundation, Annual Review (2007/2008), p. 7.
153. C. Barnett, N. Clarke, P. Cloke and A. Malpass 'The political rationalities of fair-trade consumption in the United Kingdom', *Politics and Society*, 35.4 (2007), p. 595.
154. Ibid., pp. 583–607.
155. A. Ahmed Khan and L. Thaut, *An Islamic Perspective on Fair Trade* (Birmingham: Islamic Relief Worldwide, August 2008), p. 12. Available http://policy.islamic-relief.com/wp-content/uploads/2014/05/Islam_and_Fairtrade.pdf
156. Ibid.
157. At the end of December 2012 there were over 7,000 faith groups (mainly churches, church networks and dioceses, also 44 synagogues, 3 mosques, 1 Hindu temple and 1 Bahá'í community). Quoted in: 'The Fairtrade Foundation, Annual Report and Financial Statements for the year ended 31 December 2012'. Available http://www.fairtrade.org.uk/what_is_fairtrade/annual_reports.aspx
158. Christian Aid, *Partnership For Change: The Power to End Poverty* (March 2012). Available http://www.christianaid.org.uk/resources/corporate_reports/2012-plus-strategy.aspx
159. Fairtrade Foundation, *Fairtrade Churches Newsletter* (June 2009). The three goals a Fairtrade church (or other place of worship) must fulfil are: 1. Use Fairtrade

tea and coffee after services and in all meetings for which, they have responsibility; 2. Move forward on using other Fairtrade products such as sugar, biscuits and fruit; 3. Promote Fairtrade during Fairtrade Fortnight and during the year through events, worship and other activities whenever possible.

160. FMR Research, 'Final Report August 2005: Traidcraft Stakeholder Research', Available http://researching.co.uk/pdfs/traidcraft_stakeholder_research.pdf
161. E. F. Schumacher, *Small is Beautiful: A Study of Economics as If People Mattered* (London: Blond & Briggs, 1973).
162. C. Fager, 'Small is Beautiful, and So Is Rome: Surprising Faith of E. F. Schumacher', *Christian Century,* 6 April 1977.
163. Ibid.
164. Ibid.
165. McLeod, *Secularisation in Western Europe,* p. 289.
166. A. Bose and P. Burnell, *Britain's Overseas Aid Since 1979: Between Idealism and Self-interest* (Manchester: MUP, 1991).
167. House of Commons International Development Committee, *Fair Trade and Development* (14 June 2007).
168. Prochaska, *Christianity & Social Service in Modern Britain,* p. 13.

3 The Co-operative Difference: Co-operation among Co-operatives?

1. 'Fairtrade choc', *Co-operative News* (5 April 1994).
2. The Co-operative Group, *Inspiring Through Co-operation: Sustainability Report 2011,* (Manchester, 2012). p. 16. Available online: http://www.co-operative.coop/Corporate/sustainability-report-2011/downloads/sustainability-report-2011.pdf
3. Ibid.
4. Tesco, Asda, Sainsbury's and Morrison's had a combined market share of 76.2% of the UK grocery market in the 12 weeks ending 17 February 2013 (Kantar Worldpanel). The Co-operative Food market share was 6.2% over the same period.
5. The Co-operative Group, *Setting New Sights: Our Ethical Plan 2012–14 (and beyond...),* (Manchester, 2011). Available online: http://www.co-operative.coop/Corporate/CSR/Our_Ethical_Plan_2012-2014.pdf
6. The Co-operative Group, *Sustainability Report 2011,* p.11.
7. A. Nicholls and C. Opal, *Fair Trade: Market-Driven Ethical Consumption* (London: Sage, 2005) p. 20.
8. 'Where have all the academics gone?', *Co-operative News* (6 November 1990).
9. W. Sidney and W. Beatrice, *The Consumers' Co-operative Movement* (London: Longman, 1921).
10. *New Statesman* (15 January 1921).
11. S. Pollard, 'Nineteenth-Century Co-operation: From Community Building to Shopkeeping', in A. Briggs and J. Saville (eds), *Essays in Labour History* (London: Macmillan, 1960).
12. S. Yeo (ed.), *New Views of Co-operation* (London: Routledge, 1988).
13. P. Gurney, *Co-operative Culture and the Politics of Consumption in England, 1870–1930* (Manchester: Manchester University Press, 1996).

14. J. Birchall, *The International Co-operative Movement* (Manchester: Manchester University Press, 1997).
15. W.P. Watkins, *The International Co-operative Alliance 1895–1970* (London: ICA, 1970).
16. A. Nicholls and C. Opal, *Fair Trade: Market-Driven Ethical Consumption* (London: Sage, 2005); M. Hilton, *Consumerism in 20th Century Britain* (Cambridge: Cambridge University Press, 2003); R. Harrison, T. Newholm and D. Shaw, *The Ethical Consumer* (London: Sage, 2005).
17. L. Black and N. Robertson (eds.), *Taking Stock: The Co-operative Movement in Twentieth Century Britain*, (Manchester: Manchester University Press, 2009).
18. World in Action: 'Cost of a Cup of Tea' (Granada: 24 September 1973).
19. Ibid.
20. Ibid.
21. M. Gillard, 'Ceylon's starving tea girls', *The Observer* (23 September 1973).
22. 'Tea slaves', *Co-operative News* (12 October 1973).
23. 'Sri Lanka horror', *Co-operative News* (5 October 1973).
24. War on Want, *The State of Tea* (London: 1974); Cambridge World Development Action Group, *Tea: The Colonial Legacy* (Cambridge: 1975); Oxfam, 'A bitter taste to your cuppa' in *Consumer Affairs Bulletin* (No. 7, 1977); World Development Movement, *The Tea Trade* (London: 1979).

    In 1976 the idea of an International Tea Agreement was supported by the fourth United Nations Conference on Trade and Development. Tea was included as one of the 18 commodities in its Integrated Commodities programme, which aimed at establishing a stable price on a range of products from developing countries.
25. War on Want, *The State of Tea* (London: 1974).
26. Oxfam, 'A bitter taste to your cuppa' in *Consumer Affairs Bulletin* (No. 7, 1977).
27. Ibid.
28. Ibid.
29. 'Biggest ever share of the tea market', *Co-operative News* (16 November 1977).
30. 'Tea prices are cut', *Co-operative News* (9 November 1977) and 'Co-op cuts tea price again', *Co-operative News* (8 March 1978).
31. *Co-operative News* (16 November 1977).
32. World Development Movement, *The Tea Trade* (London, first published 1979, second edition 1982).
33. Ibid.
34. Birchall, *The International Co-operative Movement*, p. 46.
35. Article 3: *Objects of the International Co-operative Alliance* (London: ICA, 1895).
36. Ibid., p. 44.
37. Watkins, *The International Co-operative Alliance*, p. 143.
38. Ibid., p. 143.
39. The Plunkett Foundation, established in 1919 by Horace Plunkett, works to support the development of rural co-operatives in the UK and worldwide.
40. M. Digby. 'Producers and Consumers', in *The Year Book of Agricultural Co-operation in the British Empire* (London: Plunkett Foundation, 1928).
41. Ibid.
42. Ibid.

43. Watkins, *The International Co-operative Alliance,* p. 264.
44. Ibid.
45. ICA Conference, Vienna, 1966.
46. J. Brazda and R. Schediwy (eds), *Consumer Co-operatives in a Changing World* (Geneva: ICA, 1989).
47. Ibid.
48. C. Job (Director of Royal Arsenal Co-operative Society), *Multi National Corporations, The Co-operative Alternative* (Warsaw: ICA Congress, 1972).
49. Ibid.
50. Ibid.
51. M. V. Madane, 'International Co-operative Trade in Asia Retrospect and Prospect', in *The Year Book of Agricultural Co-operation* (Oxford: ICA and The Plunkett Foundation, 1978).
52. Ibid.
53. Ibid.
54. In Canada, three small worker-owned co-operatives (Planet Bean, La Siembra, Just Us!) played a significant role in developing Fair Trade networks in the mid to late 1990s and continue to offer an alternative vision of Fair Trade. See G. Fridell, *Fair Trade Coffee: The Prospects and Pitfalls of Market-Driven Social Justice*, (Toronto: University of Toronto Press, 2007).
55. Ibid.
56. C. Job, (Director of Royal Arsenal Co-operative Society), *Multi National Corporations, The Co-operative Alternative* (Warsaw, ICA Congress, 1972) p.32.
57. In 1864, Friedrich Wilhelm Raiffeisen, set up the first thrift and loan Society in Heddesdorf, Germany. This is often credited as being one of the first rural co-operatives. Raiffeisen's, *Credit Unions as a Remedy for the Poverty of Rural and Industrial Workers and Artisans*, published in 1866, was considered by many as the manual for rural co-operative development.
58. Saxena, *The World of Co-operative Enterprise.*
59. Bodleian Library, Oxford, MSS.AAM1, 'Letter to Mr Okunnu from J. Bailey Co-operative Union Secretary' (14 July 1959).
60. 'Promotion of S. African goods should stop', *Co-operative News* (29 August 1975).
61. 'S. African boycott move has mixed reception', *Co-operative News* (4 April 1964).
62. 'Co-op Bank – supporters of apartheid?', *Co-operative News* (19 January 1973).
63. There are some parallels with V. Packard, *Hidden Persuaders* (London: Longman, 1957).
64. *Co-operative News* (29 August 1975).
65. Packard, *The Hidden Persuaders.*
66. G. Alder, 'The Role of Voluntary Aid Agencies', *Co-operative Review* (18 March 1972).
67. B. Murphy, *Help the Hungry to Help Each Other* (Manchester: Co-operative Press, 1966).
68. K. Mayhew, *Catholic Herald* (5 August 1966).
69. Oxford, Bodleian Library, Oxfam archive (uncatalogued), 'R1492', report by the Information Office, 'Oxfam Aid to Co-operative Schemes', Mar 1967.
70. Murphy, *Help the Hungry to Help Each Other.*

71. Oxford, Bodleian Library, Oxfam archive (uncatalogued), 'R1492', report by the Information Office, 'An Ideal Lives', Mar 1967.
72. Oxford, Bodleian Library, Oxfam archive (uncatalogued), 'BOT 6 2011 VOL I', report by M. R. Harris, Field Director Central and Southern Africa, 2 Jul 1968.
73. '£21,000 cheque for Oxfam', *Co-operative News* (3 June 1967).
74. 'Divided Views on Oxfam Divi', *Co-operative News* (5 August 1967).
75. *Co-operative News* (3 June 1967).
76. Oxford, Bodleian Library, Oxfam archive (uncatalogued), 'R1492', report by B. Murphy, 'Progress Report of the Co-operative Project Appeal', 1967.
77. Murphy, *Help the Hungry to Help Each Other*, p. 5.
78. Murphy, 'Progress Report of the Co-operative Project Appeal'.
79. Brazda and Schediwy (eds), *Consumer Co-operatives in a Changing World*, p. 131.
80. Ibid.
81. H. W. Whitehead, 'President's Address' (Co-operative Union Congress, 1981).
82. Ibid.
83. Ibid.
84. 'Green Issues – opportunity knocks for the Co-op', *Co-operative News* (16 January 1990).
85. 'The Co-op movement and the environment', *Co-operative News* (22 January 1991).
86. *Co-op Action Guide for the Environment* (Manchester: Co-operative Press, 1989).
87. *Ethical Consumer Magazine* (ECRA Publishing Ltd, May/June 1989).
88. Ibid.
89. P. Crouchman, 'Exit the "green" consumer - enter "green" citizens', *Co-operative Retail Marketing and Management* (June 1990), p. 4–6.
90. 'Bank woos the carers', *Co-operative News* (5 May 1992).
91. As was seen in its decision to operate Barclaycard despite pressure from anti-apartheid campaigners.
92. T. Thomas, 'The Co-operative Bank's Ethical Stance', *Review of International Co-operation*, 86:4 (1993), p. 71–75.
93. CA/PUBS-CAN/3: 'Trade for Change', *Christian Aid News*, No 77 (October/December 1992).
94. 'Customers don't want Fair Trade products', *Co-operative News* (26 September 1995).
95. Ibid.
96. *Co-operative News* (5 May 1992).
97. 'Customers don't want Fair Trade products', *Co-operative News* (26 September 1995).
98. Ibid.
99. Social Intrapreneurs are defined as corporate changemakers that work inside big business, to innovate and deliver market solutions to social and environmental challenges. SustainAbility (2008) 'The social intrapreneur: a field guide for corporate changemakers'. Available online: <http://www.sustainability.com/library>
100. J. Bowes (ed.) *The Fair Trade Revolution* (London: Pluto Press, 2011).
101. Ibid.
102. CWS, Press Release, 'Co-op Boosts Fairtrade Products', www.co-op.ac.uk (1999).

103. M. Newman, *The Financial Times* (11 October 1990).
104. C. Heath and D. Heath, *Made to Stick: Why Some Ideas Take Hold and Others Come Unstuck* (London: Arrow Books, 2008). Chip and Dan Heath identify six principles of sticky ideas: (1) Simplicity, (2) Unexpectedness, (3) Concreteness, (4) Credibility, (5) Emotions, (6) Stories.
105. Brad Hill quoted in H. Lamb, *Fighting the Banana Wars and Other Fairtrade Battles: How We Took on the Corporate Giants to Change the World* (New York: Random House, 2009), p. 65.
106. Watkins, *The International Co-operative Alliance*, p. 3.
107. Pollard, 'Nineteenth-Century Co-operation: from Community Building to Shopkeeping'.
108. Bowes (ed.) *The Fair Trade Revolution*, p. 138.
109. G. Holyoake, *The History of the Rochdale Pioneers, 1844–1892*. (London: G. Allen & Unwin, 1893).

4 International Trade Unionism: Labour Solidarity?

1. TUC Press Release (14 June 2007) available http://www.tuc.org.uk/international/tuc-13394-f0.cfm.
2. Memorandum submitted by the TUC, House of Commons International Development Committee, Fair Trade and Development (14 June 2007), Ev. 127.
3. H. J. Frundt, *Fair Bananas: Farmers, Workers, and Consumers Strive to Change an Industry* (Tucson: University of Arizona Press, 2009).
4. J. McIlroy, *Trade Unions in Britain Today* (Manchester: Manchester University Press, 1988); R. Martin, *TUC The Growth of a Pressure Group 1868–1976* (Oxford: University Press, 1980); G. Eley, *Forging Democracy: The History of the Left in Europe, 1850–2000* (Oxford: University Press, 2002); A. J. Reid, 'Trade unions a foundation of political pluralism?' *History and Policy* (May 2002), available http://www.historyandpolicy.org/archive/policy-paper-05.html (17 July 2007).
5. P. Pasture, 'A century of International Trade Unionism, review essay', *IRSH* (2002), p. 47.
6. Ibid., p. 288.
7. Ibid.
8. P. Pasture, *The Lost Perspective?: Trade Unions between Ideology and Social Action in the New Europe* (Aldershot: Avebury, 1996).
9. R. O'Brien, 'Workers and world order: The tentative transformation of the International Union Movement', *Review of International Studies*, 26 (2000), p. 533.
10. Ibid., p. 553.
11. Ibid., p. 554.
12. J. Harrod and R. O'Brien (eds.), *Global Unions?: Theory and Strategies of Organized Labour in the Global Political Economy* (London: Routledge, 2002), p. 6.
13. Ibid.
14. P. Waterman, *Globalization, Social Movements and the New Internationalists* (London: Mansell Publishing Limited, 1998).

15. The International Confederation of Free Trade Unions (ICFTU) was established in 1949 following a split within the World Federation of Trade Unions (WFTU). In October 2006 the ICFTU merged with the World Confederation of Labour (WCL) to form the International Trade Union Confederation (ITUC).
16. Waterman, *Globalization, Social Movements and the New Internationalists*, p. 113.
17. Ibid., p. 111.
18. Ibid.
19. Ibid., p. 5.
20. D. Della Porta and M. Diani, *Social Movements: An Introduction* (Oxford: Blackwell Publishing, first edition 1998, second edition 2006), p. 213.
21. Ibid., p. 212.
22. R. Cox, 'Civil society at the turn of the millennium: Prospects for an alternative world order', *Review of International Studies*, 25 (1999), p. 19.
23. R. Martin, *TUC The Growth of a Pressure Group 1868–1976* (Oxford: University Press, 1980), p. viii.
24. J. McIlroy, *Trade Unions in Britain Today* (Manchester: Manchester University Press, 1995), p. 22.
25. Ibid., p. 26.
26. M. Stewart, *Britain and the ILO: The Story of Fifty Years* (London: HMSO, 1969), p. 110.
27. J. P. Windmuller, 'ICFTU after ten years: Problems and prospects', *Industrial and Labor Relations Review*, 14.2 (January, 1961), pp. 257–272.
28. Ibid.
29. MSS.292D/931/5 'ICFTU development charter – Towards a New Economic Order' (17–18 May 1978), p. 3.
30. Ibid.
31. Ibid.
32. P. H. Werhane, 'Moral imagination and the search for ethical decision-making in management', *Business Ethics Quarterly*, Ruffin Series, 1 (1998), pp. 75–98.
33. MSS.292D/954.9/1: ICFTU/ITS Working Party on Multinational Companies (11–12 September 1975).
34. C. Wilms-Wright, 'Our unacceptable capitalism in Sri Lanka,' *Socialist Commentary* (March 1975).
35. Ibid.
36. MSS.292D/954.9/1: Role of International trade union movement, BGB/DG (31 July 1975).
37. Ibid.
38. MSS.292D/905.234/1: Patrick Wintour, The TUC's 'foreign policy' *New Statesman* (2 March 1979).
39. War on Want was founded following a letter from Victor Gollancz to *The Guardian* in February 1951. Gollancz's letter asked people to join an international struggle against poverty. Harold Wilson MP was invited to chair the committee and in 9 June 1952 they published their report, 'War on Want: A plan for World development'.
40. E. Bond, *The State of Tea* (London: War on Want, 1974), p. 14.
41. D. Thompson, *Where Were You, Brother? An Account of Trade Union Imperialism* (London: War on Want, 1978), p. 1.

42. Ibid., p. 133.
43. Ibid.
44. Ibid.
45. Ibid., p. 28.
46. Ibid., p. 29.
47. Ibid., p. 32.
48. MSS.292D/905.234/1: War on Want, 'Wanted one hour of your pay' (1981).
49. In 1992, the World Development Movement became one of the founding members of the Fairtrade Foundation in the United Kingdom.
50. MSS.292D/931/4: TUCICD 'Submission to the parliamentary Select Committee on overseas development,' (21 July 1977).
51. Ibid.
52. In December 1976 the Minister for Overseas Development announced the intention to allocate £150,000 annually to help finance education and information work on development matters in the United Kingdom by non-governmental organisations.
53. MSS.292D/931/4: TUC Inter-departmental Correspondence, 'Trade Union Committee for International Co-operation and Development (TUCICD)' (19 April 1978).
54. Ministry for Overseas Development, *The Changing Emphasis in British Aid Policies: More Help for the Poorest* (London: HMSO, 1975).
55. MSS.292D-931.3-1, letter by John Grant, Parliamentary Under Secretary ODM, 1 September 1975.
56. Ibid.
57. MSS.292D/931.3/1: Trade Union Foundation, Memorandum of Association (December 1976).
58. MSS.292D/931/5: Bilateral Aid and Rural Development Department, 'ICFTU Development Charter' (July 1978).
59. Ibid.
60. MSS.292D/931.3/1: Letter by Anthony Beattie (ODM) to J. A. Hargreaves (TUC) re: ODM Grant (12 February 1979).
61. Thompson, *Where Were You, Brother?*, p. 102.
62. J. Lloyd, 'TUC fears cut in £1.6m grant', *Financial Times* (26 August 1982).
63. MSS.292D931/8: Oxfam, Evan Luard letter to Len Murray, General Secretary TUC (20 January 1981).
64. B. Towers, 'Running the Gauntlet: British trade Unions under Thatcher, 1979–1988', *Industrial and Labor Relations Review*, 42.2 (January 1989), pp. 163–188.
65. The Report of the Independent Commission on International Development Issues under the Chairmanship of Willy Brandt, *North-South: A Programme for Survival* (London: Pan Books, 1980).
66. MSS.292D931/7: TUC, 'The Brandt report' (12 March 1980).
67. Ministry for Overseas Development, *The Changing Emphasis in British Aid policies: More Help for the Poorest* (London: HMSO, 1975); Neil Marten, Hansard, 20 February 1980 Cols 464–465.
68. MSS.292D/931/8: Report by Adrian Moyes, 'Brandt and the poor', Oxfam (12 May 1980).
69. Ibid.

70. MSS.292D/931/7: TUC, 'The Brandt report' (12 March 1980), p. 10.
71. A. Sampson, 'Young and wise in surge to Brandt,' *The Observer* (7 December 1980).
72. Ibid.
73. Ibid.
74. TUAC, Trade Union Advisory Committee to the Organisation for Economic Co-operation and Development (OECD), an interface for the labour unions with the OECD.
75. MSS.292D/931/8: Otto Kersten, General Secretary ICFTU, correspondence with Mr A. Sampson (10 December 1980).
76. MSS.292D/931/7: TUC, 'The Brandt report' (12 March 1980), p. 9.
77. Ibid.
78. Ibid.
79. MSS.292D/931/8: Evan Luard, Oxfam, correspondence with Len Murray, General Secretary TUC (20 January 1981).
80. MSS.292D/905.234/1: Tracey Lacey, General Secretary, War on Want correspondence with Len Murray, General Secretary, TUC (20 November 1979).
81. Ibid.
82. Twin and Twin Trading, 'Fair Trade at the Crossroads: Annual Report 2004/05', Available: www.twin.org.uk/downloads/AnnualReport0405.pdf.
83. TWIN, *Bridges Not Fences: Report of the Third World Trade and Technology Conference* (London, February 1985), p. 8.
84. Twin Trading has been responsible for a number of developments and innovations that have contributed to the growth of Fair Trade in Britain. In particular, Twin Trading helped launch two of the most successful and recognisable Fairtrade brands in the United Kingdom: Cafédirect, in 1991 and Day Chocolate, in 1997.
85. '*Statement of Principles for Developing Trade and Technology Exchange*', adopted at closing plenary, Bridges Not Fences (February 1985).
86. TWIN, *Bridges Not Fences*, p. 11.
87. Ibid., p. 24.
88. Olivier Le Brun, Director of Twin Trading, *Bridges Not Fences* (February 1985), Part 5, Paper 9.
89. Ibid.
90. K. Young and L. Grayson, *Abolition: The Reform of Metropolitan Government in England 1983–1986* (Letchworth, Technical Communications, 1988) pp. 80, 84.
91. Ibid., p. 154.
92. Ibid.
93. *Bridges Not Fences* (February 1985), part 2, paper 5.
94. M. Barratt Brown, 'Twin: The first 20 years', Twin Trading Annual Report 2004/05: Fair Trade at the Crossroads.
95. Third World Information Network, *The Network*, III.3 (July–October 1990), p. 4.
96. L. Raynolds, D. Murray and J. Wilkinson (eds.), *Fair Trade: The Challenges of Transforming Globalisation* (London: Routledge, 2007), p. 216.
97. This has been referred to as the 'plantation vs. small farmer debate'.
98. Frundt, *Fair Bananas*.
99. Ibid., p. 115.

100. Ibid.
101. Ibid., p. 187.
102. Ibid., p. 215.
103. Fairtrade International defines a smallholder as a producer who is dependent on family labour, as opposed to non-family labour.
104. A. Nicholls and C. Opal, *Fair Trade: Market-Driven Ethical Consumerism* (London: Sage Publications 2004).
105. Raynolds, et al., *Fair Trade*, p. 150.
106. Ibid.
107. Ibid., p. 213.
108. Ibid., p. 201.
109. Ibid., p. 212.
110. 'The Fairtrade fresh fruit and empowerment consultation forum', Grabouw, South Africa (24–25 May 2004).
111. G. Fridell, 'The co-operative and the corporation: Competing visions of the future of fair trade', *Journal of Business Ethics*, 86.1 (2009), pp. 81–95.
112. Retail employees from ten Starbucks outlets in Vancouver, unionized under one master collective agreement as a member of the Canadian Auto Workers, Local 3000.
113. Fridell, 'The co-operative and the corporation'.
114. G. Fridell, *Fair Trade Coffee: The Prospects and Pitfalls of Market-driven Social Justice* (University of Toronto Press, 2007).
115. BBC News, 'Banana firm exploits migrants', (23 May 2007) Available: http://news.bbc.co.uk/1/hi/uk/6682689.stm
116. 'Fairtrade in spotlight after claims of abuse', *The Grocer*, (4 June 2007) Available: http://www.thegrocer.co.uk/fmcg/fairtrade-in-spotlight-after-claims-of-abuse/119722.article
117. 'Banana factory finally recognises union', *Luton Today*, (23 April 2008) Available: http://www.lutontoday.co.uk/news/local/banana-factory-finally-recognises-union-1-1029271
118. Memorandum submitted by the Fairtrade Foundation, House of Commons International Development Committee, Fair Trade and Development, 14 June 2007, Ev. 98.
119. Thompson, *Where Were You, Brother?*
120. John P. Windmuller, 'ICFTU after ten years: Problems and prospects', *Industrial and Labor Relations Review*, 14. 2 (January 1961), pp. 257–272.
121. Ibid., pp. 257–272.
122. Ibid.
123. Waterman, *Globalization, Social Movements and the New Internationalists*, p. 111.
124. W. Hutton, 'Davos man thrives while the rest of us pay for his excesses', *The Observer*, Sunday 20 January 2013. Available http://www.guardian.co.uk/commentisfree/2013/jan/20/davos-world-economic-forum-bad-capitalism
125. A. Bullock, Report of the Committee of Inquiry on Industrial Democracy, Cmnd 6706 (HMSO: London, 1977).
126. P. Davies, Lord Wedderburn, 'The Land of Industrial Democracy', *Industrial Law Journal*, 6.1 (1977), pp. 197–211.
127. History & Policy, 'Democracy in the workplace – the Bullock Report revisited' Published online: Available http://www.historyandpolicy.org/forums/union/meeting_090710.html#jackjones

128. Ibid.
129. Fairtrade International, 'Hired labour standards', available http://www.fairtrade.net/944.html.
130. Oxfam briefing paper, *Made at Home: British Homeworkers in Global Supply Chains* (May 2004), available http://www.oxfam.org.uk/resources/policy/trade/downloads/bp63_homeworkers.pdf, 20 May 2008.
131. An IDS impact study of the first eight years of the ETI found that workers were being denied membership of trade unions in the all of the countries chosen for investigation – the United Kingdom, Costa Rica, India, South Africa and Vietnam. S. Barrientos, IDS, Ethical Trading Initiative Impact Assessment (October 2006) available http://www.ids.ac.uk/ids/pvty/pdf-files/ETI-impact-1-main.get.pdf, 20 May 2008.
132. Memorandum submitted by the TUC, House of Commons International Development Committee, Fair Trade and Development (14 June 2007), Ev. 131.
133. 'Unlocking the power of the many', Fairtrade International's 2013–2015 Action Plan.
134. Fairtrade International, 'Hired Labour Standards' (2014). Available http://www.fairtrade.net/hired-labour-standards.html.
135. 'Powering up Smallholder Farmers to Make Food Fair: A Five Point Agenda', A Fairtrade Foundation Report, February 2013.

5 Ethical Consumerism: 'Shopping for a Better World'

1. Oxford, Bodleian Library, Oxfam archive (uncatalogued), Bridge Committee minutes and papers, B. Yates, 'From the Margins to the Mainstream', Sept 1990.
2. I. Hudson, M. Hudson and M. Fridell. *Fair Trade, Sustainability and Social Change* (Basingstoke: Palgrave Macmillan, 2013). p. 111.
3. Arguably many of these gains where short-lived and involved significant compromises for the environmental movement.
4. Multatuli (Douwes-Dekker) *Max Havelaar: Or the Coffee Auctions of a Dutch Trading Company*, first published 1860 (London: Penguin Classics, 1986).
5. 'Green labelling' *Which?* (January 1990), p. 12.
6. To use the Max Havelaar name roasters had to pay a license fee of 1.6% and fulfil minimum criteria including: payment for coffee of 5%–10% above the international markets, a minimum 60% advance payments and offer long-term contracts.
7. 'Now the supermarkets do what we tell them', *The Independent* (9 March 1991).
8. R. Adams personal archive, FTF/Europe/EC-Fund2, 'Fair Trade Marks: translating consumer education and consciousness into consumer behaviour through mainstream business participation' (3 January 1992), p. 9.
9. Ibid.
10. Hudson et al., *Fair Trade, Sustainability and Social Change*, p. 102.
11. Ibid.
12. A. Nicholls and C. Opal, *Fair Trade: Market Driven Ethical Consumption* (London: Sage Publications, 2004).
13. Ibid., p. 13.
14. Ibid.

15. L. Raynolds, D. Murray and J. Wilkinson (eds.), *Fair Trade: The Challenges of Transforming Globalisation* (London: Routledge, 2007), p. 103.
16. S. Barrientos and S. Smith, 'Mainstreaming Fair Trade in global networks', in L. Raynold, D. Murray and J. Wilkinson (eds.), *Fair Trade: The Challenges of Transforming Globalisation* (London: Routledge, 2007).
17. M. Sandel, *What Money can't Buy: The Moral Limits of Markets* (London: Macmillan, 2012).
18. R. Scott, *Church Times*, Fair Trade Fortnight Issue (7 March 2003). Available http://www.onevillage.org/fairtrade-history.htm.
19. At this point the UK Fair Trade market was dominated by two ATOs: Oxfam Bridge and Traidcraft. Both of these organisations were supportive of Fairtrade certification and became founding members of the Fairtrade Foundation.
20. Oxford, Bodleian Library, Oxfam archive (uncatalogued), Bridge Committee minutes and papers, report by E. Millard, 'Fair Trade Mark (FTM): Update report', 9 Apr 1991.
21. *Bridge News*, 'Trading for change', Caroline Lucas, Issue 8, October 1990.
22. C. Barnett, N. Clarke, P. Cloke and A. Malpass, 'The political rationalities of Fair-Trade consumption in the United Kingdom', *Politics and Society*, 35.4 (2007), pp. 583–607.
23. R. Mitchell, B. Agle, and D. Wood, 'Toward a theory of stakeholder identification and salience: Defining the principle of who and what really counts', *Academy of Management Review*, 22.4(1997), pp. 853–886.
24. Ibid.
25. J. Holiman, *Consumers' Guide to the Protection of the Environment* (London: Friends of the Earth, Pan /Ballantine Books, 1971).
26. Ibid., p. 119.
27. Ibid., p. 206.
28. J. Elkington, 'Costing the earth – The urgent need to meet the challenge of securing a greener environment', *The Guardian* (27 November 1987); H. Thomas, 'Growing demand from the new conscious consumers', *The Guardian* (6 January 1988); B. Laurance, 'The greening of supermarkets as shoppers get the message' *The Guardian* (13 September 1988); R. North, 'Consumed with various shades of green' *The Independent* (23 September 1989); M. McCarthy, 'New force in the land: The Green Consumer', *The Times* (5 June 1989).
29. H. Thomas, 'Growing demand from the new conscious consumers', *The Guardian* (6 January 1988).
30. Elkington and Hailes, *The Green Consumer's Supermarket Shopping Guide.*
31. Ibid.
32. Between 1961 and 1984, the number of greengrocers dropped by nearly two-thirds, the number of butchers and poulterers was cut in half, and the number of bakers also fell by nearly a third. Cited in Elkington and Hailes, *The Green Consumer's Supermarket Shopping Guide*, p. 7.
33. Elkington and Hailes, *The Green Consumer's Supermarket Shopping Guide.*
34. *Bridge News*, 'Trading for change', Caroline Lucas, Issue 8, October 1990.
35. Ibid.
36. Adams, 'Corporate social responsibility and the progressive market'.
37. R. Adams, J. Carruther and C. Fisher, *Shopping for a Better World: A Quick and Easy Guide to Socially Responsible Shopping* (London: Kogan Page, New Consumer, 1991).

38. Adams, 'Corporate social responsibility and the progressive market'.
39. *Bridge News*, 'Trading for change', Caroline Lucas, Issue 8 (October 1990).
40. 'Now the Supermarkets do what we tell them', *The Independent* (9 March 1991).
41. 'Trade facing shocks from ethical consumerism', *The Grocer* (22 September 1990).
42. 'Now the Supermarkets do what we tell them', *The Independent* (9 March 1991).
43. *Ethical Consumer (EC)*, Issue 1 (March 1989).
44. Ibid.
45. *EC* Issue 2 (May/June 1989).
46. *EC* Issue 17 (December 1991/January 1992), p. 2.
47. Ibid.
48. Ibid., p. 23.
49. Ibid.
50. R. Mitchell, B. Agle and D. Wood, 'Toward a theory of stakeholder identification and salience: Defining the principle of who and what really counts', *Academy of Management Review*, 22.4 (1997), pp. 853–886.
51. FTF/Tea/Premier: Meeting with Philip Mumby (26 June 1992).
52. FTF/Tea/CaseIntr: R. Adams, 'Premier Teas – The Typhoo quality assurance project' (8 January 1991).
53. FTF/TEA/FTFZ: FTF Executive Group, 'The Fairtrade Foundation and Premier Teas' (23 July 1992).
54. Ibid.
55. FTF/Tea/Premier: Meeting with Philip Mumby (26 June 1992).
56. Philip Mumby later became the founding Director and Chair of the Ethical Trading Initiative in 1997/1998.
57. FTF/Tea/Premier: Meeting with Philip Mumby (26 June 1992).
58. Oxfam: Bridge Information, 'Withdrawal of Darjeeling, Nilgiri and Assam Teas from the OT range' (1989).
59. FTF/Tea/Premier: Meeting with Philip Mumby (26 June 1992).
60. FTF/Tea/Kenya92: R. Adams, 'Visit to Kenyan tea estates' (August 1992).
61. Social Intrapreneurs are defined as corporate changemakers that work inside big business, to innovate and deliver market solutions to social and environmental challenges. SustainAbility (2008) 'The social Intrapreneur: A field guide for corporate changemakers'. Available http://www.sustainability.com/library.
62. Oxford, Bodleian Library, Oxfam archive (uncatalogued), Cafédirect papers 'R1244', project document, '*Establishing a New Ethical Coffee Brand for the UK*', 1 Nov 1990, p. 1.
63. Ibid., p. 2.
64. A. Jack, 'Fair Trade set to join free-range as a USP', *Financial Times* (11 October 1990).
65. Ibid.
66. Oxford, Bodleian Library, Oxfam archive (uncatalogued), Fairtrade Foundation papers 'R0716', Action guide no. 4, '*Why "Shopping for a Fairer World"?*', 1992.
67. Oxford, Bodleian Library, Oxfam archive (uncatalogued), Cafédirect papers 'R1244', 'Minutes of Cafédirect Consortium Meeting at Twin Trading', 12 Nov 1991.
68. CA/PUBS-CAN/3: 'Trade for Change', *Christian Aid News*, No 77 (October/December 1992).

69. Weak sales proved to be an issue when Cafédirect was introduced into Co-op stores. See Chapter 3.
70. Minutes of the Meetings of Directors of The Fairtrade Foundation: Special General Meeting (6 January 1994).
71. C. Sams, 'Case history: Green & Black's', in S. Wright and D. McCrea (eds.), *The Handbook of Organic and Fair Trade Food Marketing* (Oxford: Blackwell Publishing, 2007), p. 117.
72. In 1991 the sector was already worth £92 million and by 1997 annual sales had reached £250 million.
73. Support for smallholder farmers was reinforced by the Fairtrade Foundation in its recent strategy report: available http://www.fairtrade.net/fileadmin/user_upload/content/2009/news/2013-05-Fairtrade_Smallholder_Report_FairtradeInternational.pdf.
74. Sams, 'Case history: Green & Black's', p. 116.
75. C. Sams and J. Fairley, *Sweet Dreams: The Story of Green & Blacks* (London: Random House, 2009). p. 91.
76. Sams notes that they increased the price paid for cocoa to BZ$1.75 per pound – a few cents higher than originally agreed. Cited in Sams and Fairley, *Sweet Dreams*, p. 90.
77. Sams, 'Case history: Green & Black's', p. 117.
78. The announcement that Green & Black's intended to switch its entire worldwide food and beverage range to Fairtrade only came in January 2010 (four years after Green & Black's was sold to Cadbury and one month before Kraft's takeover of Cadbury). In March 2011, Green & Black's (and new owners Kraft) were able to confirm that it had met its target for full Fairtrade certification in the United Kingdom. Available http://www.guardian.co.uk/environment/2011/mar/08/green-blacks-fairtrade-pledge.
79. Sams and Fairley, *Sweet Dreams*, p. 201.
80. Ibid.
81. Ibid.
82. Sams and Fairley, *Sweet Dreams*, p. 202 (at the time there was no organic Fairtrade sugar available).
83. Sams, 'Case history: Green & Black's', p. 127.
84. The Guardian, 'How a £1.50 chocolate bar saved a Mayan community from destruction' (Sunday, 28 May 2006). Available http://www.theguardian.com/lifeandstyle/2006/may/28/foodanddrink.features1.
85. Sams, 'Case history: Green & Black's'.
86. The Guardian, 'How a £1.50 chocolate bar saved a Mayan community from destruction' (Sunday, 28 May 2006).
87. Originally the company was called The Day Chocolate Company in memory of Richard Day, a key member of the team at Twin that had helped Kuapa Kokoo develop its organisation. On 1 January 2007, Day Chocolate changed its name to Divine Chocolate Ltd to more closely align the company with its flagship brand.
88. A. Hutchens, *Changing Big Business: The Globalisation of the Fair Trade Movement* (Cheltenham: Edward Elgar Publishing, 2009).
89. Following the restructuring in 2006, Body Shop granted its shares to Kuapa Kokoo, and Oikocreadit was also brought on as a member organisation. Cited in Divine Annual Report 2005/06 available http://www.divinechocolate.com/uk/sites/default/files/img/893.pdf.

90. ECRA, *Ethical Consumer*, Issue 17 (December 1991/ January 1992), p. 23.
91. Select Committee on International Development Written Evidence, Memorandum submitted by Divine Chocolate, Trading Visions, Comic Relief and Kuapa Kokoo (February 2007). Available http://www.publications.parliament.uk/pa/cm200607/cmselect/cmintdev/356/356we03.htm.
92. B. Doherty and J. Meehan, 'Competing on social resources: The case of the Day Chocolate Company in the UK confectionery sector', *Journal of Strategic Marketing*, 14.4 (2006), pp. 299–313.
93. See Chapter 1.
94. *The Guardian*, 'Divine's sweet partnership with its supporters' (December 2011). Available http://www.theguardian.com/social-enterprise-network/2011/dec/12/divine-chocolate-supporters-social-enterprise-lesson.
95. Cited in Divine Annual Report 2005/06 Available http://www.divinechocolate.com/uk/sites/default/files/img/893.pdf.
96. Select Committee on International Development Written Evidence, Memorandum submitted by Divine Chocolate, Trading Visions, Comic Relief and Kuapa Kokoo (February 2007). Available http://www.publications.parliament.uk/pa/cm200607/cmselect/cmintdev/356/356we03.htm.
97. B. Doherty and J. Meehan, 'Competing on social resources: The case of the Day Chocolate Company in the UK confectionery sector'.
98. B. Doherty and S. Tranchell, 'Radical mainstreaming of Fairtrade: The case of The Day Chocolate Company', *Equal Opportunities International*, 26.7 (2007), pp. 693–711.
99. Ibid.
100. Ibid.
101. Father Shay Cullen, 'Fair Trade logos and marks must benefit the poor and not the rich' (2006). Available http://www.preda.org/archives/2006/r06032901.html.
102. 'Nestlé to Launch Fairtrade Coffee', (7 October 2005). Available http://www.prnewswire.co.uk/news-releases/nestle-to-launch-fairtrade-coffee-154042915.html.
103. *The Guardian*, 'Society: Environment: String-along or beanfeast?: Nestle's new brand has presented Fair Trade campaigners with a dilemma. Is it a sop or a sign of genuine reform?' (21 September 2005), p. 8.
104. Baby Milk Action Press Release, 'Fairtrade Mark and infant health could be damaged by Nestlé application warn campaigners', (6 October 2005). Available http://www.babymilkaction.org/press/press6oct05.html.
105. WDM Press Release, 'Nestlé FAIRTRADE Partners' Blend Coffee', Friday (7 October 2005). Available http://www.wdm.org.uk/news/presrel/current/nestle.htm.
106. M. Pemberton, 'Playing Fair [Trade] with Nestlé: The evolution of an unlikely partnership in the conventional coffee market', *Studies in Political Economy*, 87 (2011), pp. 65–92.
107. Ibid.
108. Fairtrade Foundation Press Release, 'Questions and answers about Nescafé Partners' Blend, (7 October 2005). Available http://www.fairtrade.org.uk/qa071005.htm.
109. M. Suchman, 'Managing legitimacy: Strategic and institutional approaches', *Academy of Management Review*, 20. 3 (1995), p. 574.

110. Twin Trading, 'Press Statement re: Launch of Nestlé Fairtrade Product', (7 October 2005). Available http://www.babymilkaction.org/action/twin trading1005.doc.
111. M. Jordan and N. Dawar. 'Nestlé Nescafe Partners' Blend: The Fairtrade decision (A)', *Ivey Case Studies* (2006).
112. Ibid.
113. Ibid.
114. Ibid.
115. In early 2004 Cafédirect, held 91.6% share in volume and 94.8% share in value of the UK Fairtrade instant coffee market. As other competitors entered, Cafédirect's share fell to 69.4% in volume and 77% in value by 2005.
116. Jordan and Dawar. 'Nestlé Nescafe Partners' Blend: The Fairtrade decision (A)'.
117. Nestlé to Launch Fairtrade Coffee (7 October 2005). Available http://www.prnewswire.co.uk/news-releases/nestle-to-launch-fairtrade-coffee-154042915.html.
118. With the delisting of Nescafé Partners' Blend from UK supermarkets Nestlé appear to be quietly discontinuing this Fairtrade coffee brand.
119. M. Pemberton, 'Playing Fair [Trade] with Nestlé: The evolution of an unlikely partnership in the conventional coffee market'.
120. Ibid., p. 85.
121. Nicholls and Opal, *Fair Trade.*
122. T. Crompton, *Common Cause: The Case for Working with our Cultural Values* (WWF, 2010). Available http://www.wwf.org.uk/wwf_articles.cfm?unewsid=4224
123. The Ecologist, 'Campaign Hero: Tom Crompton, Change Strategist at WWF-UK' (8th February 2011). Available http://www.theecologist.org/campaigning/culture_change/758398/campaign_hero_tom_crompton_change_strategist_at_wwfuk.html
124. Ibid.
125. Hudson et al., *Fair Trade, Sustainability and Social Change.*
126. The study was based on articles collected through Lexis-Nexis covering news stories from the United States, the United Kingdom, Canada, New Zealand, Australia and English-language newspapers from Japan and Spain. The decade-long sample covered the years 1997–2007.
127. Hudson et al., *Fair Trade, Sustainability and Social Change*, p. 112.
128. Ibid.
129. Ibid.
130. Fairtrade International, 'Fairtrade Theory of Change' (December 2013). Available: http://www.fairtrade.net/fileadmin/user_upload/content/2009/resources/140112_Theory_of_Change_and_Indicators_Public.pdf.

Conclusion: A New Direction for Consumer Politics

1. Fairtrade Foundation, 'Celebrating 20 years of the FAIRTRADE Mark in the UK' (10 January 2014). Available http://www.fairtrade.org.uk/en/media-centre/news/january-2014/celebrating-20-years-of-the-fairtrade-mark-in-the-uk.
2. G. Fridell, 'The co-operative and the corporation: Competing visions of the future of fair trade', *Journal of Business Ethics*, 86.1 (2009), 81–95.

3. Fairtrade Foundation, 'How businesses are going further to make International supply chains work for smallholder farmers' (February 2013).
4. D. Archibugi and D. Held (eds.), *Cosmopolitan Democracy: An Agenda for a New World Order* (Cambridge: Polity Press, 1995).
5. Ibid.
6. A. Carter, 'Nationalism and global citizenship', *Australian Journal of Politics and History* 43.1 (1997), p. 72.
7. P. Singer, 'Famine, affluence and morality', *Philosophy* and *Public Affairs* (1972), p. 232.
8. Ibid.
9. T. Lang and Y. Gabriel, 'A brief history of consumer activism', in R. Harrison, T. Newhom and D. Shaw (eds.), *The Ethical Consumer* (London: Sage, 2005), p. 53.
10. Ibid.
11. C. Gendron, V. Bisaillon and A. Rance, 'Institutionalization of Fair Trade: More than just a degraded form of social action', *Journal of Business Ethics* (Spring 2008).
12. M. Micheletti and A. Follesdal, 'Shopping for Human Rights. An introduction to the special issue', *Journal of Consumer Policy*, 30 (2007), pp. 167–175.
13. Ibid.
14. 'Is Fairtrade still fair?', *Ecologist* (1st February 2009). Available http://www.theecologist.org/News/news_round_up/270375/is_fairtrade_still_fair.html
15. B. Bowden, 'The Perils of global citizenship', *Citizenship Studies*, 7.3 (2003), p. 359.
16. Ibid.
17. Ibid.
18. Ibid.
19. I. Crewe, D. Searing and P. Conover, *Citizenship and Civic Education* (London: Citizenship Foundation, 1997).
20. This challenges Trentmann's interpretation that draws direct parallels between the nineteenth and early twentieth-century Free Trade campaigns and the late twentieth-century Fair Trade campaigns. F. Trentmann, *Free Trade Nation: Commerce, Consumption, and Civil Society in Modern Britain* (Oxford: Oxford University Press, 2008).
21. J. Vidal, 'Retail Therapy: Awareness of how and where goods are produced has soared – and so has the fair trade movement' *Guardian* (26 February 2003). Available http://www.guardian.co.uk/society/2003/feb/26/guardiansocietysupplement3.
22. D. Della Porta, *Social Movements An Introduction* (Oxford: Blackwell Publishing, second edition 2006), p. 4.
23. Ibid., p. 20.
24. For the most part the trade unions have remained on the periphery of the Fair Trade movement, but this in itself is an important finding as discussed in Chapter 4.
25. BBC News, 'Fair trade forum launch in Perth', (27 January 2007) Available http://news.bbc.co.uk/1/hi/scotland/tayside_and_central/6305673.stm
26. C. Barnett, N. Clarke, P. Cloke and A. Malpass, 'The political rationalities of Fair-Trade consumption in the United Kingdom', *Politics and Society*, 35.4 (2007), p. 602.

27. This list is not exhaustive but aims to highlight some of the most prominent and frequently cited individuals that both acted as an inspiration for early Fair Trade campaigners and developed important networks between organisations that would underpin the growth of the Fair Trade social movement.
28. J. Gabbaro, *The Dynamics of Taking Charge* (Cambridge, MA: Harvard Business School Press, 1987); N. M. Tichy and M. A. Devanna, *The Transformational Leader* (New York: John Wiley & Sons, 1986); D. Hambrick, 'The top Management Team: Key to Strategic Success', *California Management Review*, 30.1 Fall 1987, pp. 88–108; D. Nadler and M. Tushman, 'Beyond the Charismatic Leader: Leadership and organizational change', *California Management Review*, 32.2 (Winter 1990), pp. 77–97.
29. D. Nadler and M. Tushman, 'Beyond the Charismatic Leader', p. 82.
30. M. Diani and D. McAdam (eds.), *Social Movements and Networks: Relational Approaches to Collective Action* (Oxford: Oxford University Press, 2003); G. Davis, D. McAdam, W. Scott and M. Zayer (eds.), *Social Movements and Organization Theory* (Cambridge: Cambridge University Press, 2005); D. Snow, S. Soule and H. Kriesi (eds.), *The Blackwell Companion to Social Movements* (Oxford: Blackwell Publishing, 2003), K. McDonald, *Global Movements: Action and Culture* (Oxford: Blackwell Publishing, 2006).
31. M. Barratt Brown, 'Who Cares About Fair Trade?', Report of Conference on Development, and Cooperation, 4 September 1988, Conway Hall, London (Published by TWIN, December 1988), p. 3.
32. G. Dees, J. Emerson and P. Economy, *Enterprising Nonprofits: A Toolkit for Social Entrepreneurs* (New York: Wiley & Sons, Inc., 2001); C. Leadbeater, *The Rise of the Social Entrepreneur* (London: Demos, 1997); OECD, 'Fostering Entrepreneurship', *Organisation for Economic Co-Operation and Development*, 16 (1998), pp. 1–277; J. Nagler, 'The importance of social entrepreneurship for economic development policies' (3 April 2007). Available http://www.business4good.org/2007/04/importance-of-social-entrepreneurship.html.
33. J. Dees, J. Emerson and P. Economy, *Enterprising Nonprofits: A Toolkit for Social Entrepreneurs* (New York: Wiley & Sons, Inc., 2001), pp. 4–5.
34. G. Charles 'Fairtrade becomes mainstream with Cadbury initiative', *Marketing* (10 March 2009). Available http://www.marketingmagazine.co.uk/news/888519/Fairtrade-becomes-mainstream-Cadbury-initiative/
35. Carol Hanisch, 'The personal is political', in S. Firestone and Anne Koedt (eds.), *Notes from the Second Year: Women's Liberation* (New York: Radical Feminists, 1970).
36. 'What's behind Fair Trade success?', *Developments* (DFID) Issue 25, 5 April 2004.
37. A. Sheppard, 'Business women making work a greener place', *The Times* (24 June 2009).
38. Ibid.
39. B. Rosenbaum, 'Of women, hope, and angels', in K. Grimes B. Milgram (eds.), *Artisans and Cooperatives: Developing Alternative Trade for the Global Economy* (Tucson: University of Arizona Press, 2000), pp. 85–106; A. Tallontire, C. Dolan, S. Smith and S. Barrientos, 'Reaching the marginalized? Gender value chains and ethical trade in African horticulture', *Development in Practice*, 15.3/4 (2005), pp. 559–571; J. Steinkopf Rice, 'Free trade, Fair Trade and

gender inequality in less developed countries', *Sustainable Development*, Published Online: 30 March 2009, DOI, 10.1002/sd.407.

40. The NFWI were one of the early members of the Fairtrade Foundation, joining in 1993.
41. Ian Herbert, 'Women's Institute: It's not all jam and Jerusalem', *The Independent* (Friday, 11 November 2005). Available http://www.independent.co.uk/news/uk/this-britain/womens-institute-its-not-all-jam-and-jerusalem-514828.html.
42. NFWI, 'Fairtrade' Available http://www.thewi.org.uk/campaigns/current-campaigns-and-initiatives/fairtrade
43. NFWI, 'Recent mandates' Available http://www.thewi.org.uk/campaigns/resolutions-and-mandates/recent-resolutions
44. Soroptimist International is a worldwide organisation for women in management and the professions, working through service projects to advance human rights and the status of women.
45. A. Appadurai, 'Grassroots globalization and the research imagination', *Public Culture,* 12.1 (2000), pp. 1–19; M. Goodman, 'The mirror of consumption: Celebritisation, developmental consumption and the shifting cultural politics of Fair Trade', *Environment, Politics and Development Working Paper Series Department of Geography*, King's College London (2009); D. Brockington, 'Powerful environmentalisms: Conservation, celebrity and capitalism', *Media, Culture and Society,* 30.4 (2008), pp. 551–568; W. Low and E. Davenport 'Has the medium (Roast) become the Message? The ethics of marketing Fair Trade in the mainstream', *International Marketing Review*, 22.5 (2004), pp. 494–511.
46. M. Goodman, 'The mirror of consumption: Celebritisation, developmental consumption and the shifting cultural politics of Fair Trade', p. 2.
47. Ibid.
48. In 1950, only 380,000 licenses were issued but by 1968 there was more than 15.5 million; more than 90% of adults lived in homes that possessed a television set. Statistics cited in S. Glynn and A. Booth, *Modern Britain: An Economic and Social History* (London: Routledge, 1995) p. 203.
49. On 1 April 1957, a Panorama programme, narrated by Richard Dimbleby, featured a family from Ticino in Switzerland carrying out their annual spaghetti harvest. At the time, spaghetti was not a widely eaten food in the United Kingdom and was considered by many as an exotic delicacy. Hundreds of people called the corporation after the broadcast asking where they could get hold of a spaghetti bush so they could grow their own crop. Available http://news.bbc.co.uk/onthisday/hi/dates/stories/april/1/newsid_2819000/2819261.stm.
50. Interview, April 2009, with David Hart, Producer on, *Cost of a Cup of Tea.*
51. Goodman, 'The mirror of consumption', p. 3.
52. 'Black Gold' directed by Mark and Nick Francis (2005). Available http://www.blackgoldmovie.com/; 'Just Coffee' produced by Consumers International (2006). Available http://www.consumersinternational.org/Templates/News.asp?NodeID=94997; 'The Bitter Aftertaste' directed by Philip Thompson (2006). Available http://www.worldwrite.org.uk/bitter/; 'The Bitter Taste of Tea' directed by Tom Heinemann (2009). Available http://www.flipthecoin.org/the-films/the-bitter-taste-of-tea/.

53. C. Barnett, N. Clarke P. Cloke and A. Malpass, 'The political rationalities of Fair-Trade consumption in the United Kingdom,' p. 596.
54. Ibid.
55. Ibid.
56. C. Brown, *The Death of Christian Britain: Understanding secularisation 1800–2000* (London: Routledge, 2001), p. 3.
57. 'The size of the aid programme is but one reflection of an enduring feature of central government in Britain: the department responsible for development co-operation is politically weak ... In 1988 net public expenditure on overseas aid was a meagre 0.85 per cent of government expenditure.' A. Bose and P. Burnell, *Britain's Overseas Aid since 1979: Between Idealism and Self-interest* (Manchester: MUP, 1991), p. 15.
58. F. Prochaska, *Christianity & Social Service in Modern Britain: The Disinherited Spirit* (Oxford: Oxford University Press, 2006), p. 13.
59. S. J. D. Green, *Religion in the Age of Decline: Organisation and Experience in Industrial Yorkshire 1870–1920* (Cambridge: Cambridge University Press, 1996); S. C. Williams, *Religious Belief and Popular Culture in Southwark, c. 1880–1939* (Oxford: Oxford University Press,1999); M. A. Smith, *Religion in Industrial Society: Oldham and Saddleworth, 1740–1865* (Oxford: Clarendon Press, 1994); J. N. Morris, *Religion and Urban Change: Croydon, 1840–1914* (Woodbridge: Royal Historical Society, 1992).
60. G. Davie, *Religion in Britain since 1945: Believing without Belonging* (Oxford: Blackwell, 1994), p. 2.
61. Ibid.
62. Ibid., p. 43.
63. The only exception is the tensions that led to the division within Tear Craft and the formation of Traidcraft. But there is no evidence that this received any negative media coverage that would have impacted on public perceptions of either of these Fair Trade companies.
64. When asked, 'Do you think it is proper for churches to speak out on Third World problems?' Across Europe, 76% of respondents answered yes. D. Barker, *The European Values Study 1981–1990* (Gordon Cook Foundation, 1991). p. 47.
65. Fairtrade Foundation, Annual Review (2007/2008), p. 7.
66. A. Ahmed Khan and L. Thaut, *An Islamic Perspective on Fair Trade* (Birmingham: Islamic Relief Worldwide, 2008), p. 12. Available http://policy.islamic-relief.com/wp-content/uploads/2014/05/Islam_and_Fairtrade.pdf
67. Ibid.
68. CAFOD*, Christian Aid*, Methodist Relief and Development Fund, SCIAF, Tearfund, Traidcraft Exchange*, United Reformed Church. *Founder Member. Fairtrade Foundation, Annual Review (2007/2008). Available http://www.fairtrade.org.uk/includes/documents/cm_docs/2008/a/annual_review.pdf.
69. Initial studies of Fairtrade Town's suggest that the proportion of Christian volunteers is substantial. There are a series of research projects currently underway looking at Fairtrade Town campaign groups and it is expected that these will be able to shed more light on the numbers of Christian supporters.
70. There are parallels here with Traidcraft's approach: 'I was very conscious of how "Christian language" might alienate people', in R. Adams (ed.), *Who Profits?* (Oxford: Lion Publishing, 1989), p. 159.

71. J. Morris, 'The strange death of Christian Britain: Another look at the secularization debate', *The Historical Journal,* 46.4 (2003), p. 976.
72. Recent examples include: In May 2004, Archbishop of Wales, Barry Morgan backed the Wales Fair Trade Forum's initiative to make Wales the first Fair Trade nation. ('Backing for Fair Trade country bid', *BBC online,* May 2004). In April 2005, speaking at St Paul's Cathedral to mark the 60th anniversary of the Christian Aid, the Archbishop of Canterbury, Dr Rowan Williams, challenged a 'naive faith in free trade' that was stripping some countries of their economic power and hampering efforts to overcome poverty. ('Williams attacks "global scandal"', *BBC Online,* Tuesday, 26 April 2005). In October 2007, The Archbishop of York, Dr John Sentamu, called for a boycott of all chocolate that is not certified as Fairtrade. ('If that chocolate is not Fairtrade, then don't buy it, says the Archbishop of York', *The Times,* 31 October 2007).
73. IFAT, originally stood for the International Federation for Alternative Trade (1989), it changed its name to the International Fair Trade Association and in 2009 became the World Fair Trade Organisation.
74. Carol Wills cited in A. Nicholls and C. Opal, *Fair Trade: Market-Driven Ethical Consumption* (London: Sage, 2004), p. 12.
75. Although as discussed in Chapter 2, liberation theology demonstrated the possibility of a socially responsible, political, Christian ethic.
76. *Multi National Corporations, The Co-operative Alternative* (Warsaw, ICA Congress, 1972); Overseas Development Institute, *A Third Force for the Third World: A Study of the Channels for Investment of Church Trust Funds in Economic Development* (1972) CA2/D/14; Christian Aid, *The European Community and the Third World* letter to EC commissioners (25 April 1973) CA2/D/11; ICFTU, Working Party on Multinational Companies (11–12 September 1975) MSS.292D/954.9/1:ICFTU/ITS.
77. Oxford, Bodleian Library, Oxfam archive (uncatalogued), Directorate correspondence, 'HS/5 Bridge', report by R. Scott, 'What, Why, How: Bridge summarized', 1973.
78. Ibid.
79. Fairtrade Foundation Minutes, Twentieth meeting (8 March 1995).
80. In April 1999 the following statement was agreed by IFAT and FLO: 'Fair Trade is *an alternative approach* to conventional trade. It is a trading partnership which aims at sustainable development for excluded and disadvantaged producers. It seeks to do this by providing better trading conditions, by awareness raising and by campaigning.' Quoted in J. M. Krier, *Fair Trade in Europe 2001: Facts and Figures on the Fair Trade Sector in 18 European Countries* (Maastricht; EFTA, 2001). In 2009 the revised definition of Fair Trade no longer referred to 'an alternative approach' but instead called for 'greater equity in international trade'. *A Charter of Fair Trade Principles* (January 2009).
81. Carol Wills cited in A. Nicholls and C. Opal, *Fair Trade: Market-Driven Ethical Consumption* (London: Sage, 2004), p. 12.
82. Oxford, Bodleian Library, Oxfam archive (uncatalogued), Bridge Committee minutes and papers, B. Yates, 'From the Margins to the Mainstream', Sept 1990.
83. A. Nicholls and C. Opal, *Fair Trade: Market-Driven Ethical Consumption* (London: Sage, 2004).
84. M. K. Goodman, 'Reading Fair Trade: Political ecological imaginary and the moral economy of Fair Trade foods', *Political Geography,* 23 (2004), p. 901.

85. Nicholls and Opal, *Fair Trade*, p. 31.
86. T. Lang, 'A food crisis is heading our way', *The Guardian* (16 October 2008).
87. Ibid.
88. 'Looking Back, Looking Forward: lessons in choice editing for sustainability' (May 2006), research report by the Sustainable Consumption Roundtable – a joint initiative of the National Consumer Council and the Sustainable Development Commission.
89. Olivier Le Brun, Director of TWIN and Twin Trading, Bridges Not Fences: Report of the Third World Trade and Technology Conference (London February 1985), p. 7.
90. Harriet Lamb, Executive Director, Fairtrade Foundation (4 March 2009). Available http://www.fairtrade.org.uk/press_office/press_releases_and_statements/march_2009/cadbury_dairy_milk_commits_to_going_fairtrade.aspx.
91. Fairtrade Foundation, *Introducing the Fairtrade: A Guide to the Fairtrade Mark and the Fairtrade Foundation* (London: 2000).
92. Fairtrade certification: net retail value, 2007, in 000 €: UK = 704,300, USA = 730,800. Cited in, J. Krier, *Fair Trade 2007: New Facts and Figures from an Ongoing Success Story – A Report on Fair Trade in 33 Consumer Countries* (Dutch Association of Worldshops, Netherlands, August 2008), p. 18; DFID, *Eliminating World Poverty: Building our Common Future* (London: The Stationery Office, July 2009), p. 43.
93. G. Charles, 'Starbucks' UK outlets to convert to Fairtrade coffee', *Marketing* (26 November 2008). Available http://www.marketingmagazine.co.uk/news/865224/Starbucks-UK-outlets-convert-Fairtrade-coffee/
94. Starbuck's commitment to wider 'fair trade' practices came under scrutiny when it was revealed that it had only paid £8.6 million in corporation tax from 1998 to 2012 despite sales of over £3 billion. Available http://www.bbc.co.uk/news/uk-20650945
95. 'Sip Coffee with a conscience', *The Age*, Melbourne (27 May 2006).
96. Ibid.
97. October, 2010, TransFair controversially changed its name to Fair Trade USA, prompting a discussion about who owns Fair Trade. Available http://www.globalexchange.org/blogs/fairtrade/2011/01/18/who-owns-fair-trade/.
98. D. Jaffee, *Brewing Justice: Fair Trade Coffee, Sustainability, and Survival* (Berkley: University of California Press, 2007), p. 207.
99. Ibid.
100. L. Raynold, D. Murray and J. Wilkinson, *Fair Trade: The Challenges of Transforming Globalization* (London: Routledge, 2007).
101. Fair Trade USA, 'Fair Trade USA Resigns Fairtrade International (FLO) Membership', (15 September 2011) Available http://fairtradeusa.org/press-room/press_release/fair-trade-usa-resigns-fairtrade-international-flo-membership.
102. I. Hudson, M. Hudson and M. Fridell, *Fair Trade, Sustainability and Social Change* (Basingstoke: Palgrave Macmillan, 2013), p. 15.
103. Ibid., p. 43.
104. Ibid., p. 112.
105. Marlike Kocken, Manager of EFTA, 'Sixty years of Fair Trade: A brief history of the Fair Trade movement' (November 2006); Stefan Durwael, General

Director of Fair Trade Organisatie, 'The Development of Fair Trade in the Netherlands' (Fair Trade Organisatie, Culemborg, 1994); Bob Thomson, Managing Director TransFair Canada, 'A brief history of Fair Trade labels', unpublished (Ottawa, August 1995).

106. Bob Thomson, Managing Director TransFair Canada, 'A brief history of Fair Trade labels', unpublished (Ottawa, August 1995).
107. Ibid.
108. Ibid.
109. I have undertaken some preliminary archive research into the history of Oxfam Australia and Trade Winds. Although there has only been a national Fairtrade labelling initiative in Australia since 2003 the history of the movement dates back to the 1970s (as it does in Europe). But this research indicates potentially significant differences within the Australian national context that require further consideration, such as tariff barriers implemented to protect Australian farmers that produce goods such as bananas and mangoes.
110. V. Shiva, 'The living democracy movement: Alternatives to the Bankruptcy of globalization', in W. Fisher and T. Ponniah (eds.), *Another World is Possible: Popular Alternatives to Globalization at the World Social Forum* (London: Zed Books, 2003), p. 115.
111. Sybrandus Adema interview with Boudewijn Goossens, Executive Director of Fairtrade Label South Africa (FLSA), 'Q&A: The South can also be consumers of Fair Trade products', *Inter Press Service* (21 July 2009); D. Jaffee, *Brewing Justice: Fair Trade Coffee, Sustainability, and Survival* (Berkley: University of California Press, 2007).
112. Consumers International, From Bean to Cup: How consumer choice impacts upon coffee producers and the environment (December 2005).
113. M. Hilton, *Prosperity for All: Consumer Activism in an Era of Globalization* (Cornell University Press, 2009).
114. G. Fridell, *Fair Trade Coffee: The Prospects and Pitfalls of Market-Driven Social Justice* (Toronto: University of Toronto Press, 2007).
115. Oxford, Bodleian Library, Oxfam archive (uncatalogued), Directorate correspondence, 'HS/5 Bridge', report by R. Scott, 'What, Why, How: Bridge summarized', 1973.

Bibliography

1 Archival and unpublished sources

Oxfam Archive: Bicester/Bodleian Library

The Oxfam archive has recently moved to the Bodleian Library. The cataloguing of the Oxfam archive is being approached in three 18-month phases, with a tranche of the archive becoming available to researchers at the completion of each stage. The entire historic archive will become available to researchers in June 2017.

Oxfam, Bridge, HS/5
HS/5 Bridge File: Bridge Resolution 1 – The Purpose, and Motivations of Bridge, 1975
Bridge Resolution 2 – How Bridge Profits are used, 1975
Bridge Mail Order Catalogue, 1976
Bridge Inland Revenue enquiry, 1975
Future of the Helping by Selling Project by Roy Scott, 3 May 1972
Oxfam, Bridge Com – Bridge Committee Minutes, 1976–1983, 1989–1992
Oxfam, OA – Oxfam Activities Limited / Oxfam Trading: Board meeting minutes and papers 1976–1982
Oxfam, Executive Com – Executive Committee papers: April 1966 – November 1994
Oxfam, Information Department – Oxfam Information Department File 1972–1973
Oxfam, JS, R1106 – Bridge an Evaluation by Jonathon Stockland, April 1986

Oxfam, FTF, R0716 – Fairtrade Foundation reports, 1989–1996
Oxfam, CD, R1244 – Cafédirect reports, 1990–1992

Bernard Murphy, Oxfam Liaison Officer, Co-operatives & Trade Unions
R1492: 27(3) 10 – Correspondence
R1492: 27 (3) 4 – Correspondence
R1584 – Triple Agency Sub-committee papers August 1978
R1584 – Press Cuttings
PUB/166 – Robin Sharp, *Whose Right to Work? International Aspects of Employment in Britain and the Developing Countries and their Implications for UK Policy* (Oxfam 1976)
R0648 TUIREG – Trade Unions working for Development 1995 Annual Report
R0284 Nicaragua TUC Bluefields Appeal 1989
Oxfam's work with Trade Unions and other Workers' Associations overseas. 27 April 1989
R0285 TUC South African Appeal 1990
Campaigning and Fundraising on South African Trade Unions
R1497 Oxford Committee for Famine relief – conference report August 1960

R1495 VAT Proposed Amendment
R1494 UN Trade and Development Conference press cuttings

Christian Aid Archive: SOAS, London

Christian Aid Series I deposited at SOAS 27 June 1985
CA/A/1/6: Botswana: General Correspondence, 1963–1967
CA/A/11/2: Botswana: Agricultural training and development, 1966–1967
CA/C/2/5: Ceylon: General Correspondence, 1958–1968
CA/F/4/2: Food for the Hungry Campaign Extent of World Hunger, 1963–1968
CA/F/4/3: Food for the Hungry Campaign Projects for Oxfam, 1963–1968
CA/F/5/3: Food for the Hungry Campaign Committee minutes, 1963–1968
CA/I/6/3: Minutes of Social Responsibility Department, 1962
CA/I/10/9: International Council of Voluntary Agencies
CA/J/1: Britain's Role in the Second Development Decade, 1972
CA/J/2: Overseas Aid Series – The Aid Booklets, 1974
CA/J/4: One World Series, Patterns of International Trade, A Fair Slice of the Cake for tea etc.
CA/J/5: The Politics of Aid, The Christian Aid Story, Brazilian Blend etc.

Christian Aid Series II deposited at SOAS 1990
CA2/A/3/9: Botswana15: Social Action Programme, 1971
CA2/D/1/1: Charity Commissioners, 1962–1964
CA2/D/1/2: Charity Commissioners, 1965–1966
CA2/D/1/3: Christian Aid Constitution, 1964–1967
CA2/D/3/5: Christian Aid Board trading Company, 1970
CA2/D//3/8: Director – Correspondence with staff, 1969–1970
CA2/D/9/1: Director's reports, 1972
CA2/D/9/13: New Internationalist, 1972
CA2/D/11/3: Director's visit to South Africa
CA2/D/14/11: Investment Matters – A Third Force for the Third World, 1974
CA2/D/14/12: Meeting on Church investments, 2 May 1974
CA2/D/15/14: South Africa, 1974
CA2/D/22/3: Oxfam, 1975
CA2/D/24/4: South Africa, 1975
CA2/E/11/8: UK 181: Third World Road Show, 1974
CA2/I/8/1: WCC/ICA Self Help Projects, 1963–1966
CA2/I/47/6: Overseas Development Institute, 1966–1969

Christian Aid Series III deposited at SOAS 1995
Asia/Pacific:
CA/3/45: Philippines – Skillshop – Iloilo city, 1978–1983
CA/3/46: Artisans Training Project, Pakistan, 1977–1980
CA/3/59: Appropriate technology Development Unit, 1974–1979
CA/3/78: Consumers Association of Penang – Correspondence and reports, 1978–1981
Latin America/Caribbean:
CA/3/15: Handicrafts and Semi-industrial workshop, Chile, 1974
CA/3/40: FASE – Brazil (mainly Portuguese), 1976–1977

CA/3/41: FASE – Brazil, 1981–1983
CA/3/101: Development Projects and Relief, 1973–1974

Christian Aid Series IV deposited at SOAS 2005
CA5/G/147: Latin America and Caribbean: Brazil and FASE, 1985–1988
CA5/G/147A: Latin America and Caribbean: Brazil and Sem Terra, 1983–1988
CA5/C/283B: Asia: Sri Lanka, Plantation People's Welfare Trust, 1978–1986
CA5/C/247: Asia: Philippines, 1982–1988
CA5/C/145: Asia: World Council of Churches priority projects reports, 1984–1988
CA5/A/371: Africa/Middle East: South Africa, 1987–1988

TUC Archive: Modern Records Centre, University of Warwick

MSS. 292D/900-993 International, Europe, Asia, Africa, America, Australia 1970–1990

MSS.292D/901/1-39 **International Committee** 1970 October–1990 July

MSS.292D/901/1 **International Committee: Minutes** 1970 October–1971 August

MSS.292D/901/2 **International Committee: Minutes** 1971 October–1972 February

MSS.292D/901/3 **International Committee: Minutes** 1972 March–August

MSS.292D/901/4 **International Committee: Minutes** 1972 October–1973 March

MSS.292D/901/5 **International Committee: Minutes** 1973 April–August

MSS.292D/901/6 **International Committee: Minutes** 1973 October–1974 August

MSS.292D/901/7 **International Committee: Minutes** 1974 October–1975 February

MSS.292D/901/8 **International Committee: Minutes** 1975 March–August

MSS.292D/901/9 **International Committee: Minutes** 1975 October–1976 March

MSS.292D/901/10 **International Committee: Minutes** 1976 April–August

MSS.292D/901/11 **International Committee: Minutes** 1976 October–1977 August

MSS.292D/901/12 **International Committee: Minutes** 1977 October – 1978 January

MSS.292D/901/13 **International Committee: Minutes** 1978 February–August

MSS.292D/901/14 **International Committee: Minutes** 1978 October – 1979 March

MSS.292D/901/15 **International Committee: Minutes** 1979 April–August

MSS.292D/901/16 **International Committee: Minutes** 1979 October–1980 March

MSS.292D/901/17 **International Committee: Minutes** 1980

MSS.292D/901/18 **International Committee: Minutes** 1980 October–1981 March

MSS.292D/901/19 **International Committee: Minutes** 1981 April–August

MSS.292D/901/20 **International Committee: Minutes** 1981 October–1982 January

MSS.292D/901/21 **International Committee: Minutes** 1982 February–May

MSS.292D/901/22 **International Committee: Minutes** 1982 June–August

MSS.292D/901/23 **International Committee: Minutes** 1982 September–1983 February

MSS.292D/901/24 **International Committee: Minutes** 1983 March–August

MSS.292D/901/25 **International Committee: Minutes** 1983 October–1984 March

MSS.292D/901/26 **International Committee: Minutes** 1984 April–July

MSS.292D/901/27 **International Committee: Minutes** 1984 October–1985 February

MSS.292D/901/28 **International Committee: Minutes** 1985 March–April

MSS.292D/901/29 **International Committee: Minutes** 1985 June–August

MSS.292D/901/30 **International Committee: Minutes** 1985 October–1986 March

MSS.292D/901/31 **International Committee: Minutes** 1986 April–August

MSS.292D/901/32 **International Committee: Minutes** 1986 October–1987 January

MSS.292D/901/33 **International Committee: Minutes** 1987 February–August

MSS.292D/901/34 **International Committee: Minutes** 1987 October - 1988 February

MSS.292D/901/35 **International Committee: Minutes** 1988 March–July

MSS.292D/901/36 **International Committee: Minutes** 1988 October - 1989 February

MSS.292D/901/37 **International Committee: Minutes** 1989 March–July

MSS.292D/901/38 **International Committee: Minutes** 1989 October–1990 April

MSS.292D/901/39 **International Committee: Minutes** 1990 April–July

MSS.292D/905.234/1–3 **War: Famine Relief (Oxfam)** 1970–1990

MSS.292D/905.234/1 **War: Famine Relief (Oxfam)** 1970–1981

MSS.292D/905.234/2 **War: Famine Relief (Oxfam)** 1981–1985

Correspondence & reports, including fundraising for the African drought and Ethiopian famine of 1984–1985.

MSS.292D/905.234/3 **War: Famine Relief (Oxfam)** 1985–1990

MSS.292D/912–919 International Trades Union Organisations 1961–1990

MSS.292D/918/1–4 **International Trade Unions: World Federation of Trade Unions** 1961–1990

MSS.292D/918/1 **International Trade Unions: World Federation of Trade Unions** 1961–1978

MSS.292D/918/2 **International Trade Unions: World Federation of Trade Unions** 1979–1980

MSS.292D/918/3 **International Trade Unions: World Federation of Trade Unions** 1980–1985

MSS.292D/918/4 **International Trade Unions: World Federation of Trade Unions** 1986–1990

MSS.292D/919/1-3 **International Confederation of Free Trade Unions: General** 1970–1990

MSS.292D/919/1 **International Confederation of Free Trade Unions: General** 1970–1979

MSS.292D/919/2 **International Confederation of Free Trade Unions: General** 1980 January–1985 July

MSS.292D/919/3 **International Confederation of Free Trade Unions: General** 1985 September–1990 July

Includes material on subject of violations of Trade Union rights.

MSS.292D/919.12/1 **International Confederation of Free Trade Unions: minutes and papers of the ICFTU Executive Board** 1971–1972

Relating to amendments to the ICFTU's constitution.

MSS.292D/919.2/1–8 **International Confederation of Free Trade Unions: Minutes and Reports (Executive Board etc)** 1970–1990

MSS.292D/919.2/1 **International Confederation of Free Trade Unions: Minutes and Reports (Executive Board etc)** 1970–1977

MSS.292D/919.2/2 **International Confederation of Free Trade Unions: Minutes and Reports (Executive Board etc)** 1978–1982

MSS.292D/919.2/3 **International Confederation of Free Trade Unions: Minutes and Reports (Executive Board etc)** 1982–1985

MSS.292D/919.2/4i–ii **International Confederation of Free Trade Unions: Minutes and Reports (Executive Board etc)** 1988 December

Agenda items and supporting papers.

MSS.292D/919.2/5 **International Confederation of Free Trade Unions: Minutes and Reports (Executive Board etc)** 1989 May

Agenda items and supporting papers.

MSS.292D/919.2/6 **International Confederation of Free Trade Unions: Minutes and Reports (Executive Board etc)** 1985–1986

MSS.292D/919.2/7 **International Confederation of Free Trade Unions: Minutes and Reports (Executive Board etc)** 1986–1988

MSS.292D/919.2/8 **International Confederation of Free Trade Unions: Minutes and Reports (Executive Board etc)** 1988–1990

MSS.292D/919.21/1 **International Confederation of Free Trade Unions: Committee correspondence** 1970 September–1972 August

Correspondence, notices and papers relating mainly to the ICFTU Executive Board, but also other ICFTU committees.

MSS.292D/919.21/2 **International Confederation of Free Trade Unions: Committee correspondence** 1972 September–1978 December

Correspondence, notices and papers relating mainly to the ICFTU Executive Board, but also other ICFTU committees.

MSS.292D/919.26/1–7 **International Confederation of Free Trade Unions: Congress** 1970–1989

MSS.292D/919.26/1 **International Confederation of Free Trade Unions: 1972 Congress** 1970–1973

Correspondence and papers relating to the ICFTU's Tenth World Congress (London, July 1972).

MSS.292D/919.26/2 **International Confederation of Free Trade Unions: 1975 Congress** 1974–1977

Correspondence and papers relating to the ICFTU's Eleventh World Congress (Mexico City, October 1975).

MSS.292D/919.26/3 **International Confederation of Free Trade Unions: 1979 Congress** 1978–1982

Correspondence, reports and papers relating to the ICFTU's Twelfth World Congress (Madrid, November 1979).

MSS.292D/919.26/4 **International Confederation of Free Trade Unions: 1983 Congress** 1982–1984

Correspondence, reports and papers relating to the ICFTU's Thirteenth World Congress (Oslo, June 1983).

MSS.292D/919.26/5 **International Confederation of Free Trade Unions: 1983 Congress** 1983

Reports circulated for the ICFTU's Thirteenth World Congress (Oslo, June 1983).

MSS.292D/919.26/6 **International Confederation of Free Trade Unions: 1988 Congress** 1986–1988

Correspondence and papers relating to the ICFTU's Fourteenth World Congress (Melbourne, March 1988).

MSS.292D/919.26/7 **International Confederation of Free Trade Unions: 1988 Congress** 1988–1989

Correspondence and papers relating to the ICFTU's Fourteenth World Congress (Melbourne, March 1988). Includes report on and decisions of Congress.

MSS.292D/919.7/1-4 **International Confederation of Free Trade Unions: Publicity and Propaganda** 1973–1990

MSS.292D/919.7/1 **International Confederation of Free Trade Unions: Publicity and Propaganda** 1973 February–June

Includes copy of an article on 'Discrimination against women' for Free Labour World.

MSS.292D/919.7/2 **International Confederation of Free Trade Unions: Publicity and Propaganda** 1976 September–1978 October

Includes issue 19 of International Trade Union News (October 1978).

MSS.292D/919.7/3 **International Confederation of Free Trade Unions: Publicity and Propaganda** 1981 April–1985 July

Includes issues of International Trade Union News.

MSS.292D/919.7/4 **International Confederation of Free Trade Unions: Publicity and Propaganda** 1986 July–1990 August

MSS.292D/931 Overseas Development 1970–1990

MSS.292D/931/1–13 **Social and economic conditions of under-developed countries** 1970–1990

MSS.292D/931/1 **Social and economic conditions of under-developed countries** 1970–1971

Correspondence and papers relating to developing countries

MSS.292D/931/2 **Social and economic conditions of under-developed countries** 1971–1974

Correspondence and papers relating to developing countries, development aid and the Second Development Decade.

MSS.292D/931/3 **Social and economic conditions of under-developed countries** 1975–1977

Correspondence and papers relating to developing countries and development issues.

MSS.292D/931/4 **Social and economic conditions of under-developed countries** 1977–1978

Correspondence, publications and papers relating to developing countries and development issues.

MSS.292D/931/5 **Social and economic conditions of under-developed countries** 1978

Correspondence, publications and papers relating to developing countries and development issues.

Includes World Development Charter 1978 and ICFTU Development Charter.

MSS.292D/931/6 **Social and economic conditions of under-developed countries** 1978–1979

Correspondence, reports and papers relating to developing countries and development issues.

MSS.292D/931/7 **Social and economic conditions of under-developed countries** 1980

Correspondence, reports and papers relating to developing countries and development issues.

Subjects include the Brandt Report and north-south co-operation and international trade.

MSS.292D/931/8 **Social and economic conditions of under-developed countries** 1980–1982

Correspondence, reports and papers relating to developing countries and development issues.

Subjects include the Brandt Commission and its second report, north-south issues and development education.

MSS.292D/931/9 **Social and economic conditions of under-developed countries** 1983–1985

Correspondence, reports and papers relating to developing countries and development issues.

Subjects include the Brandt Commission and Reports.

MSS.292D/931/10 **Social and economic conditions of under-developed countries** 1985–1986

Correspondence, reports and papers relating to developing countries and development issues.

Subjects include north-south co-operation and international trade.

MSS.292D/931/11 **Social and economic conditions of under-developed countries** 1986–1987

Correspondence, reports and papers relating to developing countries and development issues.

MSS.292D/931/12 **Social and economic conditions of under-developed countries** 1987–1989

Correspondence, reports and papers relating to developing countries and development issues.

MSS.292D/931/13 **Social and economic conditions of under-developed countries** 1989–1990

Correspondence, reports and papers relating to developing countries and development issues.

MSS.292D/931.03/1 **Social and economic conditions of under-developed countries: Overseas Aid Select Committee 1970** 1973–1974

Correspondence and papers (including a pattern of inquiry and draft submission) relating to a House of Commons Select Committee on Overseas Development, to which the TUC General Council had been invited to submit evidence.

MSS.292D/931.04/1 **Social and economic conditions of under-developed countries: Tariff Preferences** 1970–1972

Correspondence and papers relating to tariff preferences for developing countries, with special reference to the textiles and the clothing industry.

MSS.292D/931.06/1–5 **Social and economic conditions of under-developed countries: Overseas Development Institute** 1970–1990

MSS.292D/931.06/1 **Social and economic conditions of under-developed countries: Overseas Development Institute** 1970–1974

Correspondence, memoranda and publications relating to the ODI (including annual reports and accounts).

MSS.292D/931.06/2 **Social and economic conditions of under-developed countries: Overseas Development Institute** 1973–1977

Correspondence, memoranda and publications relating to the ODI.

MSS.292D/931.06/3 **Social and economic conditions of under-developed countries: Overseas Development Institute** 1978–1987

Correspondence and publications relating to the ODI. Correspondence mainly concerns discussion meetings.

MSS.292D/931.06/4 **Social and economic conditions of under-developed countries: Overseas Development Institute** 1987–1989

MSS.292D/931.06/5 **Social and economic conditions of under-developed countries: Overseas Development Institute** 1989–1990

MSS.292D/931.07/1 **Social and economic conditions of under-developed countries: Labour Party Overseas Development Study Group** 1971–1980

Correspondence and papers relating to the formation and work of the Study Group.

The study group on overseas development was established by the Labour Party's National Executive Committee to explore aspects of development assistance.

MSS.292D/931.3/1–5 **Minimum Standards of Social Policy Overseas Development Administration (ODA – ODM) Grant to TUC** 1975–1990

MSS.292D/931.3/1 **Minimum Standards of Social Policy Overseas Development Administration (ODA–ODM) Grant to TUC** 1975–1979

Correspondence and papers relating to the establishment and administration of a substantial grant from the Ministry of Overseas Development (ODM) to the TUC and a proposed 'Trade Union Foundation'.

The three-year grant from the Ministry of Overseas Development (to begin 1977–8) was to be used to promote the training and education of trade unionists from developing countries and to increase contacts between them and British trade unionists.

MSS.292D/931.3/2 **Minimum Standards of Social Policy Overseas Development Administration (ODA – ODM) Grant to TUC** 1979–1981

Correspondence and papers relating to the administration and future of the ODM/ODA (Overseas Development Administration) grant.

MSS.292D/931.3/3 **Minimum Standards of Social Policy Overseas Development Administration Grant to TUC** 1981–1983

Correspondence and papers relating to the administration of the ODA (Overseas Development Administration) grant.

MSS.292D/931.3/4 **Minimum Standards of Social Policy Overseas Development Administration Grant to TUC** 1983–1987

Correspondence and papers relating to the administration of the ODA (Overseas Development Administration) grant.

MSS.292D/931.3/5 **Minimum Standards of Social Policy Overseas Development Administration Grant to TUC** 1988–1990

Correspondence and papers relating to the administration of the ODA (Overseas Development Administration) grant.

Michael Ward Collection: London Metropolitan Archives

LMA/4282/01/005 – GLC and Twin Trading

LMA/4282/03/002 – Thatcher and abolition of GLC

LMA/4282/02/004 – The future of the GLEB

Archive of the Anti-Apartheid Movement, 1956–1968: Bodleian Library, University of Oxford.

A Boycott Movement papers, 1959–1961
Shelfmarks: MSS AAM 1–12
Committee of African Organisations' papers concerning establishment of Boycott Movement, 1959–60
Shelfmark: MSS AAM 1

Boycott Movement minutes, 1959–1960
Shelfmark: MSS AAM 2

Boycott Movement press releases, 1959–1960
Shelfmark: MSS AAM 3

C.3.3 Papers of multi-faith conferences, 1984–1988 Shelfmarks: MSS AAM 146–148

Inter-Faith Colloquium on Apartheid convened by Archbishop Trevor Huddleston in co-operation with the United Nations Special Committee Against Apartheid, March 1984
Shelfmark: MSS AAM 146

Multi-Faith conference planning meeting, September 1985
Shelfmark: MSS AAM 147

The Religious Struggle Against Apartheid. A consultation for people of all Faiths, September 1988
Shelfmark: MSS AAM 148

O.5 Consumer Boycott, 1960–1994

O.5.1 Correspondence and committee papers, 1960–1993

Shelfmarks: MSS AAM 1556–1558
General correspondence, 1960–1992
Shelfmark: MSS AAM 1556

London Boycott Working Group minutes and papers, 1986–1989
Shelfmark: MSS AAM 1557

Consumer Boycott Unit minutes and papers, 1988–1993
Shelfmark: MSS AAM 1558

C.3 Multi-Faith Committee, 1967–1994

C.3.2 General correspondence, 1974–1994
Shelfmarks: MSS AAM 145

General correspondence on religious matters, 1974–1994
Shelfmark: MSS AAM 145

C.3.4 Files on multi-faith issues, 1967–1994
Shelfmarks: MSS AAM 149–160

British Council of Churches/Council of Churches of Britain and Ireland, 1967–1992
Shelfmark: MSS AAM 149
Includes conference 'Britain and Southern Africa: the Way Forward', February 1989.

World Council of Churches, 1970–1992
Shelfmark: MSS AAM 150

Quakers, 1975–1992
Shelfmark: MSS AAM 151
Southern African News & Views, September 1985, Black Boycott Shuts Up Shops

Methodists, 1976–1981
Shelfmark: MSS AAM 152
Includes Methodist Task Force for Co-operative Action on Southern Africa, 1976–1979

Churches – general, 1980s
Shelfmark: MSS AAM 153

Multi-faith leaflets, 1980s
Shelfmark: MSS AAM 158

Background papers from various sources concerning South Africa and religion, 1970s–1990s
Shelfmark: MSS AAM 159–160

Community Aid Abroad (Oxfam Australia) Archive: University of Melbourne

81/122 CAA (Box 15) Index No. 84 Trade Action PTY LTD
1. Minutes of Directors' Meetings 5/11/1975–8/2/1979
2. Board Meeting Papers
2/1 1969–1970
2/2 October 1975 – December 1976
2/3 1977
2/4 1978/79

81/122 CAA (Box 16) State Correspondence
81/122 CAA (Box 17) Trade Action PTY LTD Correspondence

CAA 81/122 Box 18
3. Correspondence
3/6 Sale of Trade Action 1979
4. Balance Sheets & Financial Statements
4/1 Financial Statements 1966–1976
4/2 Reports 1975–1978

CAA 81/122 Box 20 Trade Action Pty Ltd Tanzania Project
CAA 81/122 Box 24 Press Cutting Books
3. Trade and Relating Matters
CAA 81/122 Box 62 Publications Misc. 1960s–1970s
CAA 81/122 Box 63 Publications Misc. 1960s–1970s
82/50 Newspaper Cuttings 1960s and 1970s Volume 1
82/50 Newspaper Cuttings 1960s and 1970s Volume 2

2nd Accession (1986) CAA 86/152
Box 5: 5 A – Trade Action 1972–1982
1) Finance – Trade Action profits 1969–1974
2) Correspondence
3) Tanzania Project – Report Tanzania Commodity Venture, 1
4) Reports

Newspapers and periodicals

Adbusters
Ethical Consumer
Green @ Work Magazine
The Guardian
The Independent
Shopper's Guide
Social Audit
The Telegraph
The Times
Which?

Unpublished theses

Brenheny, J. C. R. (1988). 'State and international aid charities in Britain, with particular reference to Oxfam UK, 1979–1988.' Ph.D. thesis, London School of Economics.

Coates, I. (1998). 'Green ideology in theory and practice: An examination of theories of green politics in relation to a sociological investigation to the worldview of Green Party activists.' Ph.D thesis, Bristol University.

Newholm, T. (2000). 'Understanding the ethical consumer: Employing a frame of bounded rationality.' Ph.D thesis, Open University.

Rahman, B. M. (1999). 'Constructing humanitarianism: Oxfam's humanitarian culture 1942–1994. Ph.D thesis, University of Aberystwyth.

Shaw, D. (2000). 'Consumed by ethics? A model building approach to ethical consumer decision-making.' Ph.D thesis, Glasgow Caledonian University.

2 Primary books and articles

Nineteenth and early twentieth century sources

Morris, W. (1884). *Useful Work versus Useless Toil*. London.

Morris, W. (1885). *How We Live and How We Might Live*. London.

Morris, W. (1890). *News from Nowhere*. London.

Multatuli (Edward Dowes Dekker) (1860). *Max Havelaar or The Copy Auctions of the Dutch Trading Company*. Holland.

Redfern, P. (1920). *The Consumers Place in Society*. Manchester.

Redfern, P. (1913). *The Story of the CWS: The Jubilee History of the Co-operative Wholesale Society Limited, 1863–1913*. Manchester.

Ruskin, J. (1864). *Sesame and Lilies*. London.

Ruskin, J. (1862). *Unto This Last: Four Essays on the First Principles of Political Economy*. London.

Late twentieth century sources

Adams, R. and C. Fisher (1991). *Shopping for a Better World*. London, Kogan Page.
Brandt, W. (1980). *North–South: A Programme for Survival*. London, Pan Books.
Bond, E. (1974). *The State of Tea*. London, War on Want.
Elkington, J. (1997). *Cannibals with Forks: The Triple Bottom Line of 21st Century Business*. Oxford, Capstone Publishing.
Elkington, J., Hailes, J. and D. Hill (1990). *The Young Green Consumers Guide*. London, Victor Gollancz.
Elkington, J. and J. Hailes (1988). *The Green Consumers Guide: From Shampoo to Champagne – High Street Shopping for a Better Environment*. London, Victor Gollancz.
Elkington, J. and T. Burke (1987). *The Green Capitalist: How Industry Can Make Money – and Protect the Environment*. Victor Gollancz, London.
Endersbee, M. (1973). *They Can't Eat Prayer: The Tear Fund Story*. London, Hodder and Stoughton.
Fairtrade Foundation (1997). *Spilling the Beans on the Coffee Trade*, London, Fairtrade Foundation.
Fairtrade Foundation (2000). *Unpeeling the Banana Trade*, London, Fairtrade Foundation.
Fisher, W. and T. Ponniah (eds.) (2003). *Another World is Possible: Popular Alternatives to Globalization at The World Social Forum*. London, Zed Books Ltd.
Hanlon, J. and R. Omond (1987). *The Sanctions Handbook*. Harmondsworth, Penguin Books.
Hines, C. (2000). *Localisation: A Global Manifesto*. London, Earthscan.
Holliman, J. (1971). *Consumer Guide to the Protection of the Environment*. London, Ballantine Books, Pan Books.
Krier, J. M. (2001). *Fair Trade in Europe: Facts and Figures on the Fair Trade Sector in 18 European Countries*. Maastricht, EFTA.
Lamb, H. (2008). *Fighting the Banana Wars and other Fairtrade Battles: How we Took on the Corporate Giants and Changed the World*. London, Rider.
Martinelli, E. (1995). *Fair Trade in Europe: Facts and Figures on the Fair Trade Sector in 14 European Countries*. Maastricht, EFTA.
Mehta, M. (1994). 'Fair trade coffee.' *Tea and Coffee Trade Journal*, 166(11): p. 70.
Millar, R.(1963). *The Affluent Sheep*. London, Longmans, p. 6.
Pearson, L. (1969). *Partners in Development: Report on the Commission on International Development*. London, Praeger.
Ransom, D. (2001). *The No-Nonsense Guide to Fair Trade*. Oxford, New Internationalist Publications.
Roddick, A. (ed.) (2001). *Take it Personally: How Globalisation Effects You and Powerful Ways to Challenge it*. Thorsons.
Sider, R. J. (1971). *Rich Christians in an Age of Hunger*. London, Hodder and Stoughton.
Shiva, V. (1996). *Globalization of Agriculture and the Growth of Food Insecurity*. New Dehli, Research Foundation for Science, Technology and Ecology.
Thompson, D. and R. Larson (1978). *Where were you, Brother?; An Account of Trade Union Imperialism*. London, War on Want.
Watkins, K. (1995). *The Oxfam Poverty Report*. Oxford, Oxfam.

Wells, P. and M. Jetter (1991). *The Global Consumer: Best Buys to Help the Third World.* London, New Consumer, Victor Gollancz.
Whitaker, B. (1983). *A Bridge of People: A Personal View of Oxfam's First Forty Years.* London, Heinemann.

Oxfam reports: Available http://policy-practice.oxfam.org.uk/publications

Oxfam International/ Clean Clothes Campaign, *Play Fair at the Olympics: Respect Workers' Rights in the Sportswear Industry* (April 2006).
Oxfam International, *Dumping on the World: How EU Sugar Policies Hurt* Poor Countries (April 2004).
Oxfam International, *Trading Away Our Rights: Women Working in Global Supply Chains* (April 2004).
Oxfam International, *Dumping Without Borders: How US Agricultural Policies are Destroying the Livelihoods of Mexican Corn Farmers* (August 2003).
Oxfam International, *Make Trade Fair in the Americas: Three Reasons to Say No to the FTAA* (January 2003).
Oxfam International, *Europe and the Coffee Crisis: A Plan for Action* (February 2003).
Oxfam International, *Mugged: Poverty in Your Coffee Cup* (April 2002).
Oxfam International, *Rigged Rules and Double Standards: Trade, globalisation and the fight against poverty* (May 20002).
Oxfam International, *Rigged Trade and Not Much Aid: How Rich Countries Help to Keep the Least Developed Countries Poor* (May 2001).
Oxfam GB, *Submission to the Government's White Paper on Globalisation* (May 2000).
Oxfam International, *Loaded against the poor: World Trade Organisation* (November 1999).

3 Secondary books and articles

Aaker, D. (1996). *Building Strong Brands.* New York, The Free Press.
Aaker, D. A. and G. S. Day (eds.) (1978). *Consumerism: Search for the Consumer Interest.* New York, The Free Press.
Aldridge, A. (1994). 'The Construction of National Consumption in Which? Magazine: The more Blobs the Better.' *Sociology,* 28(4): pp. 899–912.
Anderson, M. (2009). 'Cost of a Cup of Tea: Fair Trade and the British co-operative movement, c. 1960–2000', in L. Black and N. Robertson (eds.) *Consumerism and the Co-operative Movement in Modern British History: Taking stock.* Manchester, Manchester University Press, pp. 240–260.
Anderson, M. (2009). 'NGOs and Fair Trade: The Social Movement Behind the Label', in N. Crowson, M. Hilton and J. McKay (eds.) *NGOs in Contemporary Britain: Non-state Actors in Society and Politics since 1945.* Basingstoke, Palgrave Macmillan, pp. 222–241.
Anderson, M. (2012). 'Fairtrade: Partners in Development? A reassessment of trading partnerships within the Fairtrade model', in J. Dine and B. Granville (eds.) *The Processes and Practices of Fair Trade: Trust, ethics and governance.* London, Routledge, pp. 79–95.
Anderson, M., Booth, P. and S. Mohan (2014). 'Crossfire: does Fairtrade have more impact than conventional trade or trade certified by other sustainability standards?' *Food Chain,* 4 (1). pp: 7–13.

Andrews, M. (1997). *The Acceptable Face of Feminism: The Women's Institute as a Social Movement.* London Lawrence & Wishart Ltd.

Atkinson, D. and L. Elliott (1998). *The Age of Insecurity.* London, Verso.

Attala, A. and M. Carrigan (2001). 'The myth of the ethical consumer: Do ethics matter in purchase behaviour?' *Journal of Consumer Marketing,* 18(7): pp. 560–578.

Bahadur, C. and R. Mendoza (2002). 'Toward free and fair trade: A global public good perspective.' *Challenge,* 45(5) (September/October): pp. 21–62.

Barnet, R. and J. Cavanagh (1994). *Global Dreams: Imperial Corporations and the New World Order.* New York, Simon & Schuster.

Barnett, P. (2001). 'Fair Trade in tourism.' *Industry and Environment,* 24(3/4): pp. 18–19.

Barnett, C., Clarke, N., Cloke, P. and A. Malpass (2005). 'The political ethics of consumerism.' *Consumer Policy Review,* 15(2): pp. 45–51.

Barnett, C., Clarke, N., Cloke, P. and A. Malpass (2007). 'Fairtrade Urbanism? The politics of place beyond place in the Bristol Fairtrade city campaign.' *International Journal of Urban and Regional Research,* 31(3): pp. 633–645.

Barnett, C., Clarke, N., Cloke, P. and A. Malpass (2007). 'The political rationalities of Fair-Trade consumption in the United Kingdom.' *Politics and Society,* 35(4): pp. 583–607.

Barratt Brown, M. (1993). *Fair Trade: Reform and Realities in the International Trading System.* London, Zed Books.

Barrientos, S. (2000). 'Globalisation and ethical trade: Assessing the implications for development.' *Journal of International Development,* 12(4): pp. 559–570.

Barrientos, S. and C. Dolan (2006). *Ethical Sourcing in the Global Food System.* London, Earthscan.

Barrientos, S., McClenaghan, S. and Orton L. (2000). 'Ethical trade and South African deciduous fruit exports – Addressing gender sensitivity.' *European Journal of Development Research,* 12(1): pp. 140–158.

Bastiaensen, J. and R. Mendoza (2003). 'Fair trade and the coffee crisis in Nicaraguan Segovias.' *Small Enterprise Development,* 14(2(June)): pp. 36–47.

Baudrillard, J. (1998). *The Consumer Society: Myths and Structures.* London, Sage.

Bauman, Z. (1998). *Globalisation: The Human Consequences.* Cambridge, Polity.

Benson, J. (1994). *The Rise of Consumer Society in Britain, 1880–1980.* London, Longman.

Berg, M. and H. Clifford (eds.) (1999). *Consumers and Luxury: Consumer Culture in Europe, 1650–1850.* Manchester, Manchester University Press.

Bevir, M. and F. Trentmann (eds.) (2002). *Critiques of Capital in Modern Britain and America: Transatlantic Exchanges 1800 to the Present Day.* Basingstoke, Palgrave Macmillan.

Bhagwati, J. (1995). 'Trade liberalisation and "fair trade" demands: addressing the environmental and labour standards issues.' *World Economy,* 18(6): pp. 745–759.

Black, M. (1992). *A Cause for Our Time: Oxfam the First 50 years.* Oxford, Oxfam.

Blackburn, S. (1993). *Practical Visionaries: A Study of Community Aid Abroad.* Melbourne, Melbourne University Press.

Blowfield, M. (2001). 'Ethical trade: Revisiting progress, developments and issues.' *Forests Trees and Livelihoods,* 11: pp. 187–206.

Bohstedt, J. (1992). 'The moral economy and the discipline of historical context.' *Journal of Social History,* 26(2): pp. 265–284.

Bonner, A. (1961). *British Co-operation: The History Principles, and Organisation of the British Co-operative Movement.* Manchester, Manchester University Press.
Boulstridge, E. and M. Carrigan (2000). 'Do consumers really care about corporate responsibility? Highlighting the attitude-behaviour gap.' *Journal of Communication Management,* 4(4): pp. 355–368.
Bowden, B. (2003). 'The perils of global citizenship.' *Citizenship Studies,* 7(3): pp. 349–362.
Broad, R. (ed.) (2002). *Global Backlash: Citizen Initiatives for a Just World Economy.* London, Rowman & Littlefield Publishers.
Brown, C. G. (2001). *The Death of Christian Britain: Understanding Secularisation 1800–2000.* London, Routledge.
Brown, C. G. (2006). *Religion and Society in Twentieth-Century Britain.* Harlow, Pearson.
Browne, A. W., Harris, P. J. C. and A. H. Hofny-Collins (2000). 'Organic production and ethical trade: Definition, practice and links.' *Food Policy,* 25(1): pp. 69–89.
Buchanan, P. (1998). *The Great Betrayal: How American Sovereignty and Social Justices Are Being Sacrificed to the Gods of the Global Economy.* New York, Little, Brown.
Burnell, P. (1991). *Charity Politics and the Third World.* London, Harvester Wheatsheaf.
Cain, P. J. (1996). *Free Trade and Protectionism.* London, Routledge/Thoemmes Press.
Carbery, T. F. (1969). *Consumers in Politics: A History and General Review of the Co-operative Party.* Manchester, Manchester University Press.
Carrier, J. G. and D. Miller (eds.) (1998). *Virtualism: A New Political Economy.* Oxford, Berg.
Charlesworth, A. (1993). 'From the moral economy of Devon to the political economy of Manchester, 1790–1812.' *Social History,* 18(2): pp. 205–217.
Charleworth, A. and A. J. Randall (1987). 'Comment: Morals, markets and the English crowd in 1766.' *Past & Present,* 114: pp. 200–213.
Chomsky, N. (1988). *Manufacturing Consent.* New York, Pantheon.
Chomsky, N. (1998). *Profit over People.* New York, Seven Stories.
Christensen, S. L. and J. Kohls (2002). 'The business responsibility for wealth distribution in a globalized political-economy: Merging moral economics and Catholic social teaching.' *Journal of Business Ethics,* 35(3): pp. 223–234.
Cohen, L. (2003). *A Consumers' Republic: The Politics of Mass Consumption in Postwar America.* New York, Random House.
Cole, M. (ed.) (1949). *The Webbs and their Work.* London, Frederick Muller.
Conti, D. (1998). *Reconciling Free Trade, Fair Trade, and Interdependence: The Rhetoric of Presidential Economic Leadership.* London, Praeger.
Creyer, E. H. and W. T. Ross (1997). 'The influence of firm behaviour on purchase intention: Do consumers really care about ethics?.' *Journal of Consumer Marketing,* 14(6): pp. 421–433.
Cross, G. (1993). *Time and Money: The Making of Consumer Culture.* London, Routledge.
Cross, G. (2000). *An All Consuming Century: Why Consumerism Won In Modern America.* New York, Columbia University Press.
Daunton, M. and M. Hilton (eds.) (2001). *The Politics of Consumption: Material Culture and Citizenship in Europe and America.* Oxford, Berg.

Davie, G. (1994). *Religion in Britain since 1945: Believing without Belonging.* Oxford, Blackwell.
Davies, I. A. and A. Crane (2003). 'Ethical decision making in Fair Trade companies.' *Journal of Business Ethics,* 45(1/2): pp. 79–92.
Dawson, E. (1998). 'The relevance of social audit for Oxfam GB.' *Journal of Business Ethics,* 17(13): pp. 1457–1469.
De Moraes, M. V. P. (2001). 'Fair globalization means Free Trade in agriculture.' *New Perspectives Quarterly,* 18(3): pp. 45–46.
Dench, G., T. Flower, et al. (eds.) (1995). *Young at Eighty: The Prolific Public Life of Michael Young.* Manchester, Carcanet Press Ltd.
Dicken, P. (1998). *Global Shift: Transforming the World Economy.* London, Chapman.
Dobbin, M. (1999). *The Myth of the Good Corporate Citizen: Democracy Under the Rule of Big Business.* Toronto, Stoddart.
Dowie, M. (2001). *American Foundations: An Investigative History.* Cambridge, Massachusetts: MIT Press.
Durning, A. (1992). *How Much is Enough? The Consumer Society and the Future of the Earth.* Norton, New York.
Durning, A. (1996). *This Place on Earth: Home and the Practice of Permanence.* Sasquatch Books, Seattle.
Edwards, M. (2000). *NGO Rights and Responsibilities: A New Deal for Global Governance.* London, Demos.
Elgin, D. (1981). *Voluntary Simplicity.* New York, Morrow.
Elliott, C. (1973). *Fair Chance For All: Money and Trade Between Unequal Partners.* New York, United Nations.
Ewen, S. (2001). *Captains of Consciousness: Advertising and the Social Roots of the Consumer Culture.* New York, Basic Books.
Fisher, W. & T. Ponniah (2003). *Another World is Possible: Popular Alternatives to Globalization at the World Social Forum.* London, Zed Books.
Forbes, J. D. (1987). *The Consumer Interest: Dimensions and Policy Implications.* London, Croom Helm.
Fournier, S. (1998). 'Consumer resistance: Societal motivations, consumer manifestations and implications in the marketing domain.' *Advances in Consumer Research,* 25: pp. 88–90.
Fox, R. W. and T. J. Lears (eds.) (1983). *The Culture of Consumption: Critical Essays in American History, 1880–1920.* New York, Random House USA.
Frank, T. (2001). *One Market Under God: Extreme Capitalism, Market Populism and the End of Economic Democracy.* London, Random House.
Freidberg, S. (2003). 'Cleaning up down South: Supermarkets, ethical trade and African horticulture.' *Social and Cultural Geography,* 4(1): pp. 27–44.
Fridell, G. (2007). *Fair Trade Coffee: The Prospects and Pitfalls of Market-Driven Social Justice.* Toronto: University of Toronto Press.
Friedman, J. (ed.) (1994). *Consumption and Identity.* London, Harwood Academic Press.
Friedman, M. (1996). 'A positive approach to organised consumer action: The "buycott" as an alternative to the boycott.' *Journal of Consumer Policy,* 19: pp. 439–451.
Friedman, M. (1999). *Consumer Boycotts: Effecting Change through the Marketplace and the Media.* London: Routledge.

Fuat Firat, A. and N. Dholakia (1998). *Consuming People: From Political Economy to Theaters of Consumption.* New York and London, Routledge.
Fukuyama, F. (1992). *The End of History and the Last Man.* London, Penguin.
Furlough, E. and C. Strikwerda (1999). *Consumers Against Capitalism: Consumer Cooperation in Europe, North America, and Japan, 1840–1990.* Oxford, Rowman & Littlefield.
Gabriel, Y. and T. Lang (1995). *The Unmanageable Consumer: Contemporary Consumption and its Fragmentation.* London, Sage.
Galbraith, J. K. (1952). *American Capitalism: The Concept of Countervailing Power.* Harmondsworth, H.Hamilton.
Galbraith, J. K. (1958). *The Affluent Society.* Harmondsworth, H.Hamilton.
Gibney, M. J. (ed.) (2003). *Globalizing Rights, The Oxford Amnesty Lectures 1999.* Oxford, Oxford University Press.
Giddens, A. (1991). *Modernity and Self-identity: Self and Society in the Late Modern Age.* Cambridge, Polity.
Giddens, A. (2002). *Runaway World: How Globalisation is Reshaping our Lives.* London, Profile.
Giddens, A. and W. Hutton (eds.) (2000). *On the Edge: Living with Global Capitalism.* London, Jonathan Cape.
Gilbert, A. D. (1976). *Religion and Society in Industrial England: Church, Chapel and Social Change 1740–1914.* London, Longman.
Glickman, L. B. (1997). *A Living Wage: American Workers and the Making of Consumer Society.* New York, Cornell University Press.
Glickman, L. B. (1997). 'Workers of the world, consume: Ira Steward and the origins of labor consumerism.' *International Labor and Working Class History,* 52: pp. 72–86.
Glickman, L. B. (1999). *Consumer Society in American History: A Reader.* New York, Cornell University.
Glickman, L. B. (2001). 'The strike in the temple of consumption: Consumer activism and twentieth-century American political culture.' *Journal of American History,* 88(1): pp. 99–128.
Goodman, M. (2004). 'Reading fair trade: Political ecological imaginary and the moral economy of fair trade foods'. *Political Geography,* 23: pp. 891–915.
Goodwin, N., F. Ackerman, et al. (eds.) (1997). *The Consumer Society.* Washington D. C., Island Press.
Gould, N. J. (2003). 'Fair Trade and the consumer interest: A personal account'. *International Journal of Consumer Studies,* 27(4): pp. 341–345.
Gray, J. (1998). *The False Dawn: The Delusions of global Capitalism.* London, Granta.
Greider, W. (1997). *One World, Ready or Not: The Manic Logic of Global Capitalism.* New York, Simon & Schuster.
Griesgraber, J. and B. Gunter (eds.) (1997). *World Trade: Towards Fair and Free Trade in the Twenty-first Century.* London, Pluto Press.
Gurney, P. (1996). *Co-operative Culture and the Politics of Consumption in England, 1870–1930.* Manchester, Manchester University Press.
Gurney, P. (2005). 'The battle of the consumer in Postwar Britain,' *Journal of Modern History,* 77: pp. 956–987.
Hale, A. (2000). 'What hope for "Ethical" Trade in the globalised garment industry?,' *Antipode,* 32(4): pp. 349–356.

Hall, S. and M. Jacques (eds.) (1989). *New Times: The Changing Face of Politics in the 1990s.* London, Lawrence and Wishart.

Harrison, R., T. Newhom and D. Shaw (eds.) (2005). *The Ethical Consumer.* London, Sage.

Harrod J. and R. O'Brien (eds.) (2002). *Global Unions?:Theory and Strategies of Organized Labour in the Global Political Economy.* London, Routledge.

Hayden, T. (ed.) (2002). *The Zapatista Reader.* New York, Thunder's Mouth Press.

Held, D. (1995). *Democracy and the Global Order: From the Modern State to Cosmopolitan Governance.* Cambridge, Polity.

Held, D. (1999). *Global Transformations: Politics, Economics and Culture.* Cambridge, Polity.

Hermann, R. O. (1993). 'The tactics of consumer resistance: Group action and marketplace exit.' *Advances in Consumer Research,* 20: pp. 130–134.

Hertz, N. (2001). *The Silent Takeover: Global Capitalism and the Death of Democracy.* London, Arrow Books.

Hilton, M. (2002). 'The fable of the sheep; or, private virtues, public vices. The consumer revolution of the twentieth century.' *Past & Present,* 176: pp. 222–256.

Hilton, M. (2002). 'The female consumer and the politics of consumption in twentieth-century Britain.' *The Historical Journal,* 45(1): pp. 103–128.

Hilton, M. (2003). *Consumerism in 20-Century Britain.* Cambridge, University Press.

Hilton, M. (2009). *Prosperity for All: Consumer Activism in an Era of Globalization.* Cornell University Press.

Hirst, P. and G. Thompson (1996). *Globalisation in Question: The International Economy and the Possibilities of Governance.* Cambridge, Polity.

Horowitz, D. (1985). *The Morality of Spending: Attitudes Towards the Consumer Society in America, 1875–1940.* Baltimore, John Hopkins University Press.

Howard, R. (1995). 'Fair trade wins: The rise of ethical shopping.' *New Statesman and Society,* 7(337): p. 18.

Howse, R. and M. J. Treblicock (1996). 'The fair trade/free trade debate: Trade, labour and the environment.' *International Review of Law and Economics,* 6:1(March): pp. 61–80.

Jaffee, D. (2007). *Brewing Justice: Fair Trade Coffee, Sustainability, and Survival.* Berkley, University of California Press.

Kapstein, E. (1999). *Sharing the Wealth: Workers and the World Economy.* New York, W. W. Norton.

Karliner, J. (1997). *The Corporate Planet: Ecology and Politics in the Age of Globalisation.* San Francisco, Sierra Club Books.

Kennan, J. and C. Stevens (2001). *The impact of the EU's 'Everything But Arms' proposal; a report to Oxfam.* London, Institute for Development Studies.

Keohane, R. and J. Nye (2000). 'Globalization: What's new? What's not? (And so what?).' *Foreign Policy,* Spring.

Keynes, J. M. (1919). *The Economic Consequences of the Peace.* London, Macmillan.

Khator, R. (2000). 'Ethical implications of World trade on the environment of developing countries.' *Journal of Social Philosophy,* 31(4): pp. 465–476.

Kingsnorth, P. (2003). *One No, Many Yeses: A Journey to the Heart of the Global Resistance Movement.* New York, The Free Press.

Klein, N. (2000). *No Logo.* London, Flamingo.

Klein, N. (2002). *Fences and Windows: Dispatches from the Front Lines of the Globalisation Debate.* London, Flamingo.

Korten, D. (1995). *When Corporations Rule the World.* San Francisco, Berrett-Koehler.
Korten, D. (2000). *The Post-Corporate World: Life after Capitalism.* San Francisco, Berrett-Koehler.
Kroll, R. J. (1991). 'Advancing the consumer interest: Traditional ideology versus a generic view.' *Advancing the Consumer Interest,* 3:1: pp. 22–26.
Kuttner, R. (1997). *Everything for Sale: The Virtues and Limits of Markets.* New York, Alfred A. Knopf.
Landes, D. (1998). *The Wealth and Poverty of Nations: Why Some Are So Rich and Some So Poor.* New York, WW Norton & Co.
Langeland, L. (1999). 'On communicating the complexity of a green message part 2: The vigilant market.' *Greener Management International,* Spring, 25: pp. 81–90.
Lasn, K. (1999). *Culture Jam: The Uncooling of America.* New York, Eagle Brook.
LeClair, M. S. (2003). 'Fighting back: The growth of alternative trade.' *Development,* 46(1), pp. 66–73.
Legrain, P. (2002). *Open World: The Truth About Globalisation.* London, Abacus.
Levi, M. and A. Linton (2003). 'Fair trade: A cup at a time?' *Politics and Society,* 31(3): pp. 407–432.
Littrell, M. A. and M. A. Dickson (1998). 'Fair trade performance in a competitive market.' *Clothing and Textiles Research Journal,* 16(4): pp. 176–189.
Littrell, M. A. and M. A. Dickson (1999). *Social Responsibility in the Global Market Fair Trade of Cultural Products,* London, Sage.
Lloyd, D. (2001). *The Protest Ethic: How the Anti-Globalisation Movement Challenges Social Democracy.* London, Demos.
Luttinger, N. (2002). 'Brewing justice: Fair trade certified tea in the U.S.' *Tea and Coffee Trade Journal,* 174(8): pp. 28–32.
Luttwak, E. (1998). *Turbo Capitalism: Winners and Losers in the Global Economy.* London, Weidenfeld & Nicolson.
Martin, R. (1980). *TUC: The Growth of a Pressure Group 1868–1976.* Oxford, Clarendon Press.
Maseland, R. and A. de Vaal (2002). 'How fair is fair trade?' *Economist,* 150(3): pp. 251–272.
McCleary, R. M. (1992). *Seeking Justice: Ethics and International Affairs.* Boulder, CO; Oxford, Westview Press.
McCulloch, N. (2001). *Trade Liberalisation and Poverty: A Handbook.* London, Centre for Economic Policy Research.
McKay, G. (ed.) (1998). *DIY Culture: Party and Politics in Nineties Britain.* London, Verso.
McLeod, H. (2000). *Secularisation in Western Europe, 1848–1914.* London, Macmillan.
Meier, T. (2000). *Organic Product and Fair Trade Products: Bringing Together Social and Ecological Issues.* IFOAM, Basle.
Mendoza, R. and C. Bahadur (2002). 'Toward free and fair trade: A global public good perspective.' *Challenge,* 45(5): pp. 21–62.
Mertes, T. (ed.) (2004). *A Movement of Movements: Is Another World Really Possible?* London, Verso.
Micheletti, M. and A. Follesdal (2007). 'Shopping for human rights. An introduction to the special issue.' *Journal of Consumer Policy,* 30: pp. 167–175.
Micheletti, Follesdal and Stolle, (eds.) (2004). *Politics Products and Markets: Exploring Political Consumerism Past and Present.* London, Transaction Publishers.

Miller, D. (ed.) (1995). *Acknowledging Consumption.* London, Routledge.
Monbiot, G. (2000). *Captive State: The Corporate Takeover of Britain.* London, Macmillan.
Monbiot, G. (2003). *The Age of Consent: A Manifesto for a New World Order.* London, Flamingo.
Monbiot, G. (2003). 'World fair trade organisation.' *Ecologist,* 33(5): pp. 42–44.
Morris, J. (2003). 'The strange death of Christian Britain: Another look at the secularization debate'. *The Historical Journal,* 46(4), pp. 963–976.
Muniz, A. and T. O'Guinn (2001). 'Brand Community.' *Journal of Consumer Research,* 27: pp. 412–432.
Mutersbaugh, T. (2002). 'Ethical trade and certified organic coffee: Implications of rules-based agricultural product certification for Mexican producer households and villages.' *Transnational Law and Contemporary Problems,* 12(1): pp. 89–108.
Nelson, V., A. Tallontire and C. Collinson (2002). 'Assessing the benefits of ethical trade schemes in cocoa (Ecuador) and brazil nuts (Peru) for forest dependent people and their livelihoods.' *International Forestry Review,* 4(2): pp. 99–109.
Nicholls, A. J. (2002). 'Strategic options in fair trade retailing.' *International Journal of Retail and Distribution Management,* 30:1: pp. 6–17.
Nicholls, A. and C. Opal (2004). *Fair Trade: Market-Driven Ethical Consumption.* London, Sage.
O'Brien, R. (2000). 'Workers and world order: The tentative transformation of the international union movement.' *Review of International Studies,* 26, pp. 533–555.
Ohmae, K. (1990). *The Borderless World.* New York, Harper Business.
Overath, D. (1997). *Fair Trade: How Does it Work?* The future agenda for organic trade, Oxford, Soil Association.
Pacione, M. (1997). 'Local exchange trading systems as a response to the globalisation of capitalism.' *Urban Studies* 34(8): pp. 1179–1200.
Panagariya, A. (2003). 'International trade the collapse of the World Trade Organization talks in Cancun amid debates over "fair trade" obscured some inconvenient facts.' *Foreign Policy,* (139): pp. 20–29.
Paulsen, O. and R. Gunasekera (1999). 'Fair trade labeling for tea from Sri Lanka.' *Tea and Coffee Trade Journal,* 171(6): pp. 80–87.
Penaloza, L. and L. Price (1993). 'Consumer resistance: A conceptual overview.' *Advances in Consumer Research,* 20: pp. 123–128.
Pilger, J. (1991). 'In defence of Oxfam.' *New Statesman & Society,* 4(151): p. 8.
Pilger, J. (2002). *The New Rulers of the World.* London, Verso.
Prochaska, F. (2006). *Christianity & Social Service in Modern Britain: The Disinherited Spirit.* Oxford, Oxford University Press.
Quested, H. (1998). 'Ethical shopping: A time when organic and fair-trade standards converge.' *Living Earth,* pp. 14–16.
Raynolds, L. T. (2002). 'Consumer-producer links in fair trade coffee networks.' *Sociologia Ruralis,* 42(4): pp. 404–424.
Raynolds, L., Murray, D. and J. Wilkinson (2007). *Fair Trade: The Challenges of Transforming Globalization.* London, Routledge.
Redclift, M. (1996). *Recovering Consumption: The Environment and the Global Economy.* London, Earthscan.
Redclift, M. (1996). *Wasted: Counting the Cost of Global Consumption.* London, Earthscan.

Renard, M. C. (1999). 'The interstices of globalization: The example of fair coffee.' *Sociologia Ruralis,* 39(4): pp. 484–500.

Renard, M. C. (2003). 'Fair trade: quality, market and conventions.' *Journal of Rural Studies,* 19(1): 87–96.

Ritzer, G. (1995). *The McDonaldization of Society.* London, Sage.

Ritzer, G. (1999). *Enchanting a Disenchanted World: Revolutionizing the Means of Consumption.* London, Sage.

Roberts, M. J. D. (1998). 'The concept of luxury in British political economy: Adam Smith to Alfred Marshall.' *History of the Human Sciences,* 11(1): pp. 23–47.

Roderik, D. (1997). *Has Globalization Gone Too Far?* Washington, D C, Institute for International Economics.

Ross, A. (ed.) (1997). *No Sweat: Fashion, Free Trade and the Rights of Garment Workers.* London, Verso.

Sassen, S. (1998). *Globalization and its Discontents.* New York, The New Press.

Scarse, T. J. (2003). 'Precarious production: Globalisation and artisan labour in the third world.' *Third World Quarterly,* 24(3): pp. 449–461.

Schor, J. (1998). *The Overspent American: Why We Want What We Don't Need.* New York, Harper Perennial.

Sen, S., Z. Gurham-Canli, et al. (2001). 'Withholding consumption: A social dilemma perspective on consumer boycotts.' *Journal of Consumer Research,* 28(3): pp. 399–419.

Singer, P. (2002). *One World: The Ethics of Globalisation.* New Haven, Yale University Press.

Smith, N. C. (1995). 'Marketing strategies for the ethics era.' *Sloan Management Review,* 36(4): pp. 85–98.

Soros, G. (2000). *Open Society: Reforming Global Capitalism.* New York, Public Affairs.

Soros, G. (2002). *On Globalisation.* Oxford, Public Affairs.

Stiglitz, J. (2002). *Globalisation and its Discontents.* New York, W. W. Norton & Company.

Strong, C. (1996). 'Features contributing to the growth in ethical consumerism: A preliminary investigation.' *Marketing Intelligence and Planning,* 14(5): pp. 5–13.

Strong, C. and T. Mottershead (2000). 'Fair trade: An illustration of its role in sustainable development?' *Global Focus,* 12(3): pp. 79–88.

Tallen, B. (2003) *What Should I do if Reverend Billy comes in my Store?* London, The New Press.

Tallontire, A. (2000). 'Partnerships in fair trade: Reflections from a case study of Cafédirect.' *Development in Practice* 10(2): pp. 166–177.

Tallontire, A. (2002). 'Challenges facing fair trade: Which way now?' *Small Enterprise Development,* 13(3): pp. 12–24.

Tallontire, A. and M. E. Blowfield (2000). 'Will the WTO prevent the growth of ethical trade? Implications of potential changes to WTO rules for environmental and social standards in the forest sector.' *Journal of International Development,* 12(4): pp. 571–584.

Thomson, B. (1999). 'Lessons for fair trade.' *Small Enterprise Development,* 10(4): pp. 56–60.

Thompson, E. P. (1971). 'The moral economy of the English crowd in the eighteenth century', *Past and Present,* 50, pp. 76–136.

Trentmann, F. (2007). 'Before "fair trade": Empire, free trade and the moral economics of food in the modern world.' *Environment and Planning D: Society and Space*, 25: pp. 1079–1102.

Trentmann, F. (2008). *Free Trade Nation: Commerce, Consumption, and Civil Society in Modern Britain*. Oxford, Oxford University Press.

Turner, A. (2001). *Just Capital: The Liberal Economy*. London, Macmillan.

Ulrich, B. (2000). *What is Globalization?* Cambridge, Polity.

Vidal, J. (1997). *McLibel: Burger Culture on Trial*. London, Macmillan.

Waterman, P. (2001). *Globalization, Social Movements and the New Internationalisms*. London, Continuum.

Welford, R., J. Meaton, et al. (2003). 'Fair trade as a Strategy for International Competitiveness.' *International Journal of Sustainable Development and World Ecology*, 10(1): pp. 1–14.

Windmuller, J. (1961). 'ICFTU after ten years: Problems and prospects.' *Industrial and Labor Relations Review*, 14(2): pp. 257–272.

Zadek, S. and P. Tiffen (1996). '"Fair Trade": Business or campaign?' *Development*, Autumn, 3: pp. 48–53.

Zweinger-Bargielowska, I. (2000). *Austerity in Britain: Rationing, Controls, and Consumption 1939–1955*. Oxford, Oxford University Press.

Index

Printed and bound by CPI Group (UK) Ltd, Croydon, CR0 4YY